Routledge Revivals

The Writing on the Wall

First published in 1987, *The Writing on the Wall* tells the story of the muddle, shortsightedness and duplicity which characterised Britain's dealings with her Pacific Dominions. It describes the reactions of each Dominion and chronicles the desultory responses of Canada, Australia, and New Zealand to the developing crises in the North Pacific. The result is an important contribution to the history of all four continents.

As the 1930s opened, the British Empire was everywhere recognised as a Great Power. Its rule extended over one-fifth of the earth's land surface; it encompassed the largest population of any 'State' in the world; it controlled one-sixth of the world's trade. In truth, the Empire was tragically fragile. Both Britain and the Dominions had disarmed to the point of impotence, so that when Japan occupied Manchuria in 1931 and attacked Shanghai, the centre of British trade in China, in the following year, they were unable to respond. British defence chiefs declared Japan's success to be 'the writing on the wall'. Despite these warnings, British politicians chose to appease the Japanese at the cost of seriously damaging the League of Nations, and to avoid spending money on defence in the Far East. Despite the concerns of the Dominions—Australia, New Zealand, and Canada—the scene was set for the total collapse of Britain's Empire in the East within a decade. This book will be of interest to students and researchers of history.

The Writing on the Wall
The British Commonwealth and Aggression in the East 1931–1935

E. M. Andrews

First published in 1987
by Allen & Unwin Pty Ltd

This edition first published in 2024 by Routledge
4 Park Square, Milton Park, Abingdon, Oxon, OX14 4RN

and by Routledge
605 Third Avenue, New York, NY 10017

Routledge is an imprint of the Taylor & Francis Group, an informa business

© E. M. Andrews 1987

All rights reserved. No part of this book may be reprinted or reproduced or utilised in any form or by any electronic, mechanical, or other means, now known or hereafter invented, including photocopying and recording, or in any information storage or retrieval system, without permission in writing from the publishers.

Publisher's Note
The publisher has gone to great lengths to ensure the quality of this reprint but points out that some imperfections in the original copies may be apparent.

Disclaimer
The publisher has made every effort to trace copyright holders and welcomes correspondence from those they have been unable to contact.

A Library of Congress record exists under LCCN:

ISBN: 978-1-032-88815-6 (hbk)
ISBN: 978-1-003-53982-7 (ebk)
ISBN: 978-1-032-88819-4 (pbk)

Book DOI 10.4324/9781003539827

The British Commonwealth and Aggression in
the East 1931-1935.

E. M. ANDREWS

ALLEN & UNWIN
Sydney London Boston

For Steven Andrews 23.11.57–13.4.75

© E. M. Andrews 1987
This book is copyright under the Berne Convention. No reproduction without permission. All rights reserved.

First published in 1987
Allen & Unwin Australia Pty Ltd
8 Napier Street, North Sydney, NSW 2060, Australia

Allen & Unwin (Publishers) Ltd
Park Lane, Hemel Hempstead, Herts HP2 4TE, England

Allen & Unwin Inc.
8 Winchester Place, Winchester, Mass 01890, USA

National Library of Australia
Cataloguing-in-publication entry:

Andrews, E. M. (Eric Montgomery), 1933–
  The writing on the wall.

  Bibliography.
  Includes index.
  ISBN 0 04 909027 5.

  1. Great Britain — Relations — Foreign countries. 2. Great Britian — Military relations — Japan. 3. Japan — Military relations — Great Britain. 4. Imperial federation — History. 5. World War, 1939–45 — Causes. 6. Commonwealth of Nations — History. I. Title.
327.41

Library of Congress Catalog Card Number: 86-071025

Printed by Singapore National Printers Pte Ltd, Singapore

Set in 10/11 pt Plantin by Vera Reyes, Inc., Philippines

Contents

Maps vii

Note viii

Acknowledgements ix

Preface x

Introduction xiv

1 **The birth of the 'Commonwealth'** 1
   From 'Empire' to 'Commonwealth' 1
   'Imperial foreign policy' and 'consultation' 6
   The machinery of consultation 11
   Canada: Skelton, King and External Affairs 19
   New Zealand: loyalty to Britain and fear of Japan 21
   Australian indifference and the weakness of consultation 24
   Imperial disarmament 25
   The Singapore base and New Zealand 33
   Imperial impotence 35

2 **The new idea tested: crisis in the East, 1931–32** 37
   Britain: political and economic problems 38
   New Zealand: the government of 'Farmer Forbes' 43
   Bennett's Canada 45
   Australia: advent of the Lyons government 49
   Shanghai, January 1932 54
   'Imperial consultation' 58

3 **Hesitation in the League, 1932–33** 66
   The importance of the League to the Commonwealth 66
   The Pacific Dominions and the League 67
   The 'Special Assembly': March 1932 70
   Sanctions and 'non-recognition' 75
   The Lytton Report—and a New Zealand maverick 81

Britain, Canada and Australia in the Assembly, December 1932 84
Repercussions in Canada 90
Australian reservations 94
The end of the affair 96
The Commonwealth, the League and Dominion influence on Britain 99

4 **The writing on the wall: problems of defence** **104**
The Disarmament Conference, Geneva 1932 104
Britain's military weakness 107
The waiting dominoes: Canada, New Zealand and Australia 110
Commonwealth at loggerheads: the possible sale of arms to China 120
Australian defence: confused policies and the appeal to Britain 126

5 **Armaments or diplomacy: The search for security** **132**
The Singapore conference and its aftermath
The Australian Eastern mission: Sir John Latham, March–June 1934 135
Britain: the defence requirements debate begins 145
Appeasing Japan 151

6 **The collapse of consultation** **156**
Defence decisions hidden from the Dominions 156
Hankey's Commonwealth tour 159
Aftermath of Hankey: divided policies and weak defence 172
The Silver Jubilee and the Dominion PMs' meetings, May 1935 176

7 **The Commonwealth fallacy exposed** **185**
The divergent Dominions 185
The significance of League failure 186
Weakness in the heart of Empire 192
The 'newspeak' behind consultation 193
Britain, Australia, Canada and New Zealand: the future 195

Appendix Comparative naval strengths in April 1931 196

Endnotes 197

Bibliography 217

Index 224

Maps

1 The British Empire/Commonwealth in the interwar years   2
2 The Pacific Dominions and Japan   29
3 The aftermath: the strategic position of the Commonwealth, 1935–39   190

Note

Both the British and New Zealand Labour Parties are so spelt. Since 1916, however, the Australian Labor Party has used the American form for its middle name. To complicate matters, if the trade unions and the party are referred to as a 'movement', it then uses the British spelling, i.e. 'the Labour movement'. Such are the vagaries of the English language, spread as it is throughout the world!

Australian readers might also note that in British usage the words 'Prime Minister' and 'Premier' are synonymous, and are used interchangeably in this book.

Acknowledgements

This book has only been made possible by the help of staff in many public institutions around the world. My thanks therefore go to the workers in the Public Record Office, the British Library and the Westminster Central Reference Library, London; the National Maritime Museum, Greenwich; the Australian Archives, the History section of the Department of Foreign Affairs and the National Library in Canberra; the Australian Archives in Melbourne; the Public Archives of Canada in Ottawa, the archives of York University in Toronto and the New Zealand Archives in Wellington.

My debt to individuals is almost unlimited, but in particular mention should be made of Mr L. F. Fitzhardinge, of the Australian National University, Neill Gow and Associate Professor J. McCarthy in Duntroon, Canberra, and, from the Institute of Commonwealth Studies in London, the late Trevor Reese. His untimely death will be felt by the profession, as well as his many friends, for years to come. Mention should also be made of the staff of Canada House and New Zealand House in London, where I. P. Puketapu was of great help. Those people who have kindly aided my researches by giving their memories of events in the past have been mentioned at the appropriate places in the footnotes. They have my gratitude, as do those who have kindly allowed me to quote from their own researches.

My thanks also go to Newcastle University and its History Department for sabbatical leave, which enabled me to go to England, and travel grants which took me to Canada and New Zealand; the History Department secretary, Jan Ebbeck and to Robyn Gay who typed—and retyped—the manuscript; and to Professor R. G. McMinn, who read the text and made many useful suggestions. Those errors which obstinately remain, however, are my responsibility.

Finally, my gratitude is due to my family, who have faithfully trailed over the earth after me, enjoying themselves part of the time, but also putting up with the vagaries of a research worker's life and temper. Tragically, my son did not live to see this book published. To him, therefore, I dedicate it.

Preface

Over the years, several books have been written about the developing crisis in the Far East which began in Manchuria in 1931. At the time and immediately afterwards many writers regarded it as the first occasion when the British government, by the policy of appeasement, betrayed the League of Nations and paved the way for later aggression by the Axis powers. After the Second World War, however, two books appeared which shed fresh light upon the subject. Gwendolen Carter looked at the influence of the British Commonwealth on foreign policy throughout the interwar period and in doing so naturally discussed Manchuria. Then Reginald Bassett dealt with the crisis in its own right, defending British policy in general and Sir John Simon, Secretary of State for Foreign Affairs, in particular. He showed quite clearly the false assumptions of many of Simon's contemporary critics and the reservations of even the most vociferous of the League's supporters about the use of force to support League decisions.[1]

In time, however, the British government abandoned the rule by which its documents only became available to historians—except the official variety—after 50 years. The period was reduced, at least on paper, to 30 years. As a result, a mass of material became suddenly available to researchers. In 1972 Christopher Thorne used it with effect in a book which will probably remain a standard text on the Manchurian crisis for a long time.[2] He looked at it, however, from the point of view of Britain, the European nations at the League headquarters in Geneva, and the United States of America. He did not consider the British Commonwealth in detail, although he mentioned it in several places.

There are, however, two problems with this approach. Britain adopted the stance of a major world Empire and claimed that her new 'Commonwealth' was an integral part of that Empire. To ignore the Commonwealth, or to play down its significance, is to miss an important factor in the equations of power and policy. On the other hand, to mention the Commonwealth without looking at it in some detail can be misleading. After carefully studying the often ambiguous documents collected by the Dominions Office (and occasionally the Foreign Office in its dealings with the Dominions) the historian needs to compare them with documents held in the Dominions themselves. To go further and to understand the nuances behind the bald statements in the documents, he or she really needs to know something of the internal history of the individual Dominions.

The documents in London cannot be taken at face value, partly because many of them have an inherent bias—being records of a situation seen from British eyes or from the personal viewpoint of Dominion representatives who were living in London and therefore were not typical of their compatriots—and partly because those that are messages from the Dominions were written with Britain in mind. Even more important, there are great gaps in the surviving collections in England. The Foreign Office kept a class of documents which it called 'Dominions Information', handled by a separate department from 1929 to 1933 while the discussions were under way that led to the Statute of Westminster. Thereafter such matters came under the 'Treaty Department'. In the same way the Dominions Office, half begun in 1925 and created as a separate entity in 1930, turned into the Commonwealth Relations Office in 1947. Then a series of changes led to its amalgamation with the Foreign Office, so creating the Foreign and Commonwealth Office in 1967.[3] In the course of these metamorphoses the British parliament, in its wisdom, decided that many documents could be destroyed. Nor did the authorities see fit to destroy them in a rational manner; material which was held by either the Foreign or the Dominions Office was destroyed, whereas material that was held in duplicate by both bodies has been preserved—still in duplicate—in the Public Record Office in London. As a result, a definitive history of the British Dominions Office can now never be produced, although Lord Garner, who worked in that office and became permanent under-secretary in the later Commonwealth Office, has written the story as he saw it.[4]

The ill-advised—indeed amazing—destruction of documents in Britain obliges the conscientious researcher in Commonwealth history to travel extensively, since Dominion archives are scattered in different parts of the globe. The new techniques of microfilming and photocopying have helped a little, but they presuppose a specific and known body of material to be copied. The researcher, therefore, has to go to Dominion archives and hunt for elusive material himself. All too often imperial historians in Britain write histories of the Commonwealth from those documents they can see in England, supplemented, where possible, with material from published and microfilm sources, while historians in each Dominion write of their own country and Britain, referring to British works for their background. There have been too few modern studies which look at several Dominions and Britain simultaneously, using the documents recently released in each country. This book remedies that deficiency and looks at Commonwealth and British policy, using archival material in London, Ottawa, Canberra and Wellington.

The aim of the book is wider than this, however. Commonwealth opinion has, on several occasions, been used as an excuse for policies followed—for their own reasons—by British politicians, especially for example in the matter of appeasement.[5] Moreover, the founding fathers of Commonwealth history, men like Sir Keith Hancock and Nicholas Mansergh, perhaps because of their connection with the Royal Institute of International Affairs, also assumed that Commonwealth opinion and interests influenced the thinking and policies of British governments, and British historians have repeated this assumption without much serious thought. Thus D. C. Watt has written of 'the psychological vulnerability of members of all governments to representations from the Dominions . . .' and 'the effect of this was to impose on those who formulated British foreign policy the need continuously to consult Dominion representatives, and, where such consultation was impossible, to operate within the limits of what they felt the Dominions would accept'.[6] A younger generation of scholars, however, tends to treat this view with scepticism. One historian has suggested, for example, that the Dominions had little effect on British policy during the Abyssinian crisis of 1935–36 and concluded that those who argue for Dominion influence will have to seek evidence for it elsewhere. Since then there has been a more detailed examination of the complex relationship between Britain, the Dominions and America which lay behind the policy of appeasement.[7]

This book is a contribution to the continuing debate. It considers the impact and implications of the Eastern crisis which began in Manchuria in September 1931. For the Commonwealth historian this is a more interesting subject than it would appear to be at first sight. For British politicians were then in the process of changing their 'Empire' into a 'Commonwealth' and, moreover, the affair was separated by its geographical position and timing from later crises in the Middle East and Europe. It therefore forms an entity which can be studied by itself, so that its effects and lessons can be the more easily judged.

The book has several major themes, both political and military. Among the former are the constitutional changes brought about in the Empire/Commonwealth and whether they signified a change of heart in either British or Dominion politicians—in short, whether the latter believed their official statements sufficiently strongly to change their political habits. Linked with this is the subject of consultation. More important, perhaps, is the disagreement which lurked behind the constitutional changes—whether there were common 'Commonwealth' interests, and therefore whether a common policy was either possible or desirable. Finally, the military and strategic situation of the Empire/Commonwealth was all-important. It was the reality of power behind the political and ceremonial stance.

Apart from dealing with Britain, the imperial centre, the book concentrates on Australia, New Zealand and Canada. It does so, not because other sections of the Commonwealth, such as South Africa, were unimportant in themselves, but because those three countries were all 'Pacific Dominions', having shores which bordered on that ocean, and were therefore concerned to a greater extent than others with threats to its peace and security.

Introduction

On 6 May 1935 the whole of Britain, and especially London, was in a state of excitement. In warm sunshine the country celebrated the Silver Jubilee of King George V. Representatives of many nations were in attendance; and all over the land, in villages and towns, streets were decorated with bunting, open-air parties and fetes were held and loyal toasts drunk.

In London itself, people began to gather at dawn outside Buckingham Palace, so that by the time the ceremonial procession started at 10 am dense crowds packed the route. The King and Queen left the palace with their escort of Life Guards, passed through Trafalgar Square and down the Strand to Temple Bar, where they received the pearl sword of the City of London from its Lord Mayor, then on to a thanksgiving service in St Paul's Cathedral—the whole way accompanied by, as *The Times* put it, 'the fervour of cheering crowds'.

As night came down the King, by touching an electric switch, set off a chain of two thousand beacons, reaching from the Channel Islands across the English countries to the Shetlands and Northern Ireland. At the same time searchlights penetrated the night sky, innumerable private bonfires were lit and firework displays and children's parties given, while town halls, churches and historic buildings were floodlit throughout the land.

Behind all these celebrations lay the theme of British imperial greatness. The cavalcade from Buckingham Palace was led, after that of the Prime Minister, Ramsay MacDonald, by the carriages of the Prime Ministers of Canada, South Africa, Australia, New Zealand, Southern Rhodesia and Northern Ireland. Tributes came in from each of the Dominions and the King replied with messages to them all; in distant corners of the earth loyal speeches were made and the occasion celebrated.

Some ambiguity can be detected in British language, however. Much was made of India; and the King, in his moving message to his peoples, did not use the new term 'Commonwealth' at all but the old-fashioned one 'Empire'—three times, on the second occasion asking the children who heard him to remember that in the days to come they would be citizens of a great Empire. In this however, as in so many other ways, he echoed what most English men and women felt. Pride in Empire was widespread.

Unfortunately, beneath all the glitter, ceremony and rejoicing the British Empire was not what it seemed. It had gone through constitutional changes formally creating the 'Commonwealth' only four years before, in an effort to hide the differences in interest and outlook of the various parts. Then had come the crisis in the Far East, when the Japanese had struck in Manchuria and Shanghai and begun to put pressure on China in earnest. The leaders of the Commonwealth/ Empire had been indulging in protracted yet desultory debates ever since. By 1935 there were ominous weaknesses both at the centre and on the outlying reaches—hidden from public view, masked by the rhetoric of politicians, but real nonetheless. MacDonald and the Dominion Prime Ministers, the latter dressed in their ceremonial uniforms on the steps of St Pauls waiting for the arrival of the King, might have remembered a previous occasion when a great and—to its own officers—apparently invincible Empire rejoiced.

> King Belshazzar gave a great banquet to a thousand of his lords . . . they drank their wine and praised their gods . . . That very hour, the fingers of a man's hand appeared, writing on the plaster of the royal palace, opposite the lampstand . . . *Mene, Tekel, Peres*. The meaning of it is: *Mene* (numbered), God has numbered the days of your kingdom and ended it; *Tekel* (weighed), you are weighed in the scales and found wanting; *Peres* (divided), your kingdom is divided up and assigned to the Medes and the Persians.[1]

1 The birth of the Commonwealth

> ... the Foreign Office were in close touch with all parts of the world, and [I] thought [I] could say that they had rarely been far from the mark in forecasting future trouble. On economic grounds alone [I] thought it was safe to say that there would be peace for ten years.
>
> ARTHUR HENDERSON, AT THE COMMITTEE OF THE IMPERIAL CONFERENCE, 1930, ON THE SINGAPORE BASE. PRO CAB 32/91

From 'Empire' to 'Commonwealth'
In 1931 the British Empire was, to all appearances, one of the greatest powers on earth. It had survived the First World War and increased its rule to extend over thirteen million square miles—one-fifth of the earth's land surface. It 'possessed the largest population of any state in the world, with 490,000,000 people (in 1931) . . . The Empire's "white" population, at 71,500,000, was greater than Germany's, one and three quarters the size of France's, and by no means incomparable with the white population of the United States'.[1] The Empire also produced a large proportion of the world's foodstuffs and raw materials, including over 60 per cent of the rubber and 50 per cent of the chrome. The Empire owned 45 per cent of the world's shipping and Britain held 17 per cent of the world's trade.

The British, moreover, faced by demands for independence in their outlying colonies, had been doing their best to modify their theory of Empire and to grant more self-government. The loss of the American colonies much earlier had alerted them to the fact that they could not control the Empire from their homeland, but the more immediate origins of the change in imperial constitutional theory are to be found at the turn of the century.

About that time the idea of some sort of federation developed. In 1884 J. R. Seeley, in his book *The Expansion of England*, suggested that it was the only way the British could equal the superpowers of the future. He was supported by the Imperial Federation League and, in 1893, by the British Empire League and the Imperial Defence Committee. All these, however, were British organisations.

The idea, however, ran counter to the growing independence felt by many people in the Dominions. They were scattered over thousands of miles of the earth's surface and naturally, despite their origins, had gradually come to see the world from their own viewpoint. Such an attitude was spurred on by the existence of racial

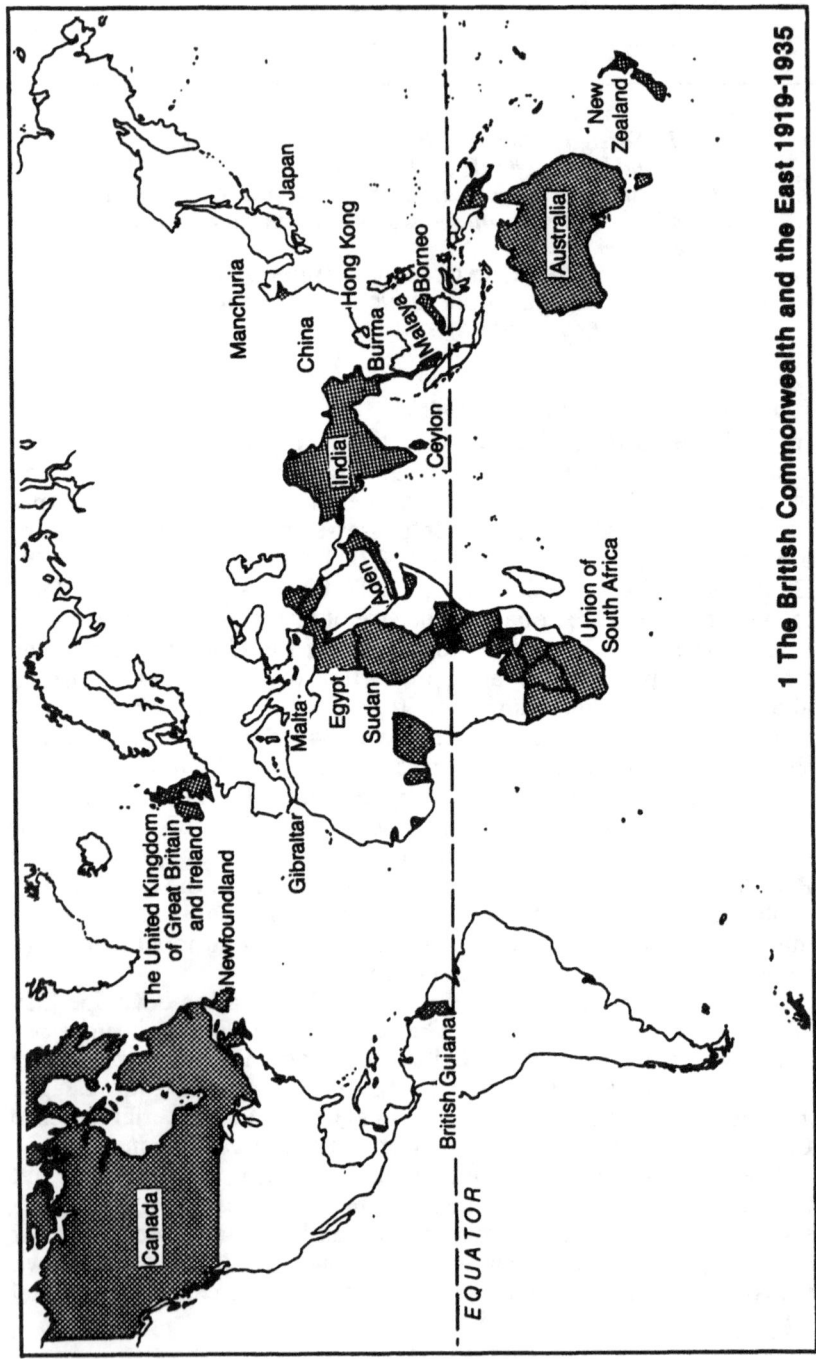

1 The British Commonwealth and the East 1919-1935

minorities in some of the Dominions, racial minorities who had been defeated by the British in the past and resented their assumption of superiority in the present. They were especially important in Canada (the French Canadians) and South Africa (the Boers).

So the rhetoric of Empire gradually changed to one stressing independence. Lord Rosebery, in a speech in Adelaide in 1884, had talked of the Empire being a 'Commonwealth of nations'.[2] Rosebery had had a grounding in Cromwellian studies, and the term 'Commonwealth' was common in the closing years of the nineteenth century. (George Bernard Shaw used it in his pamphlet *Fabianism and the Empire* in 1900.) Then in the 1907 imperial conference the term 'Dominion'—first used when applied to Canada in 1867—was adopted for all the self-governing units of the Empire, as distinct from the non-self-governing 'colonies'. And in 1909 the Dominions were called a 'Commonwealth of States within the British Empire'.

The First World War, and the part played by Dominion forces in it, encouraged English idealists to sympathise with the Dominions and to water down their talk of imperial federation. Lionel Curtis, who in 1908 had hoped for a federal system for the Empire, published his book *The Commonwealth of Nations* in 1916, and in April 1917 the Imperial War Conference resolved that after the war there should be '. . . full recognition of the dominions as autonomous nations of an imperial commonwealth'.[3]

That conference had, indeed, talked of 'continuous consultation' in forming foreign policy on matters that were of concern to all. This came near to a concept of an 'imperial foreign policy', but when the war was over the old nationalism and separatism reasserted themselves, as the representatives of the Dominions returned home and became preoccupied with their own affairs. Dominion leaders had gained a new self-confidence as a result of the war and the contribution of their countrymen to Britain's survival. Moreover, their independent status was recognised (except for Newfoundland) by their separate membership of the League of Nations, with their delegates to the League Assembly accredited by their own governments, ILO Conventions ratified by themselves, and—by 1927—with Canadian representation on the League Council.

This new independence and status in the eyes of the world, combined with anti-British feeling among the minorities in Canada and South Africa and the majority in Ireland, meant that any hope of federation was vain. The South African Jan Smuts had seen this as early as 1917 when he said to the imperial war conference, 'The circumstances of the Empire entirely preclude the federal solution . . . and to attempt to run even the common concerns of that group of nations by means of a central parliament and a central executive is to my mind absolutely to court disaster'. Smuts backed up this remark with his memorandum in 1921 which, by dismissing the idea of federation, publicised the word 'Commonwealth' instead. Accordingly, the term 'British Commonwealth of Nations' was used in the Anglo–Irish Treaty in 1921.

The meaning of the term, however, was still extremely vague. What was happening was that many of the 'imperialists' were trying to avoid the natural history of Empires. The Assyrian, Babylonian and Roman Empires had fallen. So had all the others known to have existed in the distant past. But it was unthinkable that the British Empire too should disappear.

By the time the next imperial conference was held in 1923, however, the idea even of a 'confederation' was doomed. For the Irish and Boer nationalists were joined by spokesmen from Canada. The new Canadian Prime Minister, Mackenzie King, was an anti-British isolationist, determined on Canadian independence at all costs. He therefore set out to break the idea of the Empire as an effective alliance, with a common policy decided after consultation. King wanted complete independence for Canada, and therefore opposed any talk of consultation. He had, moreover, discovered an able second for his plans in the dean of the Faculty of Arts at Queens University, Kingston, Dr O. D. Skelton. In January 1922 King had heard Skelton deliver a scathing attack on the idea of an imperial foreign policy, and had invited him to prepare the Canadian case for the 1923 conference and to be a member of the Canadian delegation. Skelton was to leave the academic world and to become permanent head of the Canadian Ministry of External Affairs.

Meanwhile, in September 1922, the Chanak crisis had occurred. The Young Turks, under Mustapha Kemal, defeated the Greek army in Asia Minor and advanced towards the Dardanelles and Constantinople. The British contingent in the neutral zone was in his path. The British government issued a warning—that if necessary it would go to war to maintain the settlement—and an appeal to the Dominions. The matter, unfortunately, was reported in the press before the telegrams arrived in the various Dominion capitals. The New Zealand government loyally promised help, the Australian was lukewarm and indignant over the lack of consultation;[4] but the governments of South Africa and Canada rejected the whole idea out of hand. To King and Skelton, the Chanak incident justified all their fears that the imperial connection with England would drag Canada into wars in obscure parts of the globe. The fact that peace was maintained in 1922 was no consolation. At the 1923 conference, therefore, King launched an attack on the very idea of a single body deciding all the foreign policy of the Empire. Some matters were common, but others were of local or particular interest to Britain or the Dominions. By implication

Europe might be considered a British concern; the South Pacific an Australian and New Zealand one.

His attitude offended the Australian and New Zealand representatives, for their answer to Chanak had been to stress the need for a common imperial policy decided by consultation. King would have none of it. The conference, therefore, was split over a fundamental issue and this disagreement spread from foreign policy to naval and military defence. None of the Dominions was willing to concede to Britain the complete decision making and control of armed forces that British politicians, especially Winston Churchill, seemed to expect. But S. M. Bruce of Australia and W. F. Massey of New Zealand did want a collective foreign policy formed by consultation, and coordination of the various navies. From reading the documents one can only draw the conclusion that King and Skelton, with those who thought like them, were completely successful: King had all his reservations, and even language, put into conference statements. The British had preserved the facade of an Empire, but its spirit was dead. This was illustrated in 1925 when the Treaty of Locarno specifically excluded the Dominions unless they chose to adhere to it.

The 1926 imperial conference was called in part to discuss Dominion adherence to the Locarno Treaty, but largely to try to define the new relations which Dominion separatism was forcing on the British. Mackenzie King again represented Canada, but this time the South African representative was—to British eyes—even worse. General Hertzog was a Boer nationalist, who demanded that the constitution of the Empire should be formally redefined or, he threatened, he would go back to South Africa to begin agitation to secede from the Empire. The British for their part adopted a policy which they later applied to the Axis powers—appeasement, combined with a search for a form of words which hid the results of that policy.

This reached its climax in the Inter-Imperial Relations Committee Report—the 'Balfour Report'—which papered over the cracks with a skill unusual even for Balfour, who has been described as producing 'beautifully phrased but intrinsically meaningless pronouncements'.[5] On this occasion he defined the Dominions in glowing, but ambiguous, terms: 'They are autonomous communities within the British Empire, equal in status, in no way subordinate one to another in any aspect of their domestic or external affairs, though united by a common allegiance to the Crown, and freely associated as members of the British Commonwealth of Nations.' This, of course, was deliberately vague. As an American observer soon afterwards put it, 'The Crown was like a sacred mystery for which British statesmanship was kept busy devising Athanasian creeds . . .' A recent historian comments that it could only be understood in the light of the 'political romanticism' of the era which produced the Locarno Pact.[6] More pungently, the Australian Billy Hughes, too old and too much a realist to be taken in by Balfour's verbiage, described his report as a 'wonderful document'.

> It took stock of everything. Nothing escaped it . . . Every prime minister went away perfectly satisfied—Mr. Bruce because it altered nothing that affected Australia, Mr. Mackenzie King because it taught Lord Byng [the Canadian Governor-General, with whom he had been involved in a constitutional crisis] where to get off, and General Hertzog because he was able to assure the burghers that the King of England was no longer the King of South Africa, although it was true that the King of South Africa was also King of England.[7]

It was not surprising, therefore, that the 1926 imperial conference marked another defeat for the idea of a coordinated Empire/Commonwealth. The Dominions did not adhere to the Locarno Treaty and the discussions on foreign policy 'amounted to no more than the familiar cant about improving liaison between England and the Dominions'.[8] Despite grave warnings by the service chiefs about British Imperial military weakness, no decisions could be made on defence matters, because of obstructionism from Canada, South Africa and Ireland. The published proceedings were full of platitudes and included no concrete decisions, except that the new definition of 'dominion status' would be incorporated into a statute.

The British continued to hide the truth with words: 'Yet all such optimistic glosses to the effect that the Commonwealth was "developing" rather than disintegrating were like claiming that at the very moment when the emperor in the fable removed his pants and finally stripped himself bare, he had really finished donning fresh raiment of miraculous beauty and utility.' Hughes remained unconvinced, and Hertzog, back in South Africa, proudly proclaimed that the old British Empire no longer existed. The defeat by Britain in the Boer War was reversed. It is difficult to avoid the conclusion that Hertzog and Hughes were right, and that 'the Commonwealth had now become just a sentimental association of sovereign states under one Crown, somewhat akin to the old Holy Roman Empire'.

'Imperial foreign policy' and 'consultation'
Like that Empire, however, the Commonwealth had alongside it countries some of which were indifferent to it and some of which were hostile. It therefore had to create a foreign and defence policy. Whether it could do so before it came under serious attack remained to be seen. It is in this sense that aggression in the East provided the

'writing on the wall'—a warning that there were dangers to be faced and that the Empire/Commonwealth was militarily weak and politically disorganised.

British leaders, however, customarily viewed the world with a woolly optimism and a fine phraseology. Perhaps, as Corelli Barnett suggests, this was the result of their predominantly classical public-school education, combined with the non-conformist religion and idealistic liberalism that was widespread in the country.[9] Those were not attitudes of mind that encouraged the hard-headed realism necessary to meet the dangers of the 1930s, or even to admit that there were dangers to be faced. For example, Balfour had opened the meetings of his Committee with a statement of his vision of the Empire and Commonwealth, ending with the remark that 'the very existence of this complex community makes for the maintenance of world peace . . . '. The Eastern crises, however, revealed that not only was the Empire *not* a force to maintain world peace, it could not even defend its own interests when threatened.

Another, and more important, assumption of Balfour's was revealed when he said that Britain had to remain the decider of foreign policy, not only while the distribution of population in the Empire remained the same, but also 'so long as the centre of difficulty is Europe'. The Manchurian crisis showed that there were 'centres of difficulty' outside Europe, made more serious because the British Empire was worldwide. As Gallagher has written, 'It is characteristic of any power which works a world system that it cannot isolate any one situation and decide it on its own individual merits. Every possible solution squeezes the trigger of another problem. Every strategic case modulates into another'. In fact the Empire/Commonwealth was, in the words of a Foreign Office man, 'a huge giant sprawling all over the globe, with gouty fingers and toes stretching in every direction, which cannot be approached without eliciting a scream'.

British politicians, however, remained Europe-oriented, and placed greater weight on events there than on other, to them, more remote parts of the world. This was only natural and was increased by the rise of Nazism in Germany, but it uncovered a flaw in the British assumption that there was a community of interest between Britain and the different Dominions.

This should have been realised. Hughes, as early as 1921, had wanted a separate representation for Australia at the Washington Conference. 'Pacific problems raise two questions both vital to us— White Australia and the safety of Australia—on which Britain cannot speak for us . . . '.[10] In Balfour's own committee in 1926 the Canadian, E. Lapointe, remarked, apropos of the Locarno Treaty, that Europe was not an area of 'primary concern' to Canada.

Accordingly, the Balfour Report made the famous statement: 'We felt that the governing consideration underlying all discussions of this problem [i.e. defence and foreign policy] must be that neither Great Britain nor the Dominions could be committed to the acceptance of active obligations except with the definite assent of their own governments.' This provided an escape clause for those Dominions who wished to use it. Henceforth, the only policy the British could pursue, if they wished to keep a united Empire behind them, was one of inaction and compromise.

Moreover, the statement implied that while Britain would remain the leader in imperial foreign policy, she would do so in consultation with the Dominions. Balfour noted this when he said: 'The principles determining the general direction of Foreign Affairs may be, and ought to be, the product of consultation; and it will be among our chief duties to make that consultation more continuous and more effective.' After mentioning, as a reservation, the demand for rapid action at times of crisis—which was to provide a perennial British excuse for failure to consult the Dominions—Balfour again returned to the need to improve the machinery of consultation, expressing the hope that improvements in technology would enable them 'to overcome more effectively the obstacles presented by Time and Space'.

In this, for once, Balfour was being realistic. The only way the Dominion Prime Ministers could personally meet one another was by long sea voyages. Meetings at short notice to deal with crises were therefore impossible. On the other hand telegrams were impersonal and radio-telegraphy was in its infancy. Those who stressed Commonwealth unity and the need for consultation therefore had to face the twin facts of the geographical dispersion of the Dominions and an inadequate communications technology. The only possible solution would seem to have been the development of air transport; but the British did surprisingly little to foster the development of civil aviation. British aircraft in the 1920s and 1930s were backward in design and construction, except in adventurous record-breaking attempts. They had nothing to compare with the German and American aviation industries. With their scattered Empire, the route mileage of their passenger planes in 1930 was not much greater than the landlocked and centralised Germany, and the number of passengers they carried was fewer. They failed to exploit the potential of air travel to bring the Empire together.[11]

Nor did the British face the problems inherent in the concept of 'consultation' between the component parts of such an empire. To begin with, the flow of information was all-important, to enable sound decisions to be made; yet, coming from the metropolitan centre, it was bound to reflect the preconceptions and interests of Britain herself. Moreover, many members of the Commonwealth had reservations about the need to discuss policy before any action—or even its desirability. Dominion politicians in Canada, South Africa and Ireland, for example, did not want effective consultation because that meant that they committed themselves to joint action and some sort of central decision-making body in the Commonwealth. They were not alone. Many British politicians and civil servants thought that the Dominions were something of a nuisance. They tended to refer to them in their debates and struggles for power, but they really regarded the interests and opinions of the Dominions as secondary. This was to be revealed later when the British government overrode New Zealand objections to their recognition of Italian sovereignty over Abyssinia.[12]

It was, therefore, hardly surprising that the Balfour Committee failed to come to any conclusion as to how 'the machinery of imperial consultation' could be improved. Lord Milner's idea that the Dominions should appoint a 'resident minister' in London had no hope of being generally accepted, and neither had the suggestion of the Australian representative, Bruce, that the Dominion High Commissioners should have the status of ambassadors in London and that consultation and communication should take place through them. He was opposed by all the British delegates, largely on the grounds that it would have made extra work for the Foreign Secretary. A cynic might have suspected that their real reason was that the High Commissioners were embarrassingly available in London, and therefore might have actually had to be consulted. There were other problems with the suggestion, however. J. G. Coates, the Prime Minister of New Zealand, opposed the idea. He seems to have feared that the High Commissioners would become divorced from their governments at home, and he therefore favoured instead the appointment of officials from each Dominion to the British Cabinet Secretariat, and for Foreign Office officials to be appointed to the personal staff of each Dominion Prime Minister. That too must have looked dangerous to many representatives, not least the British. All that was finally agreed was that the old system of sending information to the Dominion governments by the Governors-General was no longer satisfactory and that new channels of communication should be opened.

British reservations can be seen in Balfour's language. He talked about consultation over 'the general direction of foreign affairs', not actual policy in a given crisis. It is not therefore surprising that, for all its fine words, the British government did not show itself in fact very much better at consulting the Dominions after the Balfour Report than it had been before it. It was still liable to make sudden decisions for reasons of its own and then simply inform the Dominions afterwards. An example of this was soon provided.

Less than three years after the Balfour Declaration, in July 1929, the High Commissioners of Australia and New Zealand expressed in the Committee of Imperial Defence the anxiety of their governments that the British intended to cut back on Far Eastern defences, especially the promised base at Singapore. The British Prime Minister, Ramsay MacDonald, assured them that work on the graving dock would continue. Nevertheless, on 13 November—three and a half months later—the First Lord of the Admiralty rose in the House of Commons and announced that although work which had already been contracted for would continue, it would do so at a slower pace, and that where possible it would be stopped altogether until the results of the London naval conference of 1930 were known. This decision, which was a change in the spirit, if not the letter, of MacDonald's promise, was publicly announced without any prior consultation with New Zealand or Australia. As a New Zealand historian remarks, 'Notification of the decision the evening before it was made public did not appear the 'equivalent of consultation . . .'. She adds that 'a somewhat half-hearted apology was received from the British Government along with the further assurance that the slowing down would not effect the completion of the graving dock'.[13] This was typical—both the last-minute information that a change of policy was in the wind and the attempt to play down the importance of that change. The only excuse that MacDonald did not use was the assertion that there was some mystic need for a rapid decision. None of this augured well for the Commonwealth during a crisis.

For the time being, however, the developments set in train by the 1926 conference and the Balfour Report continued. The Dominions Office was not very impressed by Balfour's famous definition, and as late as January 1930 remarked: 'So far as is known, no authoritative definition of "Dominion Status" has ever been laid down.' Strictly speaking, this was correct, and the Statute of Westminster, when it finally saw the light of day, simply listed the Dominions as Australia, New Zealand, South Africa, the Irish Free State, Canada and Newfoundland. This avoidance of the problem was noted by the Dominions Office, which remarked in June 1932 that there was still no statutory definition of the term 'Dominion'.[14] It then plunged into extremely complex theorising about the relation of the Dominions to the United Kingdom and the United Kingdom to the Dominions. It is clear that in embarking on the concept of a 'Commonwealth' the British government had committed itself to complex questions of terminology, constitutional theory and diplomatic practice. The debate raged between the Dominions and Britain, and the various government departments in Whitehall, throughout the period. In 1934, indeed, George V objected to the words 'British Commonwealth' in the draft of a speech, and they were replaced by 'the countries of the British Empire'.[15] This attitude of the King was clearly behind the absence of the word 'Commonwealth' in his speech to his peoples on his Silver Jubilee, already noted.

If constitutional theory, and the terminology which expressed it, proved troublesome, so too did the creation of an imperial foreign policy. This was revealed in the 1930 imperial conference. By the time that met, the depression was preoccupying Commonwealth statesmen, so the meetings were taken up with a long debate on economic matters. Defence was completely neglected, but the representatives did get down to discussing the problem of communication and consultation within the Commonwealth. They were concerned that in treaty relations between Dominions and other nations full information should be circulated, and repeated Balfour's phrase that none of the Commonwealth governments could involve the others in active obligations without their definite assent.[16] This was probably the reason why the Dominions got more information from, and were consulted more closely by, Britain over the disarmament conference, which, if successful, would have ultimately led to some form of treaty involving obligations, than they ever did over the Manchurian crisis.

The machinery of consultation
The 1930 conference, however, did not get down to the wider problem of consultation within the Commonwealth. This problem was twofold: providing the Dominions with adequate detailed information on which they could base their judgments; and discussing with them suitable policies that reflected that information. All too often British spokesmen confused the two processes.

The method by which information was supplied to the Dominions was comparatively easy to improve, as it involved neither Britain nor the Dominions in prior commitments. A new and more effective system was therefore soon established. As early as July 1925 Leopold Amery had managed to get the Colonial Office divided into two departments, one dealing with the colonies and the other with the Dominions, although they remained under the one head.[17] With the advent of the 1930 imperial conference and the ageing of the then Secretary of State for Dominions and Colonies, Lord Passfield, the time seemed ripe to separate the two departments, and a new Secretaryship of State for Dominion Affairs was created. This handled the flow of information in London. In the Dominions, by 1931, the Governors-General had ceased to act as representatives of the British government and instead only represented the King. Therefore communications no longer went through them (except in the case of New Zealand, which obstinately clung to outdated methods) but directly from government to government. Telegrams and cables went to the Dominion Prime Ministers from London, usually via the Dominions Office. There were also the 'D' Prints, circulated to the Dominion Prime Ministers (except New Zealand, where again they went to the Governor-General) and the Dominion High Commissioners in London, keeping them informed on foreign affairs. Sometimes the Foreign Office reprinted the despatches it received from its embassies abroad, when it thought those despatches would be of interest to the Dominions. British embassies in Washington and Tokyo and the legation at Peking sent copies of some of their more important despatches direct to Australia. This had been requested by the Australians at the 1930 imperial conference, but the British government had not referred to it in the report, since it did not want such a procedure to become the general rule. Moreover, the Dominions had High Commissioners—and Australia had a liaison officer—in London, and these men had meetings, both official and social, with British ministers and officials. In addition, selected Dominion representatives were occasionally invited to attend meetings of the Committee of Imperial Defence (the CID), and of course at intervals the Dominion Premiers met the British government formally at imperial conferences.[18]

All this seemed most impressive, and a writer in 1934 spoke of 'constant communications with regard to the latest developments' and despatches sent 'by every mail'. He added: 'Thus a Prime Minister of a Dominion receives as much official documentary information on the foreign affairs of the United Kingdom as do some or all of the members of the British Cabinet.'[19]

This was simply not true, as we shall see later. Moreover, if the British government had really sent all the information at its disposal to the Dominions, it still could not, by its very nature, have been sufficient for the diverse needs of those separate countries. Adequate information on world affairs relevant to the Dominions could really only be provided by separate diplomatic services of their own. The moves in that direction, as could have been expected, came from those Dominions which had led the demand for independence from an imperial foreign policy. The Canadians had won the right to appoint a Canadian representative to Washington, seeing the importance of the United States to them, in 1920, but did not do so till 1926. They also appointed Canadian ministers to Japan and France. The Irish Free State had appointed a representative to the United States in 1924, and thereafter to France, Germany, Belgium, the Vatican and the League headquarters in Geneva. The South African government had representatives in the United States, Holland, Italy, Portugal and Geneva. The Pacific Dominions of Australia and New Zealand, however, did not follow suit. They felt more loyalty to

Britain, had a more acute sense of danger to themselves and so felt more dependent on Britain for defence.

Nor did the British quickly establish their own High Commissioners in the Dominions. Politicians feared delegating their powers, and it took the appointment of an American ambassador to Canada in 1928 to trigger the process. In that year, therefore, High Commissioners were appointed to Canada and South Africa, a 'British Migration Commissioner' to Australia—he became 'British Government Representative' in 1931—and a 'United Kingdom Liaison Officer' in New Zealand. This result came from the separatism of some Dominions and the conservatism of others and, in Britain, a struggle for influence between Amery and Neville Chamberlain which involved the Foreign and Dominions Offices and may have soured relations between those bodies in the years ahead. Moreover, the British intention behind the creation of the new posts was not just to link the various Cabinets of the Dominions, but also to spread 'discreet propaganda' and control the Commonwealth-wide press and imperial communications system. Garner comments that the British government 'did not sufficiently recognise the independence of the Dominions or the need for an effort on their part to ensure cooperation; the Dominions were regarded as subordinate and expected to conform to British views'.[20]

The word 'consultation' indeed involves more than the supply—let alone the control—of information; it also implies discussion between the various parties, *before* decisions are made. The observer of 1934 had remarked that consultation was a much more difficult problem, and that 'the procedure at present is not systematised but is elastic; at any given juncture consultation is effected at the time and by the method which appears to be most convenient'.[21] In other words, there was no *system* of consultation, as distinct from the supply of information, and without a system it was all too easy for the British government to avoid consulting the Dominions at all, as happened over the Singapore base. There was some talk of using annual attendance of Dominion representatives at the League Assembly as the basis of consultation. But even though this would have provided a venue for regular meetings, it would not have overcome the separatism of South Africa, Canada or Ireland.

If the governments of Britain and the Dominions had seriously desired to consult with one another, they would have had to reorganise their governmental bureaucratic systems with consultation in mind. Apart from Canada, whose government was motivated by separatism rather than a desire for consultation, the Dominions did not improve their departments of government which dealt with foreign affairs. Even the British move may have been the result of ulterior motives. One historian argues that Amery wanted to set up a new power base for himself, to balance the Treasury and the Foreign Office.[22] In other words, the creation of the Dominions Office was part of the internal power struggle, not concern for the Dominions as such.

Indeed, the action of the British government did not suggest that it was altogether serious in its desire for consultation. The newly formed Dominions Office was, by Foreign Office standards, a tiny department. In 1931 the politicians in charge of it were the Secretary of State for Dominion Affairs, J. H. Thomas, and the parliamentary under-secretary, Malcolm MacDonald. Under them were the permanent civil servants: the permanent under-secretary, Sir Edward Harding; one assistant under-secretary; three assistant secretaries; four principals; four assistant principals and eighteen clerical staff. In all there were only 31 persons—who were expected, among other things, to run Newfoundland.[23] This tiny department was not likely to carry much weight with either the politicians in the Cabinet or with the other civil servants in Whitehall.

If the British government had really been concerned to create the machinery of consultation, it would have given much thought to this office and put an able administrator with wide experience in charge of it. Instead, when it finally appointed a separate Secretary of State for Dominion Affairs it did so not from concern for the Commonwealth but for internal political reasons. It emasculated the new Dominions Office from the start by appointing Thomas.

Thomas was the only member of the Cabinet who came from what was then regarded in Britain as the 'working class'. Even MacDonald was a middle-class intellectual. Thomas, on the other hand, had been a locomotive fireman, and he was later in the habit of saying that the finest food he had ever tasted were bits of bacon fried on the shovel in the locomotive fire. He had become the general secretary of the National Union of Railwaymen, and from that position passed to parliament. A vulgar man, Thomas displayed an appalling lack of tact on public occasions, such as—according to one historian—'telling Rabelaisian stories to prim Catholic ladies'.[24] Nevertheless, his practical experience and self-confidence carried him through situations where his lack of formal education would appear to have been a handicap.

It was the advent of an inexperienced Labour Party to power that gave such a man his chance in politics. Tipped for the foreign secretaryship in the second MacDonald government, he was sidetracked into the Employment Department as Lord Privy Seal. There he boasted that he would remove unemployment from the country—an unfortunate statement just before the onset of a major depression. As the number of unemployed rose, Thomas came under pressure. In 1929 he made a dramatic bid to get Canada to take more British workers and manufactured goods, but failed dismally. Sixty MPs called for his dismissal; Thomas's self-confidence collapsed; he began to drink more heavily and his mastery of detail deteriorated. The problem for MacDonald's government was to relieve him without insult. The creation of the Dominions Office seemed to be the answer, for Thomas had been Secretary of State for the Colonies in MacDonald's first government in 1924, his eldest son had emigrated to Canada, and Thomas and his wife had visited that Dominion. He had also visited South Africa as head of the British delegation to the Empire Parliamentary Association in 1924. He was therefore made Dominions secretary, and the Dominions Office got its first Secretary of State separate from the Colonial Office.

It was not, however, a happy choice. Thomas had neither the intelligence, education nor temperament to deal with the self-governing Dominions. His attitude to them was wrong, to start with. He had no sympathy for their desire for independence or any realisation that they had separate interests. His raw British working-class patriotism probably jarred on them. For example, his opening remark to his staff on being made Secretary of State for the Colonies in 1924 had been 'I've been sent here to see that there's no mucking about with the British Empire'. By 1930, he probably also resented the refusal of the Canadians to support him when he faced his crisis in 1929. As time went by, therefore, his clashes with the representatives of that Dominion, as well as others, became notorious. At the 1930 conference he described the Canadian proposals as 'umbug', got drunk at an ensuing luncheon and thanked God that the New Zealand Prime Minister was soon leaving the country. The Canadian Premier issued a statement about 'language that is deeply resented by the Canadian government' and Thomas had to eat humble pie.[25]

The trouble was also, however, Thomas' method of working. It was here that his lack of formal education became a handicap. As a trade union leader he had been fond of the relaxed man-to-man approach. This worked well enough with people in Britain, whom he could meet man to man. But it did not work for a complex and diverse organisation such as the Empire/Commonwealth, scattered as it was over the globe. Thomas, moreover, was quite incapable of 'consultation': what he knew was 'bargaining'. If the Dominions wanted to discuss import quotas for their products into Britain, they would suggest a tonnage, Thomas would sneer at it and suggest a smaller figure, and a compromise would finally be worked out. But 'consultation'—discussing the world situation from the viewpoint of a Dominion—required a wide reading and study of the problem, and that was beyond him. He read little; very often he did not even read the despatches and telegrams of the Dominions Office. Instead he often called for his assistant and had him report the gist of the cables.[26]

At first sight it appears strange that such a man should have been kept in office by the conservative-dominated National government. After all, most of its members were public school educated and admired the urbane and cultivated personality. Thomas, however, was one of the few Labour men to follow MacDonald into the government. His loyalty had to be rewarded; and he would appear as a token that the government was concerned with the working classes. Moreover, he was liked by George V and also seems to have acquired some business friends in the city. The National government, therefore, felt it could afford to leave him in charge of the Dominions Office, where he could do little harm.[27]

In fact, by 1931 Thomas, like MacDonald, was in decline. He had lost his old grip on detail, and his flexibility. He still arrived in his office each day at 9 am, but paperwork irked him, and he left most of it to his private secretary, Eddie Marsh, who could draft a letter in typical Thomas phraseology, and put an undetectable imitation of his initials on state papers. The Dominions Office, indeed, had a rubber stamp of Thomas' signature, which they used on occasion. Thomas himself, after fixing his bets for the day, spent most of his time on ordinary political work for the Cabinet and on trade union matters. He was also much concerned with the Manchurian crisis, as we shall see. Of the nineteen Cabinet papers which had Thomas' name attached to them in 1932, two were on disarmament, one on the New Hebrides and fifteen on Ireland. Only one was on the other Dominions. He obviously did not devote much time to them and equally obviously was preoccupied with Ireland. (He was not the man to help matters in that quarter either, since the clash of personalities that occurred between de Valera and Thomas was—seeing the nature of the men and the political aims of each—almost inevitable. Thomas sat on the Irish Situation Committee in 1932, and in March and April of that year it is reported that there was 'an acrimonious exchange of correspondence between de Valera and J. H. Thomas.') Nor did he improve his ways in dealing with the other Dominions. His description of an incident at the Ottawa conference was typical: 'After we'd got all the bloody Dominions to initial their bloody agreements, in marched Bennett [the Canadian Prime Minister] with the whole of his Cabinet and raised some point about his bloody Dominion [etc., etc.].'

If the calibre of the man whom the British government thought fit to control its dealings with the Dominions is anything to go by, that government did not rate the Dominions or their interests very highly. What the new 'Commonwealth' desperately needed was a man at the centre of the information-supplying and consultative process with wide vision, education, experience and drive, together with some subtlety in handling men of different backgrounds, outlooks and interests. Instead, the British government seemed to regard the Dominions Office as a rubbish bin for failed politicians. It was not surprising, therefore, that from the first the Dominions Office had the stigma of being a minor government department, dealing with peripheral matters. It was not a major step in a politician's career, in the way that the Foreign Office and the Treasury were, so able and ambitious politicians steered clear of it. This had serious results, for, as Garner has written, 'in the major decisions, the D. O. could only be effective if the Minister carried weight in the Cabinet and was included in the inner circle of the decision makers'. In fact, this was rarely the case, and the DO was only in close touch with the PM's office during the Second World War. The office 'never developed the political muscle to affect British policy-making generally, as Amery had intended in 1925 . . . '.[28]

A similar criticism can be made of Dominions Office staff. If Garner is to be believed, the Foreign Office was then recruited exclusively from upper-class Etonians, whereas the men of the Dominions Office were usually from the middle classes, with the result that the Foreign Office used to treat the Dominions Office—and by inference the Dominions—with a certain amount of contempt. Moreover, it appears that the intellectual calibre of some of the civil servants of the Dominions Office did not compare with those of other departments.[29] A complete change seems to have occurred after November 1935, with the appointment of Malcolm MacDonald as Secretary of State for Dominion Affairs. But that is beyond the scope of this book.

During the Manchurian crisis the men of the Dominions Office regarded themselves as a 'post office', passing messages back and forth between the Dominions and the British government, and occasionally chivvying that government to remember the Dominions. Moreover, as Garner has written, 'the first charge on the D. O. . . . was to further the interests of Britain; the D. O. was not the representative of the Dominions. Its aim was *to secure the cooperation of the Dominions where necessary in carrying out British policies*' (emphasis added). Such an attitude would, to some extent, weaken the other functions—those of coordinating policies and transmitting ideas between the different members—of the DO. It was too one-sided. In so far as it *did* try to promote Dominion interests, the DO was weak in its dealings with the more prestigious Foreign Office. This

> . . . was probably the result of their lack of influence in F. O. circles. The poor quality of the records which they kept was probably a reflection of

their habits of work—informal, but concerned to uphold the constitutional proprieties between Dominion governments and Whitehall. They could not be seen to put words in the mouths of Dominion governments. And since the Dominion governments were uncertain about the D. O.'s functions, a vacuum was often created.[30]

This was not filled by the Foreign Office, which scrupulously left Dominion matters—except treaty ones—alone when it could. The Foreign Office seems to have harboured a certain amount of suspicion of the Dominions and resentment against their independence in foreign affairs. For example, in 1934 a meeting in the Dominions Office with the High Commissioners decided to sound out Argentina on meat quotas. This raised a veritable storm in the Foreign Office, with seven foolscap pages of memoranda fulminating over the iniquity of the Dominions Office, the Ministry of Agriculture and the Board of Trade. In the course of this it was reported that Bruce had replied to a reproach over the telephone, 'To hell with the Foreign Office'—a remark which gave great offence. Lord Stanhope, the Parliamentary Under-Secretary of State for Foreign Affairs, after considering whether to reprimand Bruce, wrote: 'It is both intolerable and impossible that our relations with foreign powers—which are more vital to our existence than a none too satisfactory Empire—should be taken out of our hands by departments whose judgements in these matters is often very faulty.'[31] The whole incident revealed not only a distrust of the Dominions Office but also a lack of sympathy, to say the least, with the new idea of a 'Commonwealth'. This did not stop members of the Foreign Office from being incensed when they were accused of failing to consult the Dominions. In January 1931, for example, A. W. A. Leeper, a second secretary, at a meeting of the Royal Institute of International Affairs, of which he was a member, took strong exception to criticism from the Canadian politician and lawyer Newton Rowell. In an outburst of irritation he asserted that the British government provided the Dominions 'with regular and full information on all matters of any conceivable interest to them, . . . without, I feared, receiving very much from them in return'.[32]

British representatives, then, were touchy about consultation, and given on occasion to making sneering references to the Dominions. The reason seems to have been that each side looked on the Empire as a source of protection and strength for itself. The British had memories of Dominion and colonial troops aiding them during the Great War. They regarded the Commonwealth as 'their' empire, and looked for 'loyalty' and 'support' from the Dominions. They were apt to resent any failures in this regard. Those Dominions who relied on the British fleet for their security, Australia and New Zealand, talked in terms of an 'imperial foreign policy'—yet did not look on that as something to which they had to contribute by military and economic aid, but as a protection provided by Britain. Both sides regarded the Empire as a sort of bank of withdrawal, from which they could draw 'security' without the necessity of making any payments into the account. The other Dominions, however, did not want consultation at all, because they were determined to foster their own independence and feared that talk of an 'imperial foreign policy' was a threat to it. Newton Rowell's criticism—as others from Canada later—were unfair, since it was largely because of Canadian obstruction that the system of consultation had not been improved. On the other hand no part of the Commonwealth was completely free from these forms of double-thinking.

Canada: Skelton, King and External Affairs
As for the Dominions themselves, the development of bureaucratic machinery for dealing with foreign policy, either 'imperial' or their own, was very uneven. Only Canada, of the three considered by this book, had by 1930 developed an effective department to deal with foreign affairs. This had been established in June 1909, and although it had been joined with the Prime Minister's Office in 1912 it at least had a rudimentary bureaucratic machine and personnel whose sole concern was with foreign policy. There was a permanent under-secretary of state, an assistant under-secretary, a counsellor, a legal advisor, a High Commissioner in London (first appointed in 1880) and ministers appointed to Washington, Paris and Tokyo. There was also a Canadian advisory officer at the League Headquarters in Geneva.[33]

The permanent civil servant in charge of this was O. D. Skelton, mentioned earlier. Under-Secretary of State for External Affairs from 1925 to 1941, Skelton's contribution to Canadian and Commonwealth history was monumental.[34] Educated at Queen's University, he had developed an interest in political science and economics and had been invited to lecture to his old university in those subjects. He wrote prolifically, and his 'endless stream of strongly nationalist books and articles established him as the leading Liberal intellectual of the day'. He wrote no books after 1921, however. He spent 1922 in Europe, but before going had spoken on 'Canada and Foreign Policy' at the Canadian Club in Ottawa, where Mackenzie King had heard him, and wrote in his diary that the address 'would make an excellent foundation for Canadian policy on External Affairs, and Skelton himself would make an excellent man for that department'.

When Skelton had joined the Department of External Affairs in 1925 it had had only three officers and he had begun a vigorous recruitment program. He decided to model the department, if possible, on the lines of the British Foreign Office. He looked for 'well-educated generalists' with university degrees in law, history, economics and political science. Indeed, between 1922 and 1944 30.5 per cent of recruits to the department had doctorates. 'Skelton thus surrounded himself with his own kind.' However, he wanted the department to be independent and professional. He was baulked of complete success by the fact that the Prime Minister remained as Secretary of State for External Affairs. As a result, there was still a tendency for the PM's Department and External Affairs to be confused, and for the department's routine and decisions to be affected by the Prime Minister's ideas and by political expediency. For example, it was difficult to persuade the Prime Ministers of the need to appoint new legations, so that by 1939 Canada still only had the three with which it started the decade.

There were weaknesses, moreover, in the position Skelton had attained. To start with, he was perhaps a little too dominant within the Department, tending not to pass on to the Prime Minister of the day anything with which he disagreed, and since he held strong views on foreign policy that left little chance for contrary opinions to be aired. This was made worse because Skelton also did much of the work now done by the secretary to the Cabinet, as well as being the Prime Minister's general deputy and advisor. Finally, Skelton had won his reforms by involving himself in politics, being closely identified with the Liberal Party and especially Mackenzie King. Indeed, his views on internal and external policy were almost identical with those of King, and this nearly proved his undoing when the new Prime Minister, R. B. Bennett, came to office. Despite these weaknesses, however, Skelton did provide a forceful head with independent ideas for the small diplomatic service that Canada was building up. He used the Canadian legations and representatives abroad as a means of gaining information on the world and making judgments on the necessary Canadian foreign policy. In 1934 he was to cable the Canadian Legation in Tokyo: 'As we do not wish to be dependent on the Foreign Office and press for our information on vital developments at Tokyo, please keep the Department advised of any important developments by cable.'[35] With its representatives abroad, the Canadian government should, in theory, have been in a better position than the other Dominions. Yet the matter was not quite as simple as this, as an investigation of the legation in Tokyo will reveal.

That legation was under the control of a minister, and had two first secretaries, a second secretary, a private secretary, three stenographers, two Japanese translators, and two Japanese office boys. The office had a tendency to send despatches by sea, which led to delays. For example, the one on the Mukden incident—which triggered the Manchurian Crisis in 1931—took thirteen days to reach Ottawa.

Some indeed took 22 days, if the sailing times for the boats were not right. It was such a delay which later led Skelton to demand that urgent matters be cabled. However, the External Affairs Department received quite regular cables from the Dominions Office in London. In the Canadian archives there are telegrams sent on 22 and 24 September, and four in October, three in November and six in December 1931.[36] Indeed, Skelton in his complaint to the Tokyo Legation used as an example of a good cable one sent by the Dominions Office. He retracted somewhat, however, when the awaited despatch eventually arrived from Tokyo, since it proved to contain much useful information. It would seem that the reports the Canadian government received from its legation in Tokyo were slower in arriving than Dominions Office cables, but were more full and gave more background information.

Both Dominions Office cables and reports from the Canadian legations and trade commissioners abroad were supplemented, however, by information, propaganda and requests coming from a variety of other sources. During the Manchurian crisis, for example, there were eminent Canadians giving their opinion, such as H. H. Stevens, Minister of Trade and Commerce, who supported the Chinese, and Newton Rowell, who advocated sanctions against Japan. The French ambassador in Canada sent a copy of the French complaint to both China and Japan under the terms of the Kellogg Pact, while the Japanese case was forwarded, at their request, by the Secretary-General of the League.[37] But the main source of information was undoubtedly the Dominions Office and the Canadian Tokyo Legation.

New Zealand: loyalty to Britain and fear of Japan

The attitude of the government of New Zealand was totally different from that of Canada. At the 1930 conference the New Zealand Prime Minister, G. W. Forbes, remarked that his government did not desire change and was quite happy with constitutional development as it was.[38] He has been castigated for this by New Zealand historians, but he was merely continuing the tradition of New Zealand Premiers. In 1922, for example, a hastily summoned Cabinet had endorsed the British action over Chanak in three minutes, and did not think it necessary to call together the New Zealand parliament. Indeed, in 1923 Sir Francis Bell, a New Zealand elder statesman, told that parliament that the standard response of the New Zealand government to a British question was 'New Zealand is content to be bound by the determination of His Majesty's Government in London'.

This loyalty to Britain, and dependence on her judgment, was partly a matter of sentiment. New Zealand's tiny population was at least 98 per cent British, without any powerful minority groups who hated British rule, such as the French Canadians in Canada or the Boers in South Africa—or even, to a lesser extent, the Irish in Australia. Nearly all New Zealanders spoke of Britain as 'home'; their education was British-centered, and most had relations in the UK. As Amery had told the British Cabinet in 1928, 'imperial sentiment . . . in New Zealand . . . is a passion, almost a religion. Alone of the Dominions, New Zealand is much more interested in her Imperial, than in her national, status'.[39]

This picture may be deceptive, however. In supporting 'imperialism' to that extent, in insisting on being a dutiful daughter of the mother country, and in their fervent British patriotism, the New Zealand governments were also following their country's interests. For New Zealand was economically dependent on Britain, being little more than 'Britain's overseas farm'. In 1930 Britain took 80 per cent of New Zealand's total exports in value. She took over 90 per cent of New Zealand's dairy products and 99 per cent of her lamb and mutton. Britain's capital investment in the country was of a similar scale and New Zealand government debts in Britain totalled nearly £174 million. Moreover, New Zealand, remote in the Pacific, was dependent on British naval power for her defence.

Forbes' obstructionism at the 1930 imperial conference in the discussions on constitutional change, therefore, was typical of New Zealand attitudes and traditions. That the New Zealanders were capable of making forceful representations on points that they felt important to them had been shown in the past over matters of economic concern and immigration. In 1930, as we shall see, Forbes' strongest representations were provoked by matters of defence and the Singapore base. That base, indeed, was the focus of New Zealand discussions on defence from its first proposal in 1921 to the outbreak of war in the Pacific twenty years later. The importance the New Zealand government attached to naval matters was illustrated by Lord Jellicoe's tenure of office as Governor-General; and by its offer of £200 000 towards the Singapore base in 1923, which it raised to £1 million in 1927. This was backed up by the vigorous New Zealand protests in 1924 and 1930 when the MacDonald governments talked of ending or slowing down the construction of the base. The CID, indeed, had long stressed the dependence of New Zealand on a British fleet and the naval base at Singapore. In March 1931 it remarked that the power most capable of damaging imperial interests in the Pacific was Japan, but continued:

> Provided that the British fleet arrives in time, and finds a properly equipped base at Singapore, New Zealand has nothing to fear beyond

sporadic attack. If, for any reason, the main fleet is unable to reach Singapore, or if the base is captured or seriously damaged . . . before its arrival, then New Zealand interests become exposed to attack on a considerable scale.[40]

'Self-interest as much as loyalty', therefore, underlay the disparagement by New Zealand leaders of the demands by other Dominions for the formal definition of their status within the Imperial framework'.

For behind its quest for security lay fear of Japan, which had begun in New Zealand after the Russo–Japanese war. This had led in 1913 to the Naval Defence Act, which authorised a New Zealand division of the Royal Navy to be controlled by New Zealand in peacetime and handed over to the Admiralty in war. The New Zealand Prime Minister, Massey, had made it clear that it was Japan that New Zealand feared.[41] The Japanese seizure of German islands in the Pacific during the First World War led to even deeper suspicions, and at the peace conference in 1919 Massey supported Hughes against Japan and demanded that New Zealand be allowed to annex Samoa. Like Hughes, he had to be content with the 'C' class mandate.

Fear of Japan was also revealed after the First World War by the anxious New Zealand questioning of British defence cuts, by the insistence on the importance of the Singapore base, and possibly too by the appointment of Sir Thomas Wilford as New Zealand High Commissioner in London in 1930. Wilford was a well-educated solicitor, with a long parliamentary career behind him. He had changed the name 'Liberal' to 'United Party' in 1929, and had become Minister for Defence and Justice in that government. He was a forceful character, with ideas of his own, who had publicly expressed concern at the Japanese threat to New Zealand, even publishing a book on the subject in 1928. His periodic suggestions that the Japanese were acquiring land overlooking the Singapore base led to an investigation by the CID. He had shown dislike for the Japanese delegation at the London naval conference, and had spoken in support of the Admiralty's position, against the British politicians. His appointment, even though the party was in electoral danger and he was one of the few members in it with any reputation, was perhaps indicative of the importance the New Zealand government put on the matter. On the other hand, doubt remains. There was 'some dislike' betweem Wilford and Forbes, and the former's appointment to London may well therefore have had the added purpose of removing a prickly member of Cabinet to a suitably distant post, and one which, because of the system of communication with the British government used by the New Zealand, cut him off from detailed information on events.

Wilford himself, moreover, had business interests, and was to resign in 1934 and pursue them in London. Many motives were therefore probably involved in his appointment as High Commissioner.[42]

Despite this, the New Zealand government was not deeply concerned with foreign affairs in general, and was content to rely on British judgment and initiative. It was not till 1943 that a separate External Affairs Department was set up: in 1931 such matters came under the Prime Minister's Department and were looked after by an 'Imperial Affairs Officer'.

Australian indifference and the weakness of consultation

The last of our three Dominions, Australia, came halfway in the scale between New Zealand and Canada in the development of a Department of External Affairs. This had been set up in 1901 as one of the original seven departments of state after Federation, but, as in New Zealand and Canada, came under the control of the Prime Minister and was abolished in 1916, its functions being taken over by the PM's Department. Although formally reestablished in 1921, it remained under the Prime Minister, and its secretaryship was always held by the secretary of his department.[43]

The Chanak crisis in 1922, however, revealed the deficiencies in Australia's knowledge of world events and British policy, and Bruce, then Prime Minister, attempted to improve the system. In 1924 Mr Alan Leeper was lent from the British Foreign Office, and on his advice the Australian government decided not to appoint its own diplomatic representatives abroad, but to use the Foreign Office and the British diplomatic service. Bruce, however, decided that there was a need for closer liaison with the British authorities, and in 1924 R. G. Casey was sent to London to establish an External Affairs Office, separate from the High Commission, in the Cabinet Offices in Whitehall. There Casey was successful in gaining the confidence of men in the British system and sending back useful inside information to his government. On his return to Australia at the beginning of 1931, V. C. Duffy was appointed officer-in-charge of this 'Liaison Office'.

Clearly Australia had taken a different course from Canada, trying to integrate her embryo Department of External Affairs into the British system. She did so with no great enthusiasm. As Casey was to say to the Australian House of Representatives later, when defending the Department against Labor Party criticism, 'The 1926 Imperial Conference . . . has meant very little to Australia. We are not much concerned about what may be the pure milk of constitutional theory in Imperial relations'. This would have horrified Mackenzie King and Skelton, as would his previous remark that 'we in Australia, although not greatly concerned with these changes, were swept along the road to dominion independence whether we liked it or not'.[44] It was not surprising, therefore, that the Department of External Affairs was unaltered when the Manchurian crisis broke out.

Nor is it surprising, seeing the inadequate means for considering foreign policy in the two Dominions which demanded consultation, and the reservations of Canada and Britain, that imperial consultation was a very spasmodic affair. This was made worse by the fact that the Dominions did not have representatives in each others' countries, only London. Thomas, as Secretary of State for Dominion Affairs, did not regularly discuss matters there with the High Commissioners, who in any case did not always enjoy the confidence of their governments. What liaison there was occurred usually between the lower ranks of the Dominions Office and the various Dominion organisations, at informal dinners, etc.[45] Any information gleaned at such meetings was not likely to be complete in matters of high state policy, nor to filter back to the higher ranks, because of the generation gap between the men involved and their superiors, and the weaknesses of the people put at the top of each organisation. As a result, the Commonwealth was not like an organism with a brain and inter-connected nerves, which could therefore come to a decision, and act on it, but more like a brain-damaged octopus, with its tentacles acting independently of each other, and no vital connections being made at the centre.

Imperial disarmament
The weaknesses in the diplomatic structure of the new Commonwealth were made more serious by equal weaknesses in its naval and military power. To start with, it was, in one historian's words, 'no well-designed product of a grand strategy of expansion; but the random debris of successive historical episodes. . . . It was a polyglot empire; a rummage-bag of an empire, united by neither common purpose in its creation, nor by language, race, religion, nor by strategic and economic design'.[46] It could be divided into the 'White Dominions' of Australia, Canada, New Zealand and South Africa, which were self-governing and advanced Western countries, albeit still economically in the developmental stage, and the 'coloured' empire—Africa, India, the West Indies and colonies in the Far East—which were primitive, often poverty-stricken, and governed from London. Of the impressive population total of the Empire, no less than 316 000 000 were in the coloured colonial part. This gave neither economic nor military strength to the British, but instead demanded much from them in the way of effort. For example, in the First World War, India provided nearly one and a half million

soldiers. This impressive figure hid the fact that it represented only 0.3 per cent of her population, compared with over 12 per cent from Britain, 11 per cent from New Zealand and 8 per cent from Canada and Australia. Almost half the Indian troops were recruited in the last year of the war. Those that went into action, apart from a dramatic incident early in France, mainly did so in the Middle East, an area which was important to the British largely because they held India. India's contribution to the British war effort therefore 'was in fact both relatively and absolutely negligible.'

Yet the white Dominions too provided little in the way of additional strength to the Empire. Their populations were tiny. Whereas in 1931 Britain had a population of just under 45 million, Canada had a little over ten million, Australia a little over six and a half million, and New Zealand one and a half million. These populations were isolated from each other and Britain, and, as we have seen, Canada and South Africa contained large anti-British sections.

> Taken as a whole, therefore, the British Empire, 'white' and 'coloured', constituted on balance a source of weakness and danger to England rather than of strength. The English in their romantic idealism about the empire had failed to see it and deal with it in terms of British power . . . There the empire stood, proud under the Union flag, a ramshackle, anomalous but immense structure of entanglements extending from the Mediterranean to the South Pacific; resting almost wholly on the human, military and industrial resources of a nation of only forty-five million people; one of the most outstanding examples of strategic over-extension in history.[46]

Nor did the British counter this situation by the careful planning and coordination of the defence forces of their sprawling dominions. The attempt to unite the Empire into a federation had clearly failed by 1930. Nor was there a common military administration. Imperial defence was supposed to be discussed in the spasmodic imperial conferences, but, as happened in 1930, was often deliberately neglected. For if the members of the Commonwealth were divided politically, they were not likely to agree on joint military aims. War, as Clausewitz noted, is a continuation of politics by other means.

In the intervals between the conferences, the responsibility for ensuring the safety of the Commonwealth and Empire rested with the Committee of Imperial Defence. This, tentatively founded in 1902, had been remodelled in 1904, had stopped meeting during the First World War, and was revived in 1922. The chief architects of its revival were Stanley Baldwin and Lord Haldane. The latter was an imperialist, and thought that only such an organisation, headed by a Prime Minister, could draw the different interests of the Dominions, India and the colonies together.[47] Baldwin, as Prime Minister, took over the active chairmanship of the CID. From 1924 subcommittees were formed from its members: the Chiefs of Staff Committee, which became the hub of the organisation, and, soon after, the Principal Supply Officers Committee. The Prime Minister was *ex officio* the president of the CID, and he had under him a small secretariat. Apart from them, he could summon whomever he wished, but the usual members were the Chiefs of Staff of the three fighting services; those Cabinet ministers whose departments were concerned with defence (the Secretaries of State for War and Air and the First Lord of the Admiralty); representatives of the Treasury, which had to provide the money for any defence measures (the Chancellor of the Exchequer, and also the permanent secretary to the Treasury); those ministers responsible for foreign policy and the Empire (Secretaries of State for Foreign Affairs, the Dominions and India); and the senior Cabinet members (The Lord President of the Council and the Lord Privy Seal).

It can be seen that though the technical experts—representatives of the professional military, naval and air forces which had to defend the Empire if it were attacked—were included in the CID, they were heavily outnumbered by the politicians. Moreover, the CID had only an advisory and consultative capacity. The full responsibility for decisions, and the decisions themselves, rested with the Cabinet. If therefore the British politicians refused to face facts in the defence of their empire, the CID could hardly *force* them to do so. Constitutionally it was simply an advisory body to the Cabinet. Harsh reality did sometimes break through in the discussions in the various subcommittees which were formed, in particular the Overseas Defence Committee and the Chiefs of Staff Committee, which brought out annual reports on the imperial military situation. Those committees were formed from the service chiefs, however, not politicians. Their reports could always be overridden and modified, first in the CID itself and then in the various Cabinet committees before they reached the full Cabinet. In any case, the Chiefs of Staff reports tended to ignore the Dominions in the period up to 1930.

Representatives of three Dominions—Australia, New Zealand and South Africa—were sometimes invited to attend CID meetings when matters of particular concern to them were to be raised. As for Canada, although Mackenzie King attended a CID meeting during the 1926 imperial conference and Bennett one in 1930, they were, despite their political differences, in general agreement that Canadian representatives should not attend the CID. Skelton was particularly opposed to it, and 'it was undoubtedly felt in Ottawa that attendance at the CID might have implied some general commitment to British military arrangements and some limitation on Canadian freedom of action'.[48] It was not only reluctance on the part of Canada—and Ireland—however, that kept them away. The British did not trust the Irish and were wary of taking even the other Dominions fully into their confidence. Dominion representatives had no *right* to be present, and this allowed the British to hide awkward facts and unpopular policies from them.

The CID system, the weakness of the Dominions Office, the predilections of the British politicians, Dominion separatism, and differing strategic situations and interests, meant that there could be no general planning and direction of the defence needs of the Empire/Commonwealth as a whole. This was seen most clearly in the matter of naval defence.

As early as 1905, in the wake of the Japanese victory over the Russians, Australian governments had been concerned with security against Japan in the Pacific. Whereas the British had stressed the security provided by a British fleet sailing to the East, the Australians had not been impressed, and had insisted, against Admiralty advice, in building up their own squadron. The British, however, faced by the growing power of Germany in European waters, had withdrawn their battleships from the Pacific in 1905 and reneged on a promise to build up a Pacific fleet in 1909. Led by Churchill, they had increasingly turned to European waters and left the security of the Pacific Dominions to depend on the Anglo–Japanese Alliance.[49] An open rupture between the Australian and British governments was prevented by the outbreak of the First World War, during which Japan remained an ally of Britain, although it took advantage of the situation in the Far East.

The clash of interests between Britain and Australia was revealed once again after 1918. Following that year Britain disarmed more than any of the other powers. When Lord Jellicoe, who had been Commander-in-Chief of the Grand Fleet at Jutland, was sent to advise the Dominion Premiers on naval organisation in 1919, he drew up a scheme for a British Far Eastern fleet of sixteen capital ships. He was disowned by the Admiralty, for disarmament was the order of the day.[50] In 1919 Lloyd George told the service chiefs that they need not expect a major war for at least ten years. It was not, therefore, surprising that not a single new warship was laid down between that time and the Washington conference of 1921, although by then the Japanese had gained mandates over the Mariana, Caroline and Marshall groups of islands in the Pacific, and so gained naval dominance in the central and western parts of that ocean. Nevertheless, the British government, at that conference, and despite warnings from the Admiralty, accepted the 5:5:3 ratio between the British, American and Japanese fleets. This was a fatal error. The British with their Empire had commitments all over the globe, and therefore faced the possibility of needing warships in the North Sea, North and South Atlantic Oceans, the Mediterranean and Red Seas, and Indian

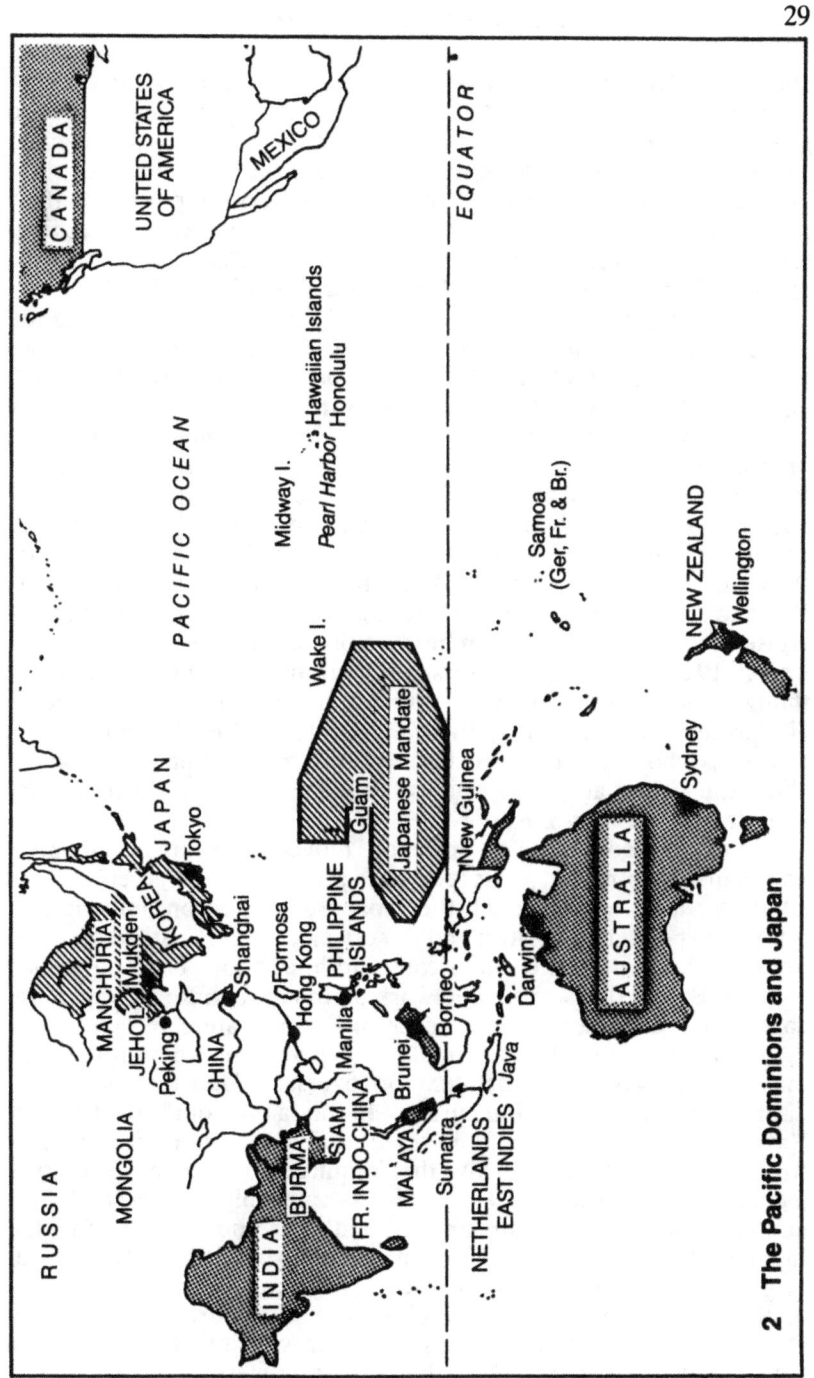

2 The Pacific Dominions and Japan

and Pacific Oceans. The Japanese, on the other hand, were a single-ocean power. The effect of the Washington Treaty, therefore, was to give the Japanese overwhelming naval superiority in the Pacific. Even worse, the acceptance of the ten-year 'naval holiday' in shipbuilding meant that the older British ships were not replaced, so their fleet was obsolete before those of their rivals. Finally, the Washington Treaties, by replacing the Anglo–Japanese Treaty, made possible an ultimate struggle between Britain and Japan in the Pacific.

British politicians, however, convinced that the war had made the world 'safe for democracy', and realising Britain's weakened economy after the First World War, continued to disarm. Between 1925 and 1927 they repeated their advice to the service chiefs that there would be no war for ten years, and in 1928, on Winston Churchill's prompting, made it automatic. On the basis of this 'Ten Year Rule', British disarmament continued. Before the London Naval Conference of 1930 the Labour government decided to reduce its cruiser strength to fifty. This brought a protest from Jellicoe, who was by then Governor-General of New Zealand. At the request of the New Zealand government he pointed out that the Royal Navy had had 114 cruisers in 1914, and that number had proved insufficient during the war; in 1929 they had 54 cruisers, and four more were being built. He thought the reduction of their number still further was dangerous. His protest was backed by the New Zealand High Commissioner, Wilford, who on the instructions of his government complained about the lack of advanced warning of the proposals and stressed the need for the base at Singapore.[51]

The British government, however, moved by pacifist and internationalist sentiment, ignored the protests and accepted the 50-cruiser level, even though the Japanese insisted on building to a ratio of 70 per cent of British and American cruisers, instead of the 60 per cent the British and Americans had hoped for. That, combined with the British decision to stop work on the naval base at Singapore, condemned their fleet to impotence in Pacific waters.

In April 1931 the Director of Naval Plans at the Admiralty, noted that Britain was still dependent on overseas foodstuffs, and had disarmed to the point of insecurity.[52] In the same month, the Chief of Naval Staff, in a memorandum to the Cabinet, reported that naval strength was 'definitely below that required to keep our sea communications open in . . . war' and was safe only as long as 'international conditions remain undisturbed'. On the other hand, 'the Japanese have increased notably in strength since 1914'. The figures he gave in an appendix, however, compared the Japanese fleet with a total for 'the British Commonwealth'. They therefore looked reasonable to the uninitiated, and possibly even weakened his case.[53] In fact, however, most of the British naval forces were elsewhere than in the Pacific, while *all* the Japanese were located there. As a result, the British Far Eastern fleet would have been totally unable to hold the Japanese in check.

This fact had been illustrated much more clearly in the preceding month, March 1931, when the CID had presented a paper on 'Imperial Defence as Affecting New Zealand'. In the appendix to this they estimated that in 1933 a British Pacific fleet of one aircraft carrier, seven 8" (203 mm) cruisers, six 6" (152 mm) cruisers, nine destroyers, and twelve submarines would oppose a Japanese fleet of three aircraft carriers, six battleships, three battlecruisers, twelve 8" cruisers, seventeen 6" cruisers, 72 destroyers and 67 submarines.[54]

Nor were the British in a stronger position as regards land and air forces. In 1931 the British army, to meet its worldwide commitments, numbered 147 764 men in Europe and 60 000 in India. The Royal Air Force had been reduced by economy measures to number less than 50 squadrons in England and 24 overseas. Even those figures grossly overestimate the strength of the RAF, since many of the planes were barely operational and nearly all were obsolescent, at a time when immense strides were being made in aircraft development.

The British government, however, put its faith in the League of Nations and assumed that Britain should set an example by further measures of disarmament. The Japanese aggression in Manchuria did not have any immediate effects on this thinking. The budget which Chamberlain presented in April 1932 included the lowest defence estimates of any between the wars—£103 million. This represented little more than 2.5 per cent of the national income, compared with 3.5 per cent in 1913.[55]

Nor could the British supplement their own naval and military forces with automatic and strong reinforcements from the Dominions. The attempt of the Admiralty in 1918 to set up an imperial navy with central control had been rejected by Dominion Premiers, even in the enthusiasm created by victory. The Canadians and South Africans, who did not feel menaced, and the Irish, who felt menaced only by Britain, steadfastly rejected any idea of an imperial force commanded from England. The 1923 imperial conference, therefore, laid it down that each Dominion was primarily responsible for its own defence, and the Admiralty had to be content with the promise that the Dominion navies would standardise their equipment.

Since they controlled their own defence forces, the Dominions could economise on them—and they therefore began to mirror British weakness. The Chiefs of Staff pointed out in 1930 that the Dominions left Britain with a disproportionate share of the burden of imperial defence. For example, they thought it absurd that the garrison from Singapore should come from England, 'when it could be sent far more expeditiously, from, say, Australia, which is at least as interested in its defence as ourselves'.[56] However, for political as well as economic reasons the 1930 imperial conference did not discuss defence measures in detail and the chance to reassess defence spending and responsibilities was lost.

With the advent of the depression, the British and Dominion governments cut back their defence establishments still further, and the naval forces and expenditures of the three Dominions most concerned with Japanese expansion in the Pacific became pathetically small. The Australian navy, on which the government spent only £1 391 991 in 1932–33, then comprised two cruisers and one destroyer in commission (plus a variety of craft on reserve) and 3186 men. New Zealand merely helped maintain two cruisers and some lesser craft of the Royal Navy, had 1097 personnel of its own, and spent £400 800 (together with another £100 000 on the Singapore base). Canada had four destroyers—two on each coastline—and some lesser vessels in commission, a force of 870 men on which £2 462 000 was spent.[57]

Worse still, the Dominions had failed to develop military air power. According to a report by the Chief of Air Staff after the 1930 imperial conference, the Australian air force numbered about 800 men together with some part-time help, and had 62 planes, mostly outdated (25 were Moths). Canada had also about 800 men, and 188 planes. The Canadian government used the RCAF for developmental work, forest-fire protection, customs patrols, etc., and therefore did not economise on it to the extent that it would otherwise have done. New Zealand had 54 men and 21 unspecified planes. (This last figure, however, was probably an overestimate. In 1928 the New Zealand permanent air force had consisted of five officers and seventeen other ranks, and its personnel wore army uniforms until April 1931). By 1932, according to figures provided by the Dominions to the League of Nations, Australia had 52 planes, New Zealand none, and Canada 355 (which, however, would not have been available for general imperial defence purposes).[58]

As for land military forces, they were, if anything, even weaker. Australia, having abolished compulsory national training, had a permanent force of 1515 officers and men and a militia of 1059, a combined total of 2574 men, although it talked hopefully of raising the militia reserves, in a crisis, to 30 000 men. New Zealand had a permanent army of 336 officers and men together with a territorial force of 6938. Canada's regular army was 3600 men, with a citizen reserve for home defence of 136 000.[59]

It largely rested with Britain and her forces, therefore, to defend the Empire, in the same way that it was left to the British public to pay for that defence. Bruce, then Australian Prime Minister, had pointed out to the 1926 imperial conference that during the previous year the British had spent 51s 1d per head of population on defence, Australia 25s, New Zealand 12s 11d and Canada 5s 10d. The situation had not improved by 1932, when Coates, the New Zealand Minister for Public Works, remarked in the New Zealand parliament that Britain's taxation for the navy amounted to £1 10s per head of population as against New Zealand's 7-8s per head.[60]

It was not surprising, therefore, that the British government was reluctant to spend money, especially on the navy. It was estimated in 1934 that the cost of a battleship was between £5 million and £7 million. To modernise and increase the whole British fleet was therefore a major economic undertaking. The desire to economise was reinforced by the pacifism and the horror of war in England in the 1930s. According to his biographers this fear affected Baldwin, especially after the dramatic swing against the government in the East Fulham by-election in October 1933. He may very well have misjudged this as an indicator of public opinion, but his assessment, combined with the hatred of war felt by many people, and especially MacDonald, swayed the government. Any talk of rearmament and strategic and military realities became distasteful.[61]

The Singapore base and New Zealand
This was illustrated most clearly by the history of the Singapore base. British governments of all complexions had long been determined to spend as little as possible and over as long time as posssible on it. They had first agreed to build the base while Lloyd George was Prime Minister, at the 1921 imperial conference, probably as a sop to keep the Dominions quiet. Thereafter they had adopted a very cautious stop-go policy. At the 1923 conference they had at last agreed to start work, provided it was not during the 1923-24 financial year. Then, in March 1924, MacDonald's Labour government decided against any expenditure on Singapore, on purely ideological grounds. It 'would exercise a most detrimental effect on our general foreign policy of international co-operation, and the creation of conditions which will make possible a comprehensive agreement on limitation of armaments'.[62] As a result, staff were withdrawn and most of the equipment was offered for sale. New Zealand's protest on that occasion had been drafted by no less a person than Jellicoe himself and was naturally, therefore, the strongest of the Dominion reactions.[63] Baldwin's second government reversed the decision, in theory, when it came to office in November 1924, but in fact plunged into a series of economies, spurred on by a prolonged and bitter argument between the Admiralty and the Air Ministry over the relative merits of coastal guns and torpedo planes as means of defence, and Winston Churchill's withering scorn of all those who

thought that Britain might have to fight Japan in that generation.

When the second Labour government came to office in 1929, therefore, the Singapore base was still in a rudimentary state, with only a floating dock and a few unfinished defences. As we have seen, the new government once again tried to stop everything, despite the fact that of the little over £2 million spent till then, £1 294 000 had come from the Federated Malay States, Hong Kong and New Zealand, while the Straits Settlements has donated the land. The British government had only spent £739 000, on a £7.75 million 'truncated scheme'. Nevertheless, ideological reasons were reinforced by the urgent need for governmental economies during the depression. When the government found that to cancel the Jackson contract for the graving dock and other installations would have been too expensive, it simply slowed down the work as much as possible. At the same time, it also had the nerve to insist that the various Dominions and colonies should keep up the payments that they had promised for the base, even though Britain was now spending little money on it. The High Commissioner for the Federated Malay States protested several times, but was in the end categorically ordered by the British government to pay over the money nevertheless.[64]

After vigorous New Zealand protests, the British eventually submitted the policy to a Special Committee of the 1930 imperial conference. At this P. Snowden, then Chancellor of the Exchequer, remarked that 'all present indications seemed to show that we should have freedom from war on an extensive scale for a good many years'. This happy view was bluntly and insistently challenged by the New Zealand Prime Minister, Forbes, who stressed the great importance attached by New Zealand to a defended naval base at Singapore. When Arthur Henderson pointed out that Japan had pledged herself to settle disputes by pacific means, 'Mr Forbes questioned whether much weight could, in reality, be attached to the signing of documents like the Kellog Pact'. J. H. Scullin, the Australian Labor Prime Minister, was more ideologically in tune with the British government and intervened to prevent a deadlock. He doubted talk of a Japanese threat to the Pacific Dominions. He seems to have been influenced by Forbes' arguments, however, for by the time of the final memorandum be commented on the proposals to slow down work on Singapore that he felt himself 'unable to do otherwise than concur', in view of the financial arguments, but added that 'any suggestion for abandoning the base would be viewed with concern by a considerable section of public opinion in Australia'. Forbes, however, had stuck to his guns throughout the discussions. He doubted Henderson's assurance that there would be peace for ten years and added that the advice given to the Dominions over a number of years had been unanimous in regarding the Singapore base as essential to defence in the Pacific. Without it, the fleet would be powerless in Far Eastern waters. He was ungracious enough to use Foreign Office documents to cast doubt on the British government's optimism over international affairs, and ended by remarking that only the financial difficulties made him hesitate to 'press his objections to the point of disagreement'.[65]

This strong stand, however, was not so much a reflection of the New Zealand government's thinking and concern as the work of a small group within the British bureaucracy who wished to strengthen the navy and support an 'imperial' policy. Forbes was helped with his statement by Sir Maurice Hankey, secretary to the cabinet and also to the CID. The use of a Dominion statesman by the 'imperialists' is interesting, but it was still not enough to push the British government into completing the Singapore base, given the economic situation and the government's ideology. The committee simply agreed that a naval base should ultimately be established at Singapore, and therefore the Jackson contract continued, but added that apart from that contract, other expenditure, such as the equipment in the docks and the defences (that is, everything that made it a base as distinct from a mere port) should be postponed for five years, after which 'the matter could again be reviewed in the light of relevant conditions then prevailing'. The critics of MacDonald's disarmament of Britain's Far Eastern empire had been totally defeated.[66]

Imperial impotence
The Empire/Commonwealth was therefore militarily weak when the Japanese struck in Manchuria in 1931. The British and Dominion governments had disarmed to the point of impotence, and based their security on isolation from dangerous areas of the world, the support of powerful neighbours, the growth of international understanding and the efficacy of the League of Nations. Yet the League itself might involve them in war—at a time and in a place where they had no military or naval power. Moreover, Britain and the Dominions were not only militarily weak, they were politically uncoordinated, for the Japanese move coincided with the effort to clarify the constitution of the Empire. The British government had promised a statute to do this at the imperial conference of 1930. Thomas therefore produced a Cabinet memorandum on the subject on 4 September 1931—fifteen days before the Mukden incident—and subsequently the Westminster Bill passed through both Houses of Parliament and received the royal assent on 11 December 1931. The Manchurian crisis thus occurred during the legal and statutory birth of 'the Commonwealth'. The events in Manchuria, however, had serious implications for the survival of such an organisation. Whether British

and Dominion politicians could see the crisis for what it was—a warning that the world was not as gentle and idealistic a place as they had imagined—and could react in time to coordinate their foreign policies and restore their economic and military strength, remained to be seen.

2 The new idea tested: *crisis in the East, 1931–32*

> ... by reason of our geographical situation, we in Australia are particularly interested in what happens in the United States, Japan and China.
> CASEY TO VANSITTART, 6 NOVEMBER 1930
> [PRO FO 372/T1207/1207/384]

> New Zealand, by virtue of her situation on the Pacific . . . is much concerned at the war now being waged between Chinese and Japanese there.
> SIR THOMAS WILFORD TO THE DISARMAMENT CONFERENCE,
> 16 FEBRUARY 1932. [NZA PM 111/12/8 (ii)]

In September 1931 sections of the Japanese army in Manchuria staged an 'incident' on the South Manchurian railway near Mukden, and thereafter quickly proceeded to occupy large areas of Manchuria. Within days the Chinese government brought the matter before the League, citing Article 11 of the Covenant, and at the same time appealed to the United States, as a signatory of the Nine Power Pact outlawing war. This action involved in the crisis the major Western powers. Their problem was made worse by the complex legal rights of both China and Japan in Manchuria, the inability of the Japanese government to control its military men, and the weakness of the British and American forces, especially in fleets and naval bases, in the Far East.

The British Empire/Commonwealth was bound to be concerned, for both strategic and economic reasons. Britain had possessions in the East, such as Hong Kong, Singapore and Malaya; the Dominions of Australia and New Zealand lay off the Asian mainland in the Pacific, while the western seaboard of Canada was on the northern parts of the same ocean. Britain also had considerable trade in the area, particularly with China, where she had treaty rights in Shanghai and other ports. Her trade with Japan was almost as valuable, the Japanese trade balance with India being almost two to one in India's favour. Japan was also a trading partner of the Dominions, to a small extent with New Zealand and South Africa, but a much greater one with Canada. The latter's trade balance with Japan was similar to that of India. But the most important trading partner of Japan was Australia. From 1929 to 1933 Japan doubled its imports of raw wool, taking 96 per cent of the increase from Australia. In 1931–32 Japan was taking nearly a quarter of the Australian wool supply and importing from Australia nearly three and a half times as much as it sold to her. This increase in Japanese trade was vital to Australian primary producers during the worst part of the depression. By 1932 Japan was taking 12.1 per cent of the total Australian exports. Nor did this aspect of the situation go unnoticed in Australia.[1]

Not only did the Manchurian affair therefore have serious economic and strategic implications for Britain and the Commonwealth, it also came at a very bad time for their governments. They were uniformly preoccupied with internal political crises and the economic depression, and so found it difficult to give Far Eastern matters deep consideration, or to ponder the long-term effects of their policies.

Britain: political and economic problems
The government of Britain was in a confused state when the Manchurian crisis broke out in September 1931. In the previous month the Labour Party had split over the need for economies to deal with the depression, and Ramsay MacDonald and three other Labour men had formed the 'National' government in alliance with a few Liberals and the Conservatives. MacDonald's Labour colleagues had felt betrayed, and accusations and counter-accusations filled the air. The new Cabinet numbered ten: four Labour men, two Liberals and four Conservatives. The Conservatives, however, were determined to force an early general election and secure their position by putting themselves forward as essential to the economic survival of the country. It soon became clear that MacDonald, without the support of his erstwhile Labour followers, was a prisoner of the Conservatives, and an election was called for 27 October 1931.[2] The Manchurian crisis, which broke before then, was not discussed by the inner Cabinet. Its members were preoccupied with their own political survival. 'No Cabinet Committee was set up to watch the matter; scarcely a mention of it appears in the diaries and letters of senior politicians . . . What exactly Britain's line should be . . . was for the moment left entirely to the Foreign Secretary and his permanent officials'.[3] They were divided on some aspects of the crisis, but the weight of opinion was against any British involvement in the dispute and, indeed, expressed some sympathy for Japan.

In the election of 1931 the 'National government' candidates won an overwhelming victory, and the Labour party was annihilated at the polls. The leading personalities of the returned National government Cabinet were the Prime Minister, James Ramsay MacDonald; the Lord President, Stanley Baldwin; the Secretary of State for Foreign Affairs, Sir John Simon; and the Chancellor of the Exchequer, Neville Chamberlain.

The Prime Minister, Ramsay MacDonald, was in decline by 1932. He had broken with his former colleagues, and had to suffer their scorn; he was in charge of an increasingly conservative administration, with whose temper he was out of sympathy, and he nearly suffered a nervous breakdown in the autumn of 1931. His health was failing—his eyes being particularly troublesome—and his speeches, never very lucid, became more convoluted still.

> Not surprisingly, this final period of his political career was to show up, besides the courage of the man in the face of a painful illness, his vanity and extreme sensitivity to criticism, his substitution of eloquence for analysis, and his tendency to dissemble . . . His skills as an international negotiator were not entirely gone . . . and in Cabinet, too, he could still push through business with expedition and shrewdness. But his general decline was unmistakable.[4]

The Lord President, Stanley Baldwin, had himself twice been Prime Minister and was to have a third term of office when MacDonald retired in 1935. Although his early career had been that of a manufacturer, in manner he appeared a quiet countryman. 'Baldwin, stocky of figure, rubicund and jowly of face between his bowler hat and his wing collars, with a slightly bulbous nose . . . *looked* the epitome of the simple, old fashioned virtues.'[5] His stance was that of the man of plain common sense, without guile, a moderate. Nevertheless, beneath the cartoonists' picture of the countryman puffing on his pipe there lay an astute politician.

Baldwin's weakness, however, was his preference for doing nothing —for letting problems settle themselves. A lazy man who liked reading and crossword puzzles, and contemptuous of intellectuals, he was not fitted to face the major economic and strategic problems that faced Britain in the 1930s. He was too content to follow events and wait, and by that time waiting was dangerous. So too was his habit of riding with public opinion, of trying always to calm the public, never to make it face unpleasant realities. He possibly understood the long-term threat to Britain's security from a resurgent Germany, but he seemed little impressed by the urgency of the matter. He sat on the fence in Cabinet discussions between the service chiefs and his colleagues, and his public statements of policy remained extremely cautious. His weaknesses were becoming more pronounced with age. Even his somewhat adulatory biographers agree that 'it would be wrong to underestimate Baldwin's reliance on Chamberlain in the years 1932–5. His own distaste for detail appears greater than in the 1920s . . .'.[6]

There is little doubt, indeed, that the National government was increasingly dominated by the sparse figure of Chamberlain.

Those who have written the story of the early 1930s have acknowledged Chamberlain as the dynamic element in MacDonald's last Government . . . No aspect of politics could be quite outside the purview of a man who controlled both the Nation's pursestrings and the Party's thinking machine. [Chamberlain set up the Cabinet Conservative Committee in 1934.][7]

All this was a little unfortunate, seeing the limitations of the man. He had a clear mind, within the limits of his vision, and great energy and self-confidence. His weakness lay not so much in his forbidding features, his dark clothes, and his harsh voice, which struck contemporaries, as in his preoccupation with financial affairs, ignorance of and blindness towards strategic matters, and his lack of imagination. It was these qualities that made Lloyd George describe him once as 'a good mayor of Birmingham, in a lean year'. Moreover, Chamberlain was already beginning to show arrogance and a desire to dominate the Cabinet. He greatly enjoyed putting forward his views on matters which were not his responsibility. In October 1932, for example, he wrote to his sister, 'It amuses me to find a new policy for each of my colleagues in turn'. He dismissed MacDonald as 'worn out' and Baldwin as 'useless'.[8] It was inevitable that, as Chancellor of the Exchequer, he should be drawn into discussions of defence expenditure, and so of foreign policy, which, as we shall see, he increasingly dominated as time went on.

The nominal director of British foreign policy was Sir John Simon, who had brought a bloc of tariff Liberals into the National coalition. Simon had many enemies, and by the end of 1934 even the Chief Whip described him as the government's biggest liability.[9] He seemed to be the caricature of the 'stiff-upper-lip' reserved Englishman. His manner was cool and excessively correct, although, beneath the exterior he might, as has since been asserted, have wished to be liked and merely lacked the imagination to bring that about.

More serious, however, was Simon's inability to give decisive leadership. As Foreign Secretary he regarded himself too much as a lawyer, putting each side of the case in turn. He could sum up the intricacies of any situation with great clarity—and then fail to come to any conclusion. An observer described Simon as 'one of the most prominent representatives of that typically British mentality which prefers a bad compromise to a straight solution, if that solution involves the assumption of any responsibility'[10] and Lloyd George said that 'the right honourable Gentleman has sat so long on the fence that the iron has entered his soul'. Simon's specious arguments in the League Assembly, when faced with the need for action against Japan, may therefore not have been the result of sympathy for Japan as such, which was suspected at the time, as his usual lawyer's ability to see both sides, combined with the wish at all costs to avoid offending Japan. Chamberlain summed up Simon in his diary: 'Simon's weakness has given rise to much criticism . . . He can always make an admirable speech in the House, to a brief, but . . . the fact is that his manner inspires no confidence, and that he seems temperamentally unable to make up his mind to action when a difficult situation arises.'[11] It may be, as Watt has argued, that a forceful Foreign Secretary, acting as an initiator of foreign policy, is incompatible with an imperial foreign policy resting on consultation with the Dominions.[12] Nevertheless, the contrary, a weak Foreign Secretary who regards himself merely as a delegate of the Cabinet, does not necessarily imply consultation with the Dominions either. The weakness of Simon at this time allowed decisions on foreign policy to be left at first to the Foreign Office, and then to drift into the hands of Chamberlain.

This was helped by the preoccupation of the Cabinet with economic and financial matters, especially the policies needed to bring the country out of the depression—over which they were deeply divided. The conservatives, for example, were convinced that British industry needed the protection of tariffs; the old-guard Liberals were equally convinced free-traders. A split in government ranks was only avoided by Lord Hailsham's suggestion that the rule of collective Cabinet responsibility should be relaxed on the matter. It could not last, however, especially in view of the forthcoming 'Imperial Economic Conference', which was to be held in Ottawa in July and August 1932. This, after bitter arguments, ended with twelve agreements between Britain and the Dominions (except Ireland). Britain promised to continue and in some cases increase imperial preference on some Dominion goods, merely in exchange for the imposition of even heavier Dominion tariffs on foreign imports than they were already levying against British goods. Lord Snowden resigned, as did two of the Liberals. The 'National' government was becoming increasingly Conservative.

This government, with all its weaknesses, also had many distractions in its early years:[13] the problem of Ireland; the disarmament conference planned for 1932; German reparations to the Allies and their repayment of war debts to the United States; reduction in judges' salaries, which their lordships had objected to as unconstitutional; the agriculture and fisheries policy; and the creation of the new 'Commonwealth'. The Cabinet, therefore, did not even discuss the Far Eastern crisis till 11 November.

On that date, Simon warned it of the danger that China might move the grounds of her complaint to the League from Article 11 of the Covenant (which stipulated vague and unspecified 'action') to Article 16 (which stipulated sanctions). The Cabinet agreed that though the League should be upheld, sanctions were neither 'suitable' nor 'practicable'. Every effort should be made to prevent the Chinese from appealing to Article 16 and instead to adopt a policy of conciliation without implied or open threats to Japan.[14] Seeing Britain's military weakness in the Far East, and economic troubles at home, this may have been a sensible initial response, but the Cabinet also gave no indication that it perceived any long-term threat to British interests in the East or of the need for contingency planning. Even the CID, at its meeting of 7 December, did not discuss the Far Eastern situation, nor did the Cabinet discuss the broader issues of the crisis. It simply tried to avoid any initiative of its own, hoping to use the League, if that body were involved, for the purposes of conciliation.[15] Simon wanted the League to get the matter over with quickly. If the Council failed to persuade the two parties to behave, then it should simply inform Japan that it disapproved of its actions, and wash its hands of the situation. Yet his attitude wavered; on 19 November he apparently even suggested that the League should act under Article 16, and on 23 November he submitted a memorandum to the Cabinet suggesting that the League president should reaffirm the 'fundamental principle' that states did not take the law into their own hands, and that if he did not Simon himself should do so. The Cabinet, however, opposed any 'special and separate attitude' on Simon's part, and thought he should simply ask the president privately to reaffirm League principles.[16] This toying with a firmer stand is interesting, in the light of Simon's later attitude. Thorne suggests that Simon was moved by his concern for the League's prestige, and was also trying to manoeuvre the Americans into making a clear statement of their own policy. In their own discussions, however, Simon and the rest of the Cabinet ruled out any thought of sanctions from the beginning. In this they were supported by Hankey, the CID and the Foreign Office, where 'Vansittart, Wellesley and the rest [regarded] any suggestion of economic sanctions as dangerous in itself, premature in its implied judgement and strenuously to be avoided'.[17]

In the same way the British did not support the new American policy of strong protests—conciliation having apparently failed— early in 1932. On 7 January the American Secretary of State, H. L. Stimson, sent a note to China and Japan informing them that America could not recognise any de facto situation that might impair her rights or those of her citizens in China, especially those which concerned the sovereignty, independence and territorial integrity of China and the Open Door policy, or which had been brought about by force contrary to the Pact of Paris. This 'Stimson Note', in short, elaborated the policy of 'non-recognition'. Stimson had suggested to the British and French ambassadors that their governments should take similar steps. The Foreign Office merely issued a communiqué citing Japanese assurances about the Open Door policy and remarking that the British government saw no need to address any formal note to the Japanese. This has since led to the British government being accused of rejecting an American offer of cooperation against Japan. Recent research, however, has revealed that a bold declaration of rights was as far as the American government was prepared to go. It had no intention of following such a declaration by sanctions, let alone war.[18] Stimson adopted an even 'firmer' pose after the attack on Shanghai, in his open letter to Senator Borah, 23 February 1932. In this he mentioned the use of force. He was, however, bluffing, for he admitted to a correspondent that Congress would not support even an economic boycott of Japan. Baldwin's reaction was therefore correct. 'You will get nothing out of Washington but words, big words, but only words.' The British government entertained a deep suspicion and dislike of America, which came into the open after the Stimson note. Hankey's mistrust of America went back to 1927–29; Sir Robert Vansittart and the Foreign Office thought the Americans 'unreliable', a judgment in which Simon and Chamberlain concurred, while Sir Warren Fisher at the Treasury hated the Americans as much as Vansittart hated the Germans.[19] The British and American governments were therefore unable to cooperate with one another, a fact which was unfortunate, and regretted by most of the Dominions.

New Zealand: the government of 'Farmer Forbes'

The British attitude of non-involvement and avoidance of sanctions was echoed in the Dominions, all of whom had their own preoccupations at the time. Typical of this was New Zealand, the Dominion with the smallest population and the least-developed foreign affairs bureaucracy. Its government had just changed, for a new coalition to save the country from the depression, that of the United and Reform Parties, was announced on the day of the Mukden incident. The Prime Minister was again G. W. Forbes, a nonentity who continued as leader simply because the more able and forceful members of the discordant coalition had made bitter enemies. Forbes had not been active enough to make them. Indeed, till 1928 he had been a politician of the second rank, whose pride and delight was in farming. 'Farmer Forbes' had been in the limelight at the 1930 imperial conference, but, as we have seen, he was briefed for his part there by Hankey. He usually revealed a much weaker grasp of events. Indeed, he has been described as 'New Zealand's most improbable premier'.[20] Although he had some qualities as a leader, such as humour and a conciliatory temper, Forbes has been treated with derision by most historians. The kindest remark seems to have been to describe him as a man of 'dogged sincerity and limited imagination'.[21] He was certainly not able enough to cope with the problems that confronted New Zealand at the time. He obstinately clung to orthodox economic policies during the depression, and accordingly went to a crushing electoral defeat in 1935, when his party was reduced from 51 to nineteen MPs.

Despite its concern with Japan's southward movement and the weakness of the British, or perhaps because of it, the New Zealand government made no statement of policy at all in the early days of the Manchurian crisis. In the New Zealand archives there are thick files containing information sent there from the Dominions and Foreign Offices in Britain, the Japanese Consul-General in Sydney, and the League secretariat. As C. A. Berendsen, the secretary of external affairs in the PM's Department, wrote, 'We have been bombarded here, as of course you have, with shoals of material from Geneva'.[22] However, there is in this mass of material not one comment giving the government's own opinion, or even that of the public servants. Nothing seemed capable of provoking a comment from Forbes, not even a letter from the French consul in Auckland hinting that New Zealand should join the signatories of the Nine Power Treaty in making a protest to both China and Japan. He simply acknowledged the letter.[23]

This was probably due to Forbes' indifference to foreign affairs— as we have seen, the Prime Minister's Department then dealt with foreign policy. The only statement of opinion by anyone connected with the New Zealand government came from Sir Thomas Wilford, in Geneva. On 16 February 1932 he told the disarmament conference that though the League Council had failed, he hoped the League would be used as 'a rallying point' to prevent future troubles.[24] Even this comment was suitably vague, and Wilford had not committed his government to anything, or, probably, been instructed by them on the issue.

It cannot be denied, however, that in many ways Forbes reflected the lack of concern in New Zealand. No questions were raised in the New Zealand parliament by members of the opposition, despite Forbes' silence on the issue. Indeed, it was perhaps indicative of New Zealand attitudes at the time that Japan was then listed on the index to the New Zealand Hansard under the title 'Eastern Markets'. The public seemed equally apathetic. T. H. McCombs, the New Zealand High Commissioner in 1974, said that in the early 1930s New Zealanders deprecated Japanese actions, but they were all a very long way away, and simply involved yellow men fighting yellow men.[25] Nor did the New Zealand press imply, as some Australian newspapers did, that Japanese expansion into Manchuria had decreased the danger of a southward advance. This apathy was partly the result of distance, which made the whole affair seem irrelevant to New Zealand, and partly the minute volume of trade the country then had with either China or Japan. In 1932 Japanese imports only comprised 1.94 per cent of the New Zealand total, and exports to Japan were only 0.67 per cent of the total.[26] There were thus no vested interests to draw the attention of New Zealanders to the long-term implications of Japanese action; government and people remained apathetic.

Bennett's Canada
A comparison between New Zealand and Canada is most interesting. To start with, Canada was not solely a Pacific power. Her vast land mass extends 3223 miles (or 5187 kilometres) from east to west, and the largest and most influential section of the population live on the eastern seaboard, facing the Atlantic. As a commentator in 1933 put it, 'That Canada is a Pacific Power is only gradually being realised in the central and eastern provinces of the Dominion. Once one comes east from British Columbia and the prairies to Ontario, Quebec and the maritime provinces, the Far East becomes ever more remote.' This had its effect on public attitudes. 'It is significant that during the Sino-Japanese crisis the eastern press has on the whole tended to be pro-Japanese, the western press pro-Chinese.[27]

If the British High Commissioner in Canada, W. H. Clark, was correct, editorial opinion was non-committal in the opening days of the crisis.[28] Nor were any comments made or questions raised in the Canadian House of Commons. Canadian newpapers did, however, cover events adequately, since, unlike New Zealand, Canada had close economic ties with the Far East.

Canadian exports to Japan had increased from $7 million in 1920 to $42 million in 1929, while her exports to China had increased from $6 million to $24 million. This was, of course, still only a small proportion—5 per cent—of all Canadian exports, and represented only 3 per cent of Japanese and only 1 per cent of Chinese imports. Trade with Britain was nine times as valuable and with the United States seventeen times as valuable.[29] However, even this trade was useful, and the government did its best to encourage it, including the establishment of a legation in Tokyo in 1928. In return, the Japanese had appointed a minister to Ottawa in 1929. He was to send long accounts of the Japanese viewpoint to External Affairs early in 1931, during the Shanghai crisis and into 1933. The link with Japan had been illustrated in April and May 1931, when Their Imperial Highnesses, Prince and Princess Takamatsu, visited Canada (after the United States), and were naturally fêted in the Canadian capital. That the Japanese felt that Canada was of interest to them was seen in October 1931, when they appointed a military attaché to Ottawa, somewhat to the consternation of the British Admiralty.[30]

The government in power during the Manchurian crisis was the Conservative ministry of R. B. Bennett, which had taken office in July 1930, 'laden to the gunwale with exuberant pledges that it would find remedies for the serious unemployment which was then afflicting the country . . .'. This government was comparatively inexperienced and closely linked with Britain. 'London was Bennett's second home. He had been there at least once in each of the past 15 years, attending to his growing business interests and on occasion pleading to a client's case before the Judicial Committee of the Privy Council.' For Bennett was a millionaire lawyer, whose 'physical appearance was that of the cartoonists' traditional capitalist, lacking for completeness only the dollar signs on the waistcoat'.[31] Not surprisingly, therefore, Bennett was a strong supporter of a British-led Commonwealth. Such views were, needless to say, at complete variance with those of Skelton. Many conservatives, moreover, disliked the very idea of an activist Department of External Affairs, since it implied disloyalty to Britain. Bennett did not go so far as this, but he meant to replace Skelton. He was, however, entirely taken up with the depression, and by the time he got around to looking at the problem, Skelton had made himself indispensable. Thus he escaped the consequences of his political attitude and Canada gained a bipartisan Department of External Affairs, by chance.[32] Moreover, the views of Bennett and Skelton on the Manchurian crisis, though different in emphasis, could be reconciled in a coherent course of action through the League, as will be seen in the next chapter, and both were aware of the need to keep on friendly terms with the United States. Skelton may have wished for this primarily for political reasons, Bennett for economic ones, but the result was the same; Canadian policy was to reconcile membership of the British Commonwealth with close ties with the United States. This was sometimes difficult, but always kept in mind. Sir George Perley, the chief delegate of Canada at the disarmament conference, was thus entirely typical in expressing satisfaction that they had 'worked in concert' with the United States in the Manchurian crisis,[33] even though the grounds for his judgment seem a little obscure.

The Manchurian crisis is, indeed, interesting, in that Canada had more sources of information than New Zealand, a more highly developed Department of External Affairs to assimilate that information, and should therefore, perhaps, have found it easier to adopt an independent policy. There were, however, complicating factors.

The minister in Tokyo, Sir Herbert Marler, had been appointed by the previous Mackenzie King administration in 1929. He was an ardent Canadian nationalist and concerned in particular with promoting Canadian trade, which, he was convinced, was the most important part of his mission. This was seen in 1932, when he wrote to Skelton apologising for not keeping him informed of the Shanghai crisis. He had assumed that the DEA had the facts from the newspapers and London, and 'I have been particularly engaged in the preparation of some important matters relating to our trade organisation in the Far East'. And, on another occasion, 'I have always thought that nowadays an Envoy's principal duty should be the promotion of economic intercourse'.[34] Marler, moreover, was a prickly man, much concerned with his official standing. As the British High Commissioner rather unkindly put it, 'He has the pomposity of manner and a voice of a rather lecturing quality which are slightly ridiculous on social occasions, and he has not yet got over the thrill of finding himself a member of so august an institution as the *corps diplomatique*'.[35] He seems to have felt very keenly the fact that he was merely the head of a legation, and not a full embassy, and also was much taken up with his rank and the deference due to it. He seems to have developed bad relations with some of the staff at the legation, preventing them accepting honours, although he insisted on full honours for himself. In 1934 one of the staff thought that he had not fully recovered from the nervous breakdown he suffered, and regained 'his practical good sense and old considerateness and thoughtfulness'. On the other hand, it does seem that he succumbed to the temptations of power and office. He was, moreover, on bad terms with his British counterparts, such as Sir Robert Clive, the British ambassador to Japan. The British in Tokyo had worried about the appointment of a Canadian minister, and were to be worried again in 1931 when Marler tried to have a Canadian minister and trade commissioners appointed to China. Despite Skelton's vigorous support, the idea lapsed for a time.[36]

One of the first secretaries at the Tokyo legation was Dr H. L. Keenleyside. He was a product of Skelton's recruitment program for a professional external affairs service, and had risen to the rank of second secretary in the Department of External Affairs in Ottawa in 1929. In that year he had gone to Tokyo to establish a legation there, and was in fact chargé d'affaires when the Manchurian crisis broke out.

Keenleyside sent a series of most percipient despatches to his superiors in Ottawa. For example, as early as 23 September he reported, quite correctly, that evidence suggested that 'the military authorities of Japan have carried out their policy . . . with comparatively little reference to the decisions of the Government in Tokyo'. On 25 September he cast doubts on the official Japanese explanation of the incident, thinking it merely a pretext, and followed this with reports which were critical of Japanese excuses, and of the so-called 'independence movement' in Manchuria.[37]

On 24 October, however, Marler returned to Tokyo, and the character of the despatches that arrived in Ottawa changed. They became simple long accounts of further developments, without any observations or judgments. Then Marler himself sent a 41-page despatch on 1 December 1931. The contrast with those of Keenleyside could hardly have been more striking. The latter had a literate style of writing, and was a shrewd observer, who analysed the situation clearly. Marler's despatch, in contrast, was disjointed, and full of rambling asides and rhetorical questions. It was more than style which revealed the man's mental incapacity, however. He totally misjudged the situation in the Far East, the position of the Japanese government and army, and the rights and wrongs of the issue, and came out with naive support for the Japanese action. He criticised the League and, even more bitterly, China and defended the right of Japan to 'civilise' Manchuria.[38] This almost incredible despatch was not answered by Skelton till 23 January, when he politely thanked Marler for his 'extremely interesting' report. He agreed that League intervention had been unwise, and doubted if the European nations would come to the assistance of Canada in similar circumstances. But he balked at the main points of Marler's judgment.

> I am inclined to think . . . that you have given Japan rather too clean a bill of health. [Granted that she had real grievances,] the question remains whether she did not violate her treaty engagements . . . I am inclined to think that she has, and that other . . . powers have taken similar action in the past does not justify a breach of the higher code of international conduct which the world has been endeavouring to build up since the Great War.[39]

The whole episode is interesting, since it shows that legations in themselves did not automatically provide accurate information for the Dominions. This depended on the calibre of the men they appointed to their overseas posts. With poor or inadequate staff, they could be less reliable than British sources of information. A split, indeed, seems to have developed within the Canadian external affairs department. Marler did not seem to like Keenleyside, preventing him being honoured on his retirement from the legation[40] and totally disagreeing with him on the political situation. Skelton later forwarded to a third party a despatch 'prepared by a member of the Legation Staff in Tokyo', which contradicted all Marler's arguments. While admitting that the Japanese had a strong case against China, it added that they had resorted to direct action, in clear violation of the Covenant, the Nine Power Treaty and the Kellogg Pact. 'The intervention of the League of Nations was both inevitable and desirable. If the League is to develop and maintain its authority in the future it was essential that it should not side-step this issue.'[41] It seems, therefore, that there was a clear division of opinion within the legation and that Skelton, on political matters, agreed with his protegé Keenleyside.

As for the impact of all this information on the Canadian government, in the early days of the crisis it made no more public statements of its policy than the New Zealand government. Historians may be grateful for the legation because it at least shows them what some members of the governmental bureaucracy were thinking, but, at the same time, its practical effect was minimal. Skelton was made uneasy by the Japanese action, but disliked the idea of League intervention, and his Prime Minister, Bennett, withheld judgment and occupied himself with other matters until later events obliged him to consider the Far East more fully. This in practice was little different from the policy adopted by the government of New Zealand, or even Australia.

Australia: advent of the Lyons government
In Australia, the Labor government, led by J. H. Scullin, was uninterested in foreign policy, being instead preoccupied with the economy and its own survival. Desperately divided over ways of escaping the depression, and with an erstwhile Labor leader in New South Wales, J. H. Lang, leading a vociferous opposition to the federal Labor Party, and that party itself about to split over the measures needed to cure the economic situation, foreign affairs were to them a peripheral matter.

This applied equally to the Manchurian crisis itself. Australia is unusual in that questions were actually asked in its parliament about the Manchurian crisis in its early days, but too much need not be read into that. They were asked by the supporters of Lang in the federal parliament, with the design of embarrassing the Scullin government. For example, on 14 October E. J. Ward demanded an undertaking that no Australian lives would be sacrificed in any war. Scullin parried this by remarking that he hoped that it would not come to a war, and they would be wise not to anticipate trouble and aggravate the situation.[42] Scullin steadily declined to make a public statement, and although Keith Officer in the External Affairs section of Scullin's Department provided a series of detailed and non-commital notes for answers to possible parliamentary questions, they were not used. Duffy from London sent telegrams as the situation developed, but there is no sign in the files of government response to them. 'Mr. Scullin took no direct interest in the Manchurian affair at any time during his remaining months of office in 1931, nor was the question brought up at the regular meetings of the Federal Parliamentary Labor Party.'[43] Scullin may have been Minister for External Affairs, but he had other overriding worries. This revealed the weakness that can come in times of crisis when the Prime Minister is also in charge of foreign policy.

The government finally split. Its Treasurer, J. A. Lyons, left its ranks with five others, and after some haggling joined other opponents of Labor to form the 'United Australia Party' (UAP), which fought the Labor Party in the general election on 9 December 1931. The campaign for this was waged with particular bitterness both in the press and on the hustings, with an anti-communist scare being prominent, and dominated Australian public interest for its duration. No party seems to have thought the Manchurian crisis worth mentioning.

In the event, the Labor Party was soundly defeated, its seats in the federal parliament falling from 46 to 13, with five Lang supporters, and the UAP came to power. It spent some time distributing portfolios—the fruits of victory. The new Prime Minister was Lyons himself, but his government was hardly a 'Ministry of all the Talents'. Hankey, two years later, thought Lyons a 'man of disarming simplicity. His obvious sincerity and extreme frankness create a most agreeable impression. [Nevertheless] Mr. Lyons is apparently not a good manager of a Cabinet, and least of all of a difficult, ill-knit coalition Cabinet such as the present one. He allows too many irrelevancies and does not keep a tight hold.' Hankey, with memories of the English Cabinet, went on to remark, 'Cabinet procedure is evidently very loose and rambling. There is a nominal agenda paper, but they dont [sic] stick to it and wander all over the place. Much time is wasted in discussing quite trivial questions, such as departmental appointments'.[44] Departmental appointments were not, to that government, 'trivial matters', but Lyons, as Malcolm MacDonald was to report later, was an impressionable man, usually swayed by those around him.[45] Indeed, it was Lyons' very weakness that made him an ideal leader, for he belonged to no faction and offended none. In this respect he resembled Forbes in New Zealand.

The strong man in the Cabinet, who 'ruled Lyons with a rod of iron', according to Hankey again, was Sir John Latham, the erstwhile leader of the Nationalists. A convinced conservative, Latham had gained a BA at Melbourne University, and then, after a period of schoolteaching, went back to study law, becoming an LLB in 1902. His early career was that of a barrister, supplemented with part-time teaching in the university. After serving in the Royal Australian Navy during the war, he went with Hughes to the imperial conference in 1918 and the peace conference in 1919. He finally entered federal politics in 1922, first as a member of the 'Liberal-Union' against Hughes, and then, after 1925, as a Nationalist under Bruce. As Attorney-General in the Bruce-Page government he went to the imperial conference of 1926 and thereafter to the League Assembly at Geneva. After Bruce's defeat in the election of 1929, Latham became leader of the Nationalists. As such, he had criticised the projected Statute of Westminster.

> I do not desire such things to be made rigid by legal rules and enactments. On many . . . matters the British Constitution, as applied not only to Great Britain but throughout the Empire, has been a success largely because it has been loose and elastic and has left things to be determined by the common sense of statesmen as emergencies arise, instead of being decided with the precision of lawyers in the interpretations of written documents.[46]

By Canadian standards, of course, Latham was not a 'nationalist' at all, but a conservative imperialist. It is indeed strange how reluctant the conservative parties in Australia have been to adopt that name.

Latham was a reserved man, who gave the impression of superiority and made few friends. As the obituary writer for *The Times* later said, 'To most he was a name rather than a personality; a man who was remote and aloof even as a politician; one who compelled respect, even deference, but one who gained the affection only of that small circle of intimates who were able to penetrate the barrier of shyness . . .'.[47] It was this reserve that made Latham unsuitable as leader of the new party, with its need to make a quick electoral appeal. Instead, 'Mr. Latham served under Mr Lyons as Deputy Prime Minister, 'holding his hand' in the difficult early days. But, as one observer said, holding hands is not to be done in public, and perhaps Mr Latham tended to make it clear that he was the power behind the throne'.[48]

A break with tradition occurred, however, in that Latham became not only Attorney-General, but also Minister for External Affairs. This was the first time since the department's re-establishment in 1921 that its head had been other than the Prime Minister. The reason was partly that Lyons himself was not interested in foreign policy and devoted all his attention to economic matters, and partly, it is thought, that it was a reward to Latham for his sacrifice of the leadership. Perhaps the Manchurian crisis had a little to do with it, but probably not much. It was a background factor in what was primarily a decision for internal reasons. It marked a stage however, in the development of the department, which was reinforced in 1932 when Bruce, after attending the economic conference at Ottawa, went as 'resident minister' to London for a year, after which he became High Commissioner. Australia, as we have seen, had not followed the Canadian example, but preferred instead to join itself to the British system. It was the only Dominion with an ex-Prime Minister in London, and with Bruce and Duffy there, and Latham and Officer in Canberra, it had a capable team handling its external relations. In Latham it certainly had an able Minister of External Affairs, and one with an incisive mind. How successful the system would be, compared with that of Canada, remained to be seen.

Australia, by virtue of its geographical position, was more concerned with events in the Far East than perhaps either Canada or New Zealand. The defence chiefs of Australia had long seen Japan as the prospective enemy. As the chairman of the Australian Defence Committee wrote in July 1930, 'Japan is obviously the only country at present which can seriously threaten Empire or Australian interests in the F.E. [sic]'.[49] This fear of Japan went back to the early years of the century, with the passing of the Immigration Restriction Bill in 1901, and had resurfaced again, after the Russo–Japanese War, in 1910 and at the peace talks in 1919. In 1931 it was coupled, however, with a realisation of Australia's economic dependence on Japan during the depression, and a feeling that of all Eastern countries Japan was the one most likely to increase her consumption of Australian goods. Relations between Australia and Japan, however, were always liable to be strained by insensitive application of the White Australia policy and, even more important, by the high Australian tariffs. Latham, as Minister for External Affairs, was therefore bound to be concerned with Japan and the Far East.

Like its counterparts in New Zealand and Canada, the Australian government received regular information from a variety of sources. To start with, there were the usual cables from the Dominions Office in London. The first one after the Mukden incident arrived on 23 September and included the information that the Japanese forces appeared to have acted without the authority of their government. Thus this knowledge was passed to Australia, even without the benefit of an Australian legation in Tokyo. On the other hand, because of its distance from Britain, the fuller despatches only arrived after a considerable lapse of time. For example, the views of the British ambassador in Tokyo, Sir Francis Lindley, sent on 24 September, did not reach Canberra until 6 November.[50]

Like Canada, however, Australia received information other than from the British Dominions and Foreign Offices, this time from its representatives in London. Duffy, who as we have seen had replaced Casey as liaison officer in London, sent a regular stream of cables to supplement or correct the press news. The High Commissioner, Sir Granville Ryrie, did not apparently send any separate information in the early days. It was not until the appointment of Bruce as High Commissioner in London that a change occurred. Thereafter very full reports on British governmental attitudes and events at Geneva and throughout the world were also sent from the High Commission Office. In this respect, Bruce improved the Australian system. He had the prestige and independence to work more effectively than Duffy, although he tended to upset some of the British officials he worked with, and could give the impression of arrogance and insensitivity.[51]

The Australian Department of External Affairs, therefore, was quite well informed on world events. It had British sources in the Foreign and Dominions Offices, it had its own representatives in London, and it received, of course, the same Japanese and French representations that were made to both New Zealand and Canada. Moreover, the crisis in Manchuria had been a long time coming and Australian authorities had had ample warning. Foreign Office despatches as early as 1926 on the subject can be found in the Australian archives, and Keith Officer had been initialling them as early as 1928. The defence chiefs had been regularly sent copies of Dominions Office cables on the civil war in China, as well as Foreign Office Prints, and Army Headquarters in Melbourne had produced a twelve-page appreciation of the situation in Manchuria in July 1929, with a large-scale map of the railways attached. It was not therefore surprising that Keith Officer produced an excellent summary of Japan's interests and rights in Manchuria, and the complexities of the situation, before any cables arrived from Britain.[52] He clearly had a good background knowledge of the situation.

This casts doubt on the argument that the Dominions, to make sensible judgments on foreign affairs, needed their own sources of information, apart from the British diplomatic service. Armed with the British information, Officer could make sound judgments on the Manchurian situation for himself. Like Keenleyside in Tokyo, he noted the independence of the Japanese army authorities, and questioned Sir Francis Lindley's opinion that the active phase of the crisis was then over.[53] He was thus able to disagree with the British, even though he used their sources. Certainly Officer's picture of the situation was considerably sounder than that of Marler in Tokyo.

Information on the crisis, however, did not induce the Australian government to make any more statements on policy than the Canadian. Keith Officer reported on the discussion of sanctions and the Stimson note, without any reaction from his political masters. Latham merely remarked that Australia had only signed the Nine Power Treaty—to which Stimson had appealed—as part of the British Empire, and that in any case the treaty itself merely provided for consultation between the powers. The implication was that no action was either possible or called for under the terms of the treaty. Indeed, Thomas assured a questioner in the British House of Commons on 23 February 1932 that no representations concerning the Far East had so far been received from the Australian government.[54]

Shanghai, January 1932

On the night of 28–29 January 1932 the vague threat of the Manchurian affair was replaced by a new and much more dramatic crisis in the great Chinese trading port of Shanghai. That seaport on the central Chinese coast, near the mouth of the Yangtze river, was the largest in Asia. Over 61 per cent of British investment in China was located in the city. Moreover, it was the site of an international settlement of British, French, Japanese and US merchants and financiers, with their own municipal council. It was thus not only a vital centre of trade, but also a guarantee and a sign that the 'open door' policy was being applied in China.

The Japanese Consul-General and naval commander in Shanghai, provoked by a local boycott of Japanese goods and riots which resulted from it, first of all issued an ultimatum to the municipal council and then landed Japanese marines to occupy the city. They pushed into the slum area of Chapei, and, when they met resistance, used their air power to bomb the suburb. The wooden houses burned readily.

The emotional impact of this on the West was overwhelming. The bombing of civilians and the destruction of a city provided the newspapers with dramatic news and pictures, which were given much prominence. One correspondent wrote:

> For terrifying ghastliness . . . the aerial bombardment of Chapei is . . . appalling beyond appreciation except by those who had seen the same in the European war. . . . Outer Chapei is ruined. Larger buildings, with few exceptions, last night were bare and gaunt walls, their interiors a seething mass of glowing embers, reflecting against the night sky.[55]

Added to this were tales of Japanese atrocities, of troops firing indiscriminately into buildings as they advanced, of artillery bombardment and tanks adding to the destruction, of Japanese troops wantonly picking off the Chinese civilians who wandered, bewildered, amid the smouldering ruins. Shanghai dominated public attention, and, in Britain, aroused public interest 'to a pitch unparalleled at any other stage of the crisis'.[56]

To the Western governments, moreover, the Japanese action not only was ruthless and inhumane, it also suggested that they were about to embark on an all-out war with China. It threw further doubts on the reliability of the Japanese government and on the ability of the League to restrain Japan. That the fighting raged near the International Settlement was bad enough. Two British sailors were killed by Chinese shell-fire, and an Italian cruiser received four hits. Worse was the fear that the Japanese would occupy the city entirely and directly challenge the rights of the Western powers there. For a time a general war seemed likely.

It fact, this crisis, unlike the one in Manchuria, embarrassed not only the Japanese government but also the Army High Command. The latter therefore wished only to win a quick victory and withdraw, but the actions of their nationals on the spot, and the increased Chinese resistance, obliged it to commit more troops—to 'save face'—and so gave the appearance of wider ambitions. Left-wing critics of Japan in the West were right in one thing, however. The two crises were connected: the leader of the Mukden conspiracy in Manchuria had had a hand in provoking the original crisis in Shanghai, in order to divert attention from Manchuria.[57] He certainly succeeded.

The crisis brought the British government face to face with reality. The Manchurian affair could be ignored, or passed over to the League, in the hope that that body would do nothing drastic. The Shanghai crisis was different, for it involved the centre of British trade in China, and, if suspicions of Japan were correct, implied a direct challenge to Britain's position in the Far East, a challenge which cast an all too clear light on the realities of power in that part of the world. As one historian has written, 'the unresolved problem of Japan's position in China had exposed the fact that Britain's presence in the far east was sustained by a huge confidence trick'.[58]

To start with, the crisis caught the British forces in the area completely unprepared. The commander-in-chief of the China Station, Admiral Sir Howard Kelly, was in Java at the time on a goodwill visit. His diary records him pondering the problem whether to wear a dinner jacket for a formal occasion on the night of 29 January. It was then that the telegram concerning the crisis came. Of his small fleet of one aircraft carrier and six cruisers, the carrier and two cruisers were at Hong Kong, one cruiser was in dock and another at Hankow. Kelly himself, in his flagship the *Kent* was at Batavia (now Djakarta) and only one cruiser was on the spot in Shanghai. Kelly had to round up his matelots from the four corners of Java, and travel '3000 miles . . . against the full force of the monsoon' to rendezvous with the other cruisers at Shanghai.[59]

Even when this was done, however, his situation was extremely dangerous. According to the Kelly papers, the British China Fleet in 1932 consisted of an impressive 56 vessels. But in fact most of them were very small, being sloops, gunboats and other auxiliary craft on duty up the Chinese rivers. Apart from the aircraft carrier and six cruisers, Kelly's fleet consisted of ten destroyers and thirteen submarines. These vessels were not only few, they were also inadequate in quality. The aircraft carrier was the *Hermes*, which, at 11 126 tonnes, was the smallest in the British navy and was destined to be sunk in a twenty-minute action during the Second World War. Apart from one cruiser built in 1916, and by then obsolescent, the other five cruisers were all 'County Class', built according to the limitations laid down by the Washington Treaty, with 8" (203 mm) guns and displacing no more than 10 160 tonnes. They were lightly armoured—with no side armour in their original state—and moreover stood high in the water, offering a large target to the enemy. They were accordingly much abused by the sailors, who referred to them as 'tin clads', 'ruddy haystacks' and 'coffin ships'. All had been ordered in 1924. The calibre of the two fleets can be gleaned from a comparison of Admiral Kelly's flagship, the *Kent* and the Japanese cruiser, the *Nachi*. The *Kent* carried eight 8" (203 mm) guns, four 4" (102 mm) guns and a variety of smaller armament, eight torpedo tubes and had $1\frac{1}{2}$—3" (38–76 mm) armour on its deck over the 'vitals'. The *Nachi*, on the other hand, had ten 8" guns, six 4.7" (112 mm) guns, twelve torpedo tubes, and 3–4" (76–102 mm) armour over the deck and turrets. She also had an armoured 'belt' just below the waterline, together with a raking profile and a low position in the water.[60] It is true that in January 1932 the Japanese rear admiral only had a force similar in size to the British in Shanghai, but he could call on the whole weight of the Japanese navy to back him, a force of approximately ten battleships, three aircraft carriers, eight new heavy cruisers, nineteen light cruisers, 67 submarines and 110 destroyers. Moreover, whereas the distance from the Japanese naval base at Sasebo to Shanghai was a mere 722 km, the British main fleet would have had to sail approximately 17 600 km. Even the distance from Singapore to Shanghai was 3495 km.[61] In these circumstances, it was not surprising that the British Chiefs of Staff and their deputies took an extremely gloomy view of the situation.

The British government, however, did not need this spelt out. As early as 1 February Vansittart in the Foreign Office had written that if Japan went unchecked in the Far East 'our position and vast interests will never recover' and '*We* [*sic*] are incapable of checking Japan if she really means business'.[62] It went further than this, however. The British were incapable of even surviving in the Far East, let alone checking Japan, if war came.

For in that event, they would have had to send their main battle fleet to the Pacific. They were naturally reluctant to do so, since that would leave them defenceless in European waters. Moreover, even if they had decided to take that risk, they still had to face the technical problem of operating at such a great distance from their home ports. British capital ships and cruisers, built primarily for North Sea operations, did not have the extended steaming capacities needed for the Pacific. To be effective, as the lesson of the Russian defeat at Tzushima in 1905 revealed, their fleet needed a defended naval base, where it could find stores and equipment, and reorganise itself in safety before venturing to meet the Japanese in battle. Such a base was supposed to exist at Singapore. However, as we have seen, British governments since 1921 had steadily declined to fulfil their promises about Singapore. When trouble came in 1932, therefore, the base was totally unprepared.

Kelly himself had visited Singapore just before the Shanghai crisis broke in January 1932 and wrote in his Journal, 'I was quite frankly appalled by what I saw. The proposed naval base was practically moribund, and nothing had been done to the defences to bring them up to date'. He accordingly wrote a long report to the Admiralty: '... the present position at Singapore ... can only be described as deplorable, and the Commander in Chief would be gravely neglecting his duty if he failed to represent this fact most earnestly to the attention of H. M. Government.' He went on to list the inadequate gun defences, against both sea and air attack, and remarked that the base could be attacked by ships which would be out of range of the defence guns. As for the oil storage tanks, they 'could easily be damaged by half a dozen coolies with hand grenades, ...'[63] He went on to urge the prompt establishment of improved gun and AA defences, and a reconnaissance flight of flying boats. Kelly's warnings were underlined by the sudden Japanese attack at Shanghai.

The Admiralty was intensely worried. On 17 February a minute stated that at the completion of the Jackson Contract '... we shall have a floating Dock, a graving Dock without a caisson, and some 800,000 tons of oil, all undefended'. Another minute noted that the elaborate plans to send a fleet to the Far East were based on the assumption that Singapore would be defended, and that sooner or later such defences would have to be provided, or 'the Federated Malay States, New Zealand, the Straits Settlements, Hong Kong and probably Australia also will want to know why ...'. As it was, there were no defences to the landward, five 9.2" (232 mm) guns to the sea, six 6" (152 mm) guns and eight anti-aircraft guns. There were no boom defences or mines, while the army garrison consisted of only two battalions and local volunteer units.[64] This was why the Chiefs of Staff Sub-Committee, in its annual review for 1932, remarked: 'The first priority should be given to requirements in the Far East. ... We cannot ignore the Writing on the Wall.'[65]

This British naval weakness was admitted in the House of Commons on 7 March 1932 by the First Lord of the Admiralty, Sir Bolton Eyres-Monsell, and then stressed by Sir Austen Chamberlain: 'Let it be clearly understood that ... our Navy is not only incomparably weaker than it had been in the past ... but it is proportionately weaker as compared with the navies of other Powers.'

In this situation, with crises in the Far East and gross weakness both in the British fleet and its essential naval base, the British Cabinet met to decide its policy. It was not surprising that Simon tried 'to avoid offending the Japanese too much',[66] to use his own words. Therefore, although the British government gathered its ships on the China Station back to Shanghai, it avoided formally joining Stimson in a note of protest to Japan. Instead, it tried mediation, both through the League and in Shanghai itself. This policy ultimately bore fruit in an armistice agreement on 5 May 1932.

'Imperial consultation'
The British government regarded the Shanghai crisis so seriously that the inner circle of the Cabinet, rather than the full body, dealt with it. The government was not likely, therefore, to indulge in consultation with the Dominions, although it greatly increased the flow of information to them as the crisis developed. No archive appears to have a complete set, but 33 telegrams sent between 28 January and 10 June can be found in the Dominions Office files in London; twenty sent before 24 February are in the Australian archives, and 33 by 21 March can be found in Canadian archives. Altogether, they gave a full coverage of the Shanghai crisis and were highly critical of the Japanese. For example, one remarked:

> ... the Japanese authorities are mainly responsible both by their original action and their persistence, in spite of assurances to the contrary, in using the International Settlement as a base of hostilities. [Britain was sending reinforcements to Shanghai, to protect its own and other nationals from the danger to which they had been] ... unjustifiably—indeed, in the view of His Majesty's Government, wantonly—exposed. We have thus been brought within measurable distance of an immense catastrophe.[67]

Apart from sending regular and detailed cables to the Dominions, the British government also informed their representatives of the latest developments when they met at the disarmament conference in Geneva. According to the Canadian advisory officer there, Dr W. A. Riddell, Thomas made a long statement to Dominion representatives on 1 February 'more than hinting that the Japanese were becoming impossible'. The British Commonwealth delegations to the disarmament conference were given more details and the text of cables on 22 and 28 February, when Simon saw them.[68]

The Dominion reaction to all this information is interesting. The opinion of the New Zealand government has not survived in the archives. Forbes was still probably preoccupied with the economy, and, though disapproving of the Japanese action, did not feel it was any of his business.

Canadians were more articulate. There, the early noncommittal attitude of most leader writers for the newspapers was changed by the Shanghai crisis, if the British High Commissioner was correct. He remarked that 'criticism of Japan's action and suspicion of her future intentions have become increasingly manifest'.[69] The matter was brought before the public in a more dramatic manner when 25 members of the air force, dismissed on the grounds of economy, talked of offering their services to the Chinese government. This led to an acrimonious debate in the Canadian House of Commons, as a result of which Bennett was prevailed on to make a statement. This, vague and suitably optimistic as it was,[70] passing the matter over to the jurisdiction of the League (which Canada would, naturally, support wholeheartedly) was at least more than the New Zealand parliament gleaned from Forbes.

Behind the scenes, however, the government was much concerned lest ardent supporters of the League involve it in the application of sanctions against Japan. Indeed, Newton Rowell wrote to Skelton on 16 February and, when he received no reply, to Bennett on 29 February. He argued that the Japanese military was in complete control in Japan and was going from one excess to another. The League had at least to attempt to do something, or lose its authority and leave the world 'back where it was in 1914'. The Americans should be asked to cooperate, but even if they refused, there was no honourable course for the League members to adopt but the imposition of 'sanctions, particularly the economic boycott'. This opinion carried more weight in that Rowell had been a Unionist Cabinet minister and acting Secretary of State for External Affairs in 1920. He was too late, however. Sir George Perley, the Canadian representative at the disarmament conference, had made an opening speech referring to the League, and asserting that it could best achieve its aims 'by building up machinery for conciliation, rather than by providing for sanctions . . .'. In this, Perley was continuing the Canadian tradition of opposition to sanctions, which had been seen as early as 1924 in discussions on the Geneva Protocol. Skelton eventually replied to Rowell. He still hoped that unanimous world opinion might help the conciliatory forces in Japan, though he admitted that he was prejudiced against the use of sanctions. He doubted if France and those who thought like her would rally round to help Canada in similar circumstances. However, he added that he did not rule out the possibility of such action if flagrant violation of the Covenant continued.[71]

The Department of External Affairs was also, needless to say, receiving comments and advice from the minister in Tokyo. Marler had cabled on 30 January that the situation was 'extremely serious'. The British ambassador, Sir Francis Lindley, thought the Japanese action was 'indefensible', but Marler's own opinion was 'somewhat less emphatic'. He was anxious that Canadian delegates to the League should show caution, since a 'strong expression of opinion . . . would not serve our interests in Japan where up to the present we are considered entirely neutral'. He was told in reply that though this was recognised, a situation might develop in which the observance of international agreements was the main concern. Marler seems to have become extremely nervous at that time, thinking that Article 16 might be invoked and a state of war develop. He asked for instructions. He held long conversations with the British naval and military attachés, who stressed British military weakness in the Far East. He therefore 'urged moderation before all else'. Thus the fears of British military advisors were affecting opinions passed to the Canadian government. Marler also saw the British ambassador, and they made joint representations to their governments. Marler was torn between his reluctant admission that Japan was clearly in the wrong and that League prestige needed to be upheld, and fear of the consequences if Canada took any lead.[72]

In London, meanwhile, the Canadian High Commissioner had arranged to meet Simon to discuss the British attitude to sanctions. Marler's meeting with Lindley ought really also to have been discussed at the same time. Unfortunately, however, a deciphering error in Lindley's report of the meeting had led to Marler being designated 'the Danish Minister', so that no one in Britain had realised what had happened until it was brought to their attention by their representatives in Geneva.[73] Nevertheless, the British had, disjointedly, at least discussed their policy with Canadian representatives. This was not the same as consulting them beforehand and did not for a moment imply that they would have modified their policy if the Canadians had so wished, but some form of sharing of information and of the policy decisions after they had been made did take place.

From the Canadian viewpoint, the interesting thing about Marler's telegram is that it reveals how he changed his ideas as a result of the Shanghai crisis. Indeed, he admitted in a long cable in mid-March that in the matter of Manchuria he had been 'not unfavourable to the Japanese'. He denied, however, that there was any similarity between their actions in Manchuria and Shanghai, or the situation in those two places. While accepting that the Chinese in Shanghai were boycotting Japanese goods, he asserted that he found it 'incomprehensible' why the Japanese thought that force would change that. He listed the Japanese excuses one by one, demolished them, and then went on to describe in detail the Japanese reign of terror in the districts they occupied and the pitiful state of the Chinese civilians.[74] This report, indeed, is most interesting. It contains many of Marler's constant ideas, but modified and written in a better style. One wonders if Keenleyside had had a hand in it and whether, as a result of the Shanghai crisis, Keenleyside had managed to influence Marler, at least for a time. Indeed, Marler became suspicious of the Japanese for a while and believed, wrongly as it happened, that they had not intended to stop at Shanghai, and, more correctly, that their concept of the Open Door was so restrictive that Canadian trade interests would be badly injured if Japanese designs succeeded in the future. He did not hesitate on 30 March to tell the Japanese Vice-Minister for Foreign Affairs that it would be a matter of extreme regret if Japan left the League, but she should not be so intolerant of criticism by smaller countries. He added that Japan would lose prestige if she left the organisation.[75] This, for Marler, was strong talk indeed.

The Canadian government, however, kept its options open, neither taking the lead against Japan nor abandoning the League and the Covenant. The reason can be found in the strongly held views of Skelton: first, that Japan was undoubtedly the aggressor, and second that the League powers including Canada should not for one moment consider sanctions. These views were internally inconsistent and certainly at variance with Canada's legal obligations.[76] Not surprisingly, therefore, Skelton strove to keep Canada out of the limelight and its policy noncommittal.

The Australian government was somewhat more definite. It became aware of this crisis—like the Manchurian—at an early stage. On 30 January Keith Officer sent a memorandum to Latham emphasising the gravity of the situation; on 3 and 10 February he forwarded two others, stressing the independence of the Japanese military. The danger of war actually provoked the Australians into making a statement of policy. On 8 February Latham cabled the High Commissioner that the government was very concerned that the Empire should not become involved in war, although it recognised the necessity of protecting British lives and property. If the matter came up at the disarmament conference or the League and a statement was necessary, the High Commissioner should express the urgent hope that a pacific settlement would be attained.[77] A simple desire to avoid war, however, would not satisfy those in the community who wanted the government to support the League of Nations. For this reason Latham gave a very guarded reply to a parliamentary question on the matter. He suggested that harm might be done by going into details, and added that the government had been kept fully informed of the situation. This was true enough, but Latham was perhaps exaggerating when he added that the government 'is lending and will lend assistance to any useful effort to effect a peaceful solution'. This stress on a peaceful solution, of course, mollified those Labor members who chose to regard the Far Eastern crisis as 'nothing more than a sordid trade war' and who accordingly demanded that Australia keep well out of it. The government was, however, anxious about the proposed visit to Australia of a Japanese naval squadron, fearing incidents caused by pro-Chinese, pacifist or 'anti-imperialist' organisations.[78]

Despite the Australian government's message to its High Commissioner, none of the Dominions made specific representations to the British government. Perhaps this was because they all, for their own reasons, agreed with the British policy of avoiding war at all costs. According to a British representative the Dominions, at a meeting with Simon in February 1932, 'all expressed considerable gratification at the improvement in the position and were very congratulatory on the part taken by Sir John Simon'. On the strength of this, Simon himself reported to the Cabinet that they had kept in close touch with representatives of the Dominions and was glad to report that 'there is evident a spirit of the friendliest cooperation between all their members and ourselves'. Eden assured a questioner in the House of Commons on 4 February that the Dominions were being kept in touch with the situation and assented to British policy. The crucial question was raised on 10 February, however, when he assured another questioner that they were being constantly informed of events. He was then asked, 'Is "informed" quite the same as "consulted"?' To this he could only reply: 'Full information is being given, and I have no reason to doubt that the Dominions are in general agreement with the policy which we are pursuing.' Yet the Canadian representative at the Special Assembly of the League was told, officially by Bennett but probably by Skelton, 'I might add, for your information, that while informed by the British Government on each occasion of the action it has taken, there has been no prior consultation at any stage during the recent dispute.'[79]

The words 'prior consultation' were the key to the matter. The Manchurian crisis did not require urgent decisions and so left time for consultation, yet the British were not noticeably keen to consult. Thomas, in the Cabinet debate on Simon's memorandum of November 1931, raised the need to consult the Dominions if the discussions in the League Council made it desirable.[80] His aim, however, was to dissuade Simon from taking a stronger line in the Council. This use of the Dominions to support policies adopted on other grounds was seen later, when the CID in 1932 cited Dominion economic dependence on Japan as an argument against sanctions.[81] Yet the CID had other more weighty reasons for its opposition to sanctions, not least the desperate position of the British forces in the Far East.

On the other hand, neither were the British willing to discuss matters at length when trouble came to Shanghai. For it was one of those sudden crises in which, as the Balfour Committee had said, there was no time for protracted consultation and Britain had to take the lead for the Dominions. Nevertheless, had they wished to consult the Dominions more fully, the opportunity existed. For Thomas was not only Dominions secretary but was also well placed to give the Dominions the latest thinking of the Cabinet. As we have seen he had been much concerned with the Manchurian crisis discussions in Britain. He it was who reported to the Cabinet on his return from Geneva on 10 February 1932; five days later he attended a meeting with MacDonald, Simon, Chamberlain, the Secretary of State for War and the First Lord of the Admiralty; he was one of the small inner group of the Cabinet who met informally to consider the crisis and who eventually formed a Cabinet committee on it, which sat between February and March 1932.[82] Yet he apparently made no reference to the Dominions at its meetings and did not take the opportunity which his membership afforded of supplying them with inside information. Moreover, in his statement to the Cabinet after his return from Geneva, just mentioned, Thomas ignored the Dominions completely and merely talked as a representative of Simon.[83] While this was natural enough in the circumstances, it does suggest that his position as Dominions secretary did not dominate, or much influence, Thomas' thinking. He seems to have adopted a schizoid attitude to his several duties and not to have rated the Dominions very high on his list of priorities.

Nor did Dominion representatives gain any enlightenment from the CID. The Manchurian crisis and the Shanghai affair were not discussed in that body until 9 June 1932, and thereafter on 6 April 1933.[84]

On the other hand, it must be admitted that the Dominions, for their part, did not press their views on the British. Roskill remarks that 'telegrams from the Dominions had revealed that, although there were the usual differences of outlook, there was hardly any support for a policy which could lead to a conflict with Japan'.[85] This is a puzzling statement. He provides no references for Dominion telegrams, and the present writer has found none. Certainly the Dominions wanted to avoid war with Japan, for varying reasons of their own. The Canadian advisory officer at Geneva, for example, noted in his diary that the British Empire meeting on 2 March 1932 'revealed desire to keep out of war with Japan'.[86] But the British government and Simon shared that view completely. Whereas the Dominion governments were willing to enter into correspondence about the forthcoming economic conference which was to be held at Ottawa, they apparently did not send any messages concerning Manchuria or Shanghai. Although Latham had urged the Australian High Commissioner to stress, if asked, that the Australian government desired to keep out of war, it seems that Sir Granville Ryrie found the atmosphere at the disarmament conference at Geneva congenial enough not to have to venture an opinion. No record of any other telegram sent by the Australian government at this time survives in the archives in either London or Canberra.

More than this, however, in Canada Skelton did not wish to be consulted—though he was willing enough to be able to complain that he had not been. As we have seen, he distrusted Europe and the British potential for drawing Canada into its wars, and was thus apparently upset when he learnt that his request to the Canadian High Commissioner to cable extracts from Sir John Simon's speech on British obligations under the Covenant had been mistaken as a request for an approach to the Dominions Office, and a subsequent suggestion that the High Commissioner discuss the matter with Simon at Geneva. This savoured far too much of 'consultation' for Skelton's taste. He therefore cabled back that Perley should disregard the suggestion that he meet Simon. In the event the meeting did take place, without compromising the Canadian government as Skelton feared.[87] The whole affair throws an interesting light on Canadian complaints of the British failure to consult.

The basic reason why the Dominions did not press their opinions on Britain, however, was probably that they agreed with British policy. After all, on 15 February 1932, at the Cabinet Committee on the Far East,

> Sir John Simon said that he had never for one moment favoured the adoption by the League of any kind of sanctions, not even of an economic character. For him the application of Article XVI was quite out of the picture. The point that concerned him was lest, by a declaration, we might provoke a situation that precipitated Japanese resentment.[88]

This being so, the British needed no promptings from the Dominions to keep out of war. They were determined to do so in any case. The only use the British might find for the Dominions was to provide further arguments for the stand they intended to take. Thorne therefore seems more accurate than Roskill when he remarks:

> Even had there existed, which there did not, a desire in Commonwealth capitals to play a forceful role in helping to shape policy, it is doubtful whether much encouragement would have been forthcoming. As various unofficial pressure groups were finding, too much was seen to be at stake for anyone outside Whitehall to get much of a hearing.[89]

Although Britain provided the Dominions with a steady flow of information on the Manchurian crisis, and an impressive amount of detail on the Shanghai crisis, 'consultation' in the full sense of the word did not take place. This was partly because the British were all too well aware of the dangers inherent in the situation, and also because of the speed of events. As for the Dominions, New Zealand seems to have been still in its Imperial 'dream time', to borrow an

Australian phrase, while the Canadian and Australian governments thought and acted more fully. But none of the Dominions actively pestered the British government with advice, or indeed openly or secretly disagreed with its policy. They all had their preoccupations in the early days of the Manchurian crisis, and that affair was comparatively remote from their shores and could be shrugged off as of no concern to themselves, or even helpful in that it involved the Japanese military on the mainland of Asia. The Shanghai crisis, which did concern them much more, was too sudden for them to make any contribution to discussions on policy. War or peace would be decided elsewhere.

The situation, however, was about to change, for, the League Council having failed to bring the two parties to the dispute to the conference table, the Manchurian crisis was about to pass to the League Assembly. In that Assembly, the representatives of the Dominions would be expected to express opinions, or at the very least vote on motions put forward by others. A new phase of the crisis was thus about to begin.

3 Hesitation in the League 1932–33

> *Our friendly relations of long standing with both parties to the dispute, and our position on the Pacific, give us an especial interest in the success of the efforts for the preservation of peace which the Council of the League has undertaken.*
> R. B. BENNETT IN THE CANADIAN HOUSE OF COMMONS.
> [CANADA: HOUSE OF COMMONS *DEBATES* 19 FEBRUARY 1932. P. 368.]

The importance of the League to the Commonwealth
As a result of the change from 'Empire' to 'Commonwealth', discussed in Chapter 1, the League had steadily become more important to the British. The members of their new 'Commonwealth', the white Dominions, had, as we have seen, differing interests, and as the British granted them greater autonomy so the formation of a common foreign policy became more difficult. Support for the League seemed an answer to the problem. It could be expressed in vague idealistic terms which offended none of the Dominions and which appealed to pacifists and internationalists alike. Moreover, the Dominions themselves were independent members of the League. 'The members of the Commonwealth came therefore to have a vested interest in the maintenance of the League of Nations as an external point of reference around which their differing interests could coalesce'.[1]

Nevertheless, this support for the League was more a public stance than a carefully determined policy. Neither Britain nor the Dominions thought that they might be called on to make sacrifices for the League, let alone fight a war to support it. As a result, their attitude to the international organisation during the Manchurian crisis was equivocal, to say the least.

The British Cabinet, for example, thought it could avoid offending Japan by passing the problem of Manchuria to the League, and then using procedural and technical means to prevent that body from taking any dangerous decisions—decisions, that is, which might require the members to take effective action. Moreover, British politicians could use the fact that the League was discussing the dispute as an excuse for not providing information or making comment, on the somewhat dubious analogy of a matter being sub judice in a civil or criminal court. A typical example of this was the British reply to an Australian offer to join in representations to the Japanese as members of the Nine Power Treaty:

Throughout the dispute as regards Manchuria His Majesty's Government in the United Kingdom have as a member of the League of Nations joined in the fullest possible extent in steps taken by that body to investigate the dispute . . . It has followed from this that . . . they have felt it inadvisable to make any separate public announcement of policy . . . [T]he Manchurian dispute has necessarily to be considered as still sub judice and it has been felt impossible to prejudge the issue. . . .²

This was part of a long reply which used verbose jargon, as well as the appeal to the League, to avoid saying anything definite. Simon, indeed, won for himself something of a name for this sort of answer by the time the Manchurian crisis was over.

There was, moreover, another reason why the British wished to use the League as a means of conciliation in the Sino–Japanese dispute. On 2 February 1932 the disarmament conference—the culmination of pacifist hopes—was to open at Geneva. Planning for the conference had been in progress since February 1931 and on this matter the British government had closely consulted the Dominions. Indeed they were separately represented at Geneva; for example, the Australian government sent Latham, its Minister for External Affairs, backed up by the High Commissioner and the liaison officer, while most others sent their High Commissioners. The conference continued from February 1932 to mid-1934, while the League members simultaneously tried to solve the Manchurian crisis. The two issues therefore became connected. As a result of the Manchurian crisis the Dominions were less willing to see Britain assume obligations in Europe, even though this seemed the price of disarmament; while as a result of its drive for disarmament, the British government was not willing to build up its military strength, even if faced by a resurgent Japan in the East.³

Because the Dominions had accredited representatives at Geneva or in London, there was more opportunity than usual for the British government to discuss international affairs with them. A series of meetings of Commonwealth representatives took place throughout the period on disarmament and on several occasions the Far Eastern crisis was discussed.⁴ Had the British wished to discuss that crisis in more detail with the Commonwealth leaders, the opportunity existed to do so.

The Pacific Dominions and the League

The Dominion attitude to the League was in many respects similar to that of Britain. In New Zealand, for example, as late as February 1933, Forbes answered a request for a debate on Manchuria with the statement that while the government deplored what had happened, '. . . no useful purpose would be served by raising this matter at the present juncture . . . [since] the position of Manchuria is still under consideration by the League.' Yet by then the Lytton Report had been debated and the matter was almost over. While the crisis continued, the New Zealand parliament did not discuss Manchuria once and Forbes managed to avoid making any reference to it. The Labour opposition, however, had long been sympathetic towards the League. In 1922 H. E. Holland, the Labour Party leader from 1916 until his death in 1933, had wanted the Chanak crisis submitted to that body. In 1930 Walter Nash, the secretary of the Labour Party, had urged Forbes—off to the imperial conference—to stress support for the League. The Labour Party therefore sympathised with the League during the Manchurian crisis, and it was Holland who provoked Forbes' evasion in 1933 by requesting a debate in which parliament should express support for the League's attitude. Indeed, according to Angus Ross, 'for some Labor MPs the League virtually superseded Britain as the object of a mother-fixation'. This, however, did not influence Forbes' government, which remained quiescent and apathetic towards the League.[5]

If New Zealand was agnostic about the League, Australia was atheist. There was a lack of idealism in the country that observers noted. As Malcolm MacDonald wrote in January 1935, 'Greatly and genuinely as I like the Australian people, I am bound to say that the way to persuade an average Australian of the virtue of any principle is to show him what advantage he is going to get from its operation. It does not impress him much when he is told that someone else is going to gain from it'.[6] The only strong support for the League came, as might be expected, from the various branches of the League of Nations Union, especially its active Victorian branch. Even this, however, concentrated on the League's arbitration and ignored the possibility of the need to use force. It wanted the Australian government to cooperate with the British—a thing it had every intention of doing—apparently under the illusion that Britain would lead a successful League crusade and also support the Kellogg Pact and the United States.[7] The League of Nations Union, to say the least, did not reveal a clear understanding of the policies of the various powers.

Most members of the Australian government, moreover, did not share their idealism. Hughes remarked that the League was 'useless'. He told the Thirteenth Assembly of the League that it should either lead the nations, or confess itself unequal to the task and 'let the sceptre fall from its palsied hands'. Lyons was obsessed with the cost of the organisation. He told federal parliament that 'the advantage we gain from our representation is not commensurate with the amount that we contribute'. These remarks accurately reflected their authors' attitude to the League. It was in line with this that Keith Officer thought that no special Australian delegate should be sent to the Assembly of the League in February 1932; Duffy, who was in Geneva for the disarmament conference, would do.[8] In the end the High Commissioner, Sir Granville Ryrie, was sent, but the Australian government's lack of interest in the issue was noticeable. In the early part of 1932 it was simply prepared to follow Britain's lead in the crisis.

In Canada there was evidence of humanitarian support for the League, and in the Bennett papers there are a series of articles and letters from Canadians concerned with China's plight, especially the famine there, and with suggestions for help. The government, however, like its Australian counterpart, tended to have other ideas. Prime among these was a keen desire to keep out of entanglements overseas. This had been seen in the first Assembly of the League in 1920, when the Canadian delegate had introduced a move to delete Article 10 from the Covenant. Foiled in this attempt, Canada had then tried to modify the Article in 1922.[9] However, the Canadian government seemed to have more idealism than the Australian. As Sir George Perley said in his opening statement to the disarmament conference,

> It has at times been suggested that our own fortunate situation and our isolation in the New World have made us indifferent to the problems of the Old. We frankly admit our reluctance to become involved in political problems over which we have no control and whose solution we cannot effect, but we are not indifferent to those problems. Bitter experience has taught us that under present conditions we live in a world of interdependent States, and fifty thousand Canadians who will forever sleep in European soil are silent witnesses to that fact.

Skelton himself revealed similar mixed attitudes. In 1920 he had been hopeful of the League of Nations, even Article 10, but 'as the years went by he seemed to become disillusioned'.[10]

The Canadian government, however, had every opportunity to produce a coherent policy. It had its advisory officer stationed at Geneva, which neither Australia nor New Zealand had, and also a Canadian legation in Paris. On the other side of the world, in Tokyo, it had Marler, who was critical of League involvement and of the League's handling of the situation, and was worried by possible reactions in the League Assembly. Moreover, Skelton and Bennett could work together during the Manchurian crisis, despite their different ideas on foreign policy, including the League, for they agreed that Canada was not an important League member and 'should remain in the background in Geneva'. Bennett still did not devote much time to foreign affairs and did not inaugurate top-level discussions with Britain, which would have offended Skelton. So the latter merely had to tolerate the contacts made by minor officials in the delegations at Geneva. However, there was a fundamental difference in their attitudes.

> Bennett sent his delegates at Geneva appreciations of the situation whenever they were to make statements and he delegated a considerable amount of authority to them. Skelton would have termed the same telegrams instructions, and considered the delegates to be merely the mouthpieces of the government. In this fashion Bennett could have his Empire policy, while Skelton at the same time could have an independent Canadian policy. Since both men favoured the British policy of eschewing sanctions in favour of conciliation this system worked, so long as the delegates did not exercise their discretion too vigorously.[11]

The vital importance of this last proviso will be seen in later events. In the meantime, Bennett—like Australia and New Zealand—followed the British precedent and used the fact that the dispute was being discussed in the League as a reason why no statement of governmental policy would be made.[12]

In contrast to these three Dominions, a very different attitude to the League was revealed in the Irish Free State. Both the Cosgrove administration, which was ruling when the crisis broke, and the de Valera government, which came into office in February 1932, gave strong support to the League, 'partly as a counterbalance to the Commonwealth relation'. Indeed, on 20 October 1931 the Irish government had embarrassed British representatives in Tokyo and Peking by asking them to pass on a message to the Chinese and Japanese governments, requesting them to abide by the Kellogg Pact and remarking that the matter had already been laid before the League of Nations. This was stronger than anything the British or the other Dominions sent during the entire crisis. Lindley, in Tokyo, informed the Japanese Vice-Minister for Foreign Affairs of the message 'verbally' and 'explained the constitutional position'.[13] There is no hint in the documents of the feelings this must have provoked in the British Foreign Office. The scene, however, was set for the difference of opinion within the Commonwealth at Geneva.

The 'special assembly', March 1932

The debate in the League was passing out of the hands of the Council. It had created a commission of inquiry, the Lytton Commission, on 10 December 1931. The Japanese, however, had reserved the right to continue operations against 'bandits' and under that pretext had resumed their advance in Manchuria. This, and the fall of the Shidehara government in December, had provoked Stimson to send his note. There followed the outbreak of fighting at Shanghai. On 12 February, therefore, the dispute was referred from the League Council to the less predictable Assembly, which met in a special session on 3 March 1932.

The meeting of the Assembly presented problems for Britain and the Dominions. Till now they had managed to hide their greatest reservation about the League—the use of sanctions to enforce its judgment. For inherent in the use of the League was the weakness—in British and Dominion eyes—that if Japan in the end defied the world organisation, then some members of it might want to use the clauses in the Covenant which provided for sanctions, economic or military, against aggressors.

The British, as we have seen, had decided as early as 11 November 1931 that they should avoid sanctions, and their position on the matter, if anything, only hardened with time. On 13 November, Cecil, in a letter to Simon, assumed that 'anything in the nature of sanctions' was ruled out. Simon's remark on 15 February 1932, that he had never favoured the adoption of sanctions, has already been noted; and on 9 March the Cabinet endorsed the decision of the Ministerial Committee on the Far East, 'that sanctions against Japan were out of the question and would not be supported in this country'. This opinion was favoured, according to Roskill, by Hankey, who thought that the sanctions clauses were a source of weakness instead of strength, and that the Covenant of the League should be scrapped, especially Articles 10 and 16. The League should use conciliation, not force, and sanctions merely impeded this.[14]

This viewpoint was in complete agreement with the Canadians, whose opposition to sanctions went back to the early twenties, as has been seen. Skelton only continued a long-established policy, therefore, when he wrote to Marler in January 1932 that he wished to avoid sanctions. Suspecting the motives of France in stressing them, and thinking that the League had acted unwisely, he wished to emphasise 'the mediatory rather than the punitive functions of the League'. As the League Assembly met he wrote that 'the League's first duty is to exhaust every possible means of restoring peace by conciliatory and mediatory measures . . . before resorting to other methods whose efficiency is untried and whose consequences are incalculable'. Perley was following instructions to the letter, therefore, when at the disarmament conference he urged that the League could best succeed' by emphasising the prevention of conflict, rather than the punishment of aggression; by building up machinery for conciliation, rather than providing for sanctions'.[15]

The Australian government liked them as little as the Canadian or British, but it seems to have decided, for the time being, to avoid the issue by not commenting on the crisis. Perhaps it would not come to sanctions. Accordingly, the Australian High Commissioner, Sir Granville Ryrie, cabled his government after the Assembly opened that he was in 'close collaboration with the Secretary of State for Foreign Affairs and Dominion representatives, and will not, of course, intervene in the discussions without reference to Simon and you'. The

New Zealand government also lay very low in the matter and its representative made no statement at all during the debate. He had simply been instructed to 'cooperate as closely as possible' with the British government. This was very different from the attitude of the Canadian government, which sent detailed and explicit instructions to its representatives. They were to use their own judgment whether to take part in the debate or not, but if they did so, they should not delve too deeply into the causes of the conflict or the arguments of both sides, nor raise the issue of sanctions before other states did. The Canadian government would wait to see the outcome of events.[16]

The British, led by Simon, made some effort to form a united front of all Commonwealth representatives. On 3 March, before the Assembly's meeting, Simon saw them all and urged restraint. The Assembly 'should proceed with prudence and caution' and avoid any inflamatory action. It should therefore suspend judgment on the merits of the case and simply reaffirm the principle of conciliation. A division of opinion appeared amongst the Dominion representatives, however. The Canadian, Australian and Indian delegates strongly agreed with Simon; the New Zealand delegate simply said he would follow British policy; but the South African, C. te Water, thought that Simon's attitude might be regarded as 'weak', while Sean Lester, for the Irish Free State, doubted whether all delegations might be happy just to reaffirm a principle and might want to address a resolution to Japan alone.[17] This was exactly what Simon must have feared—independent attitudes in support of strong action.

The lines were thus drawn for the discussions at the Assembly. Simon must have been happy with its resolution of 4 March, which simply called for a cease-fire, negotiations with the aid of the powers on the spot, and an eventual withdrawal of Japanese forces. This resolution, which so carefully avoided any judgment, led however to a revolt by the smaller states. When the president called on them to express their opinions, a silence followed, in which everyone waited for somebody else to speak. This was broken by the leader of the Swiss delegation, to a storm of applause from the gallery and then the Assembly itself. One after another the smaller nations spoke.[18] The emotional atmosphere of the meeting must have effected Perley, for he cabled Skelton on 6 March that it was obvious that Japan had broken the Covenant and made a blunder in Shanghai. Would Skelton like him to say something on those lines 'in moderate but definite words?' Skelton—as Perley should have known—definitely would *not*. He cabled back instantly stressing the need for unanimity in the British delegation and arguing that such a statement would involve sanctions immediately. Perley immediately backed down, apologised for the words 'broken the Covenant' and promised to stick to his instructions. He nervously complained to the Canadian advisory officer in Geneva, W. A. Riddell, for not decoding Skelton's reply more promptly and for letting him send the first telegram in the way he did. Riddell, piqued, confided in his diary, 'As a matter of fact, he [had] never let me see the telegram'.[19]

Simon intervened in the debate on 7 March and made a long speech endorsing the principles of the Covenant, but also emphasising 'that the immediate task under paragraph 3 of article 15 was mediation'. This did not stop him adopting an apparently firm stand. He remarked that 'it would be far better for the League to proclaim its principles even though it failed to get them observed, than to forsake those principles by meaningless compromise'. This, however, left the *enforcement* of League 'principles' very uncertain. Simon, indeed, was by now widely distrusted at Geneva. Liddell-Hart noted: 'In the eyes of most foreign representatives here, Britain has come to be viewed as manoeuvring to shield Japan for the benefit of her own interests, regardless of justice. I doubt if the old idea of 'perfide Albion' has ever been more widespread.'[20]

Disunity in the ranks of the British Commonwealth was revealed the next day, 8 March, when Sean Lester, for the Irish Free State, stressed the duty of members to uphold the League Covenant and international agreements such as the Nine Power Treaty and the Pact of Paris. The force of this implied criticism of Japan was somewhat blunted by the speech of Sir George Perley of Canada. This had been written by Skelton long before and bore no relation to the drift of the debate at Geneva. The result, hardly surprisingly, was confusing. Perley claimed Canadian friendship for both countries, stressed the importance of the issue to the League, yet ended by distinguishing between the rights of a case and the manner in which they were maintained or enforced. Canadian newspapers were not the only ones unsure whether this was a 'strong' or a 'mild' speech. Some tried to link it with Stimson's doctrine of non-recognition, and this worried the Japanese minister in Ottawa. Skelton, however, had a long meeting with him and calmed him by associating Perley's statement, not with Stimson, but with the League Council's previous note to Japan.[21] Skelton's policy of rigidly detailed instructions to League delegates, however, did not seem to have worked very well.

Back in Geneva, meanwhile, te Water, the representative for South Africa, continued the debate by opposing Simon in much more blunt and open terms. He insisted that a state of war was occurring in Manchuria, with powerful Japanese armed forces on Chinese territory. Moreover, Japan had not sought to use the pacific means at its disposal under the Covenant, nor remembered its signature of the Pact of Paris. Therefore a prima facie case had been made out against her, and he urged the Japanese representatives to state their case, if they had one, for it was the duty of the League to judge it. He then turned on the great powers. The smaller nations looked to them to give 'strong leadership—leadership which can be interpreted in terms of action and not in terms of words'.[22] This last remark was a none too veiled criticism of Sir John Simon and British League policy. The attempt of the Aga Khan, for India, to pour oil on troubled waters immediately afterwards, stressing 'reconciliation' and supporting Simon's views, only revealed more clearly the fundamental difference of opinion between Commonwealth leaders.

On 11 March the Assembly adopted a resolution affirming that the Covenant indeed applied to the Manchurian crisis, and that the use of military pressure was contrary to its spirit. The resolution also referred to the Pact of Paris and supported the principle of non-recognition. The League thus came into line with Stimson in the United States. The Commonwealth, however, remained divided. Canadian reactions, for example, were mixed,[23] but in general supported Simon. They strongly opposed South Africa, a fact which was soon revealed.

For the league had also decided to set up a Committee of Nineteen to ensure the execution of its resolutions, to try to find a basis for a settlement and to report to the Assembly. This committee was to consist of the permanent members of the Council, other than China and Japan, and six others selected by secret ballot. Te Water, who stood for the committee, was defeated narrowly—according to rumour as the result of Simon's influence. The latter however denied this; and, indeed, it was reported that Perley of Canada and Sir Granville Ryrie of Australia had 'deprecated rather strongly the terms of Mr. te Water's speech' and were not likely to support him. That the rumours circulated so freely reveals the tension that the incident had created. The South African press made much of the matter, and it was even raised in the British Cabinet.[24]

Simon, however, tried to conceal these differences of opinion from the British House of Commons. When a questioner asked if Britain were pursuing a common policy with the Dominions there was concern at the Foreign Office, and they 'concerted' a reply with the Dominions Office. Because of te Water's speech at Geneva they avoided mentioning a 'common policy'. Instead, Simon on 16 March reasserted that there had been daily contact at Geneva with Dominion representatives, and that the Assembly's resolution had been voted for by all members of the Commonwealth.[25] This ignored the fact that the representatives of Ireland and South Africa undoubtedly voted for the resolution in lieu of anything better. The questioner was not to be fooled in this way and rejoined by asking whether it was not a fact that 'a much more advanced position was taken up by the South African Delegation, and some others, than the British Government?'. To this no reply was vouchsafed.

Sanctions and 'non-recognition'

The debate in the League Assembly had provoked fresh fears among some members of the British government that there might be a call for sanctions. Thomas seemed much concerned, and was even provoked into mentioning the Dominions in support of his argument. While the debate was still in progress, and before the text of Dominion speeches to the League could be produced, he presented a memorandum on disarmament and sanctions for the Cabinet Committee on the disarmament conference. This memorandum, of 10 March 1932, cited past Canadian opposition to sanctions when the Geneva Protocol had been discussed in 1924 and the remarks of Hertzog of South Africa at the time of the London naval conference, 1930. It then quoted Sir George Perley of Canada and te Water of South Africa at the opening sessions of the disarmament conference. In case some of his colleagues were slow on the uptake, Thomas added that the settled policy of the Dominions was not to be committed beforehand, by either Britain or the League, to 'hostilities' without the approval of their parliaments, and that they would favour a policy of diminishing or eliminating sanctions from the Covenant. He then drew his own conclusion, that the great value of the League was as the 'moral organiser of world opinion . . . [which] is becoming more and more the determining factor in world affairs'. Thomas' picture of the world was naively optimistic, but his estimate of Dominion opinion was probably accurate enough as far as it went. Indeed, one Canadian scholar has commented: 'From its emphasis on conciliation, its criticism of France and its belief in cooperation with the United States this memorandum might almost have been written by Skelton.'[26]

Nevertheless, the memorandum seems to have been brought out in a hurry. Thomas' examples were sketchy and diverse. He had only to wait a few more days to have been able to incorporate the speeches of Dominion representatives at the League Assembly. However, he probably produced the memorandum because he feared the debate there would end with a call for sanctions, and therefore wanted to marshal all the arguments he could before that call came. He was using Dominion opinion to support a case he passionately believed anyway. He did not think fit to seek current Dominion opinion on the matter—as he could have done by sending cables to the various Dominion premiers or to their representatives in Geneva. That such a simple course was not taken was revealing. It would have been an easy form of consultation, with replies likely to agree with the position Thomas had adopted.

The British Cabinet, however, was determined to avoid sanctions, though it also wished to avoid admitting as much. On 22 March Simon gave what could have been a caricature of a politician's speech to the House of Commons, stressing support for the League, yet remarking that Britain did not want to be involved in further 'difficulties'. 'The truth is that when public opinion, world opinion, is sufficiently strong and unanimous to pronounce a firm moral condemnation, sanctions are not needed.' The truth, as events were to show, was nothing of the sort. Simon, moreover, was equally evasive whether Britain would accept the Assembly resolution and refuse to recognise the Japanese state of Manchukuo. He began by remarking that they had to be sure of the facts; no one would rush to recognise the new government: 'We should need to be quite certain . . . that you had a responsible Government, that you had a Government which would really administer the territory . . . and that you had a Government which really was the genuine expression of the decisions of the neighbourhood to which you refer.' Then, after mentioning the Nine Power Treaty and the need not to 'encourage or countenance what might be a disregard of a violation of Chinese territorial integrity', he went on: 'At the same time, there is no law, and there is no common sense in saying, that in no conceivable circumstance can there ever be a sub-division of an enormous area like China . . .'[27] This last point was just as well, since the Western powers had in fact in the past contemplated the subdivision of China among themselves. The question was important, however, since it brought into the open British policy towards the League. To support a policy of the non-recognition of Manchukuo would offend Japan; not to do so would make Britain appear a traitor to the League. No wonder Simon retreated behind a smokescreen of words.

The matter was also important for the Commonwealth. To start with, it raised the constitutional position of the Dominions. The question whether British recognition of a country automatically implied recognition by each Dominion, since the King was common to them all, had been raised in 1931. By 1932 the Dominions themselves, as members of the League, were faced with the issue whether they should adopt sanctions, or even support the milder policy of refusing recognition to Manchukuo. In fact, most of them shared the reservations of the British government. A debate in the South African parliament on 18 and 19 April 1932, for example, revealed that, despite brave words in the League Assembly, most South African politicians had faith in the League as a moral, not a coercive force, while the Prime Minister, Hertzog, seemed completely confused.[28]

The New Zealand parliament, on the other hand, did not discuss the Manchurian crisis at all. As for the government and its agents, Sir Thomas Wilford in London, in his report on the League Assembly, presented the case both for and against Japan, and as late as July still asserted that he had taken an entirely neutral attitude in the Sino–Japanese conflict. Although he admitted its importance for the future of the League, he was not optimistic—hardly surprisingly, since he demanded a highly unlikely outcome, the settlement of the question to the satisfaction of all the parties concerned, as a test of League success. Wilford, however, probably deliberately sent vague and scanty reports to his government to hide his real feelings in the matter, and also because he did not think very highly of his colleagues in Wellington. At one stage Forbes had to ask for more information.[29]

Forbes himself seems to have been more concerned by the cost of the League than he was by the results of its meetings. He wrote to Wilford demanding that League expenditure be reduced, suggesting cuts in the number and pay of League officials and objecting to the Secretary-General singling out New Zealand calls for economy in the previous League Assembly. The letter was lengthy and strong, but in a slightly less querulous tone than that adopted by the Australians. This did not stop the government keeping a file marked 'New Zealand's contribution to the League'. It was in this spirit that, later in 1932, Wilford decided that in the interests of economy only three people from the New Zealand High Commission in London would go to the League Assembly, and they would arrive in Geneva the evening before it began to sit.[30] It was, therefore, no wonder that they neither contributed to the debate nor were fully informed of the feelings of the other delegates.

In Australia the government, despite the fact that public opinion does not seem to have been greatly roused, was much concerned with the Manchurian crisis. Mr Sato in the League Assembly had complained of the restrictions on Japanese emigration and had implied that this was one reason for Japanese action in Manchuria. This had led to a question in the British House of Commons about a Japanese attack on the White Australia policy. The exchange did not go unnoticed in the Department of External Affairs in Australia.[31] Moreover, considering the volume of trade which Australia had with Japan, the government was bound to be concerned by the suggestion that sanctions might have to be applied to that country.

In early March 1932 Duffy in London had passed on British fears of the consequences of sanctions and Keith Officer in Canberra stressed the danger that they might provoke Japan into retaliating with force. In the same month the advisory committee of the CID brought out its report on sanctions, a copy of which, together with a letter from Duffy, arrived in Australia that May. Among its conclusions the committee noted Japan's heavy purchases of raw wool in Australia and that the closure of the Japanese market would have a serious effect there. The British Commonwealth would be the first to be affected by the double-edged application of economic sanctions. It ended with a discussion of the need to declare war on Japan to enforce the embargo and the probability that Japan would declare war anyway.

Nothing less calculated to encourage the Australian government could have been sent. Indeed, Keith Officer lined the margin of Duffy's summary of the conclusions (pages 7–9 of the report) against the sections that declared that the assumptions behind economic sanctions could not be justified, that stressed the effects on the British Commonwealth and that the imposition of sanctions was part of a state of war.[32] Thus British reservations about sanctions were passed to the Australian government. It was not therefore surprising that the Australian representative in the Commonwealth meetings at the disarmament conference came out with definite opposition to any form of sanctions in any agreement, arguing that the Sino–Japanese dispute had proved sanctions to be of no effect as a deterrent.[33] The logic in this was obscure, since no sanctions had been applied, but the attitude of mind was clear enough.

At the same time Australian nervousness was revealed by the government's reaction to the possible recognition of Manchukuo. In mid-March it simultaneously received a message from the Dominions Office on that subject and was asked a question in federal parliament on its attitude to Stimson's policy of non-recognition. Sir George Pearce, like Simon, hedged. At the end of July, however, Duffy sent the first of two warnings from London that the Japanese military were in command and would soon recognise Manchukuo. He mentioned the Nine Power Treaty in these messages. As a result, Keith Officer in Canberra wrote an appreciation of the matter and suggested that as Australia was a signatory of the Nine Power Treaty, and also a Pacific State, perhaps they should advise the British government that it had their support in a difficult situation. He drew up the text of a cable to Duffy, who was to inform the Dominions Office that the Australian government was watching the situation with anxiety. It realised the difficulties caused by the internal situation in Japan and the need for caution, but as a signatory of the Nine Power Treaty it would support Britain in suggesting to Japan that there should be no recognition of Manchukuo before full consultation between the parties to that treaty, and before the Lytton Commission had reported. Canada should be invited to join this representation. Thereafter, however, news arrived of Japanese determination to recognise Manchukuo, so Officer and Latham sent a modified cable, simply remarking—after referring to the Nine Power Treaty—that they would support the British government in any representations it might consider wise. They still suggested the inclusion of Canada in such representations.[34]

Forwarded to the Dominions Office, the Australian suggestion caused consternation among the British. The terms of the Nine

Power Treaty were vague, simply stipulating 'full and frank communications' if any signatory felt that the situation warranted it. Nevertheless, the British had approached any invocation of the Nine Power Treaty very gingerly. The Americans had that April suggested a complaint to the Japanese, under the terms of the treaty, about the new customs system in Manchukuo. The British, however, were anxious not to be drawn into cooperation with the Americans in any grandiose statements in support of 'non-recognition'.

The Dominions Office was therefore unwilling to draft a letter on its own initiative and referred the matter to the Foreign Office. There, painstaking debate occurred on the exact wording of a reply. Eventually the text was approved by no less a person than Simon himself, and the reply was sent via the Dominions Office to Duffy and from him to the Prime Minister's Department in Canberra.[35] It is an interesting example, since it is almost the only one which can be traced from its beginnings in Australia through to the British end and then back again. In no other case have all the relevant documents survived. It is noteworthy that Simon and the Foreign Office thought that this was an important enough matter to warrant dictating the terms of the British answer. From the fuss this correspondence caused it also seems that this was the first message the British had received from Australia. Thereafter, the Dominions Office meticulously kept the Dominions informed of Japanese movements towards recognition. It sent circulars on 7, 17 and 20 September and held a meeting with representatives of the Australian and New Zealand High Commissions, just before the next League assembly.[36]

As for the Foreign Office, it was primarily concerned that the Australian government be persuaded to be circumspect, and not invoke the Nine Power Treaty. Its reply therefore began by remarking—once again—that the matter was before the League and so sub judice until the Lytton Report came out. However, the British government had taken every opportunity of 'reminding the Japanese government unofficially, and in a manner such as not to inflame already excited public opinion', of its obligations under the League Covenant and the Nine Power Treaty. Britain thanked the Australian government for its offer of cooperation and assured Australia that if the United Kingdom decided to work through the Nine Power Treaty it would 'not fail to consult His Majesty's Governments in the Dominions concerned'. This message was sent by cable in the first instance, and then the full text of the British memorandum was sent by mail, arriving in Australia on 6 October.[37]

The British reply virtually requested the Australian government to avoid making a public statement on policy, which was awkward—questions were likely to be asked in the Australian parliament, especially if Japan went ahead and recognised Manchukuo publicly.

When therefore Officer received warnings from Duffy that this was imminent he drew up a reply to a possible parliamentary question, using the British message as its base. The Australian government was still anxious, however, and approached the British representative in Canberra, enquiring what it could most usefully say. In the Foreign Office it was minuted that 'I think we should appreciate the fact that the Australians have consulted us'. They informed the Dominions Office that it would be premature to take up any definite attitude towards the Japanese recognition of Manchukuo until the Lytton Report was produced. A telegram was sent in those terms to Australia and Officer accordingly drew up a revised parliamentary reply. It was not needed. Not until early November was a question asked in parliament, and then Latham simply replied that the government had been represented at the various meetings of the League, had been in 'constant consultation' with the British government, and had concurred in certain action taken by that government. 'It has not considered it useful to make any separate representations.' The reply was hardly truthful—or enlightening.[38]

In contrast, in Canada Bennett was forced in the end to suffer a debate to take place in parliament. In April 1932 he had brushed aside a question by remarking that it would be unwise for Canada at the League Assembly, 'with the slight knowledge we possess as compared with those who are constantly in touch with the situation at Geneva . . . either to blame or praise this country or the other . . .'. Commentators have remarked on 'the odd admission that a country which was a member of the League and which had a Department of External Affairs and a diplomatic mission in Tokyo should have no more than a "slight knowledge" of a major international crisis'. Moreover, Canada had also a Canadian advisory officer resident in Geneva. This was only an example, however, of Bennett's deviousness in dealing with the Canadian parliament. He managed to postpone any debate on the Manchurian issue until the end of the session, when members were tired and there was hardly a 'debate' in the full sense of that term. When reproached that Canada had not supported American protests or adopted a more active and positive policy in the League Assembly at Geneva, Bennett asked what force Canada possessed to back sanctions. He read out Perley's speech to the Assembly and suggested that the League had prevented a major war in the Far East.[39] It was hardly satisfactory. Nevertheless, the Canadian government was happy with the outcome at the League, for the Assembly had in effect associated itself with the Stimson doctrine of non-recognition.

The matter came to a head, however, at the end of 1932. For on 15 September Japan formally recognised Manchukuo and entered into an alliance with it. It thus presented the League with a *fait accompli*.

Then, on 2 October, the Lytton Report came out. The timing could hardly have been worse.

The Lytton Report—and a New Zealand maverick

After the Lytton Report's publication, Simon, the Aga Khan and Marler in Tokyo[40] were one in fearing the reaction to it in the Assembly, especially seeing that the Japanese had recognised Manchukuo. Simon prepared a Cabinet memorandum in which, after giving a long account of the report, he added revealingly that the League could probably do little but accept it, but that this, 'however natural . . . brings in its train some very serious consequences'. The League, despite the remarks in the report on the complexity of the issues, might 'find it very difficult not to pronounce what amounts to a condemnation of Japan', which in turn might have embarrassing or even dangerous results. They should therefore act with extreme caution. The League declaration of March 1932, that members would not recognise any situation brought about by force, had been an abstract declaration. Now there might even be an attempt to *apply* it!

British spokesmen at the League Assembly therefore would have to keep a variety of aims in mind. They should act as loyal members of the League, while avoiding isolated or prominent action. They could not abandon loyalty to League principles, but should explain to Japan that they were '*pro*-League and not *anti*-Japan'. They should remember the serious consequences for British trade if they antagonised China, but not involve themselves in trouble with Japan. Simon's list, indeed, reveals the mixture of selfish and idealistic motives, the conflicting aims, and especially the desperate desire not to become embroiled with Japan. The Cabinet stressed this last point when it considered the memorandum on 23 November. It fearfully noted that the matter was delicate, 'and must on no account be mentioned publicly or talked about'.[41] Fear, indeed, seemed to be the dominant reaction of the British government.

The attempt to avoid involvement would, however, need Dominion support at the forthcoming Assembly meetings. Thomas therefore raised the question how Bruce and Wilford, neither of whom had gone to Geneva, could be 'kept in touch with our policy on this question'. The Cabinet agreed that Thomas could talk to Bruce and Wilford 'on the lines of the . . . Memorandum without showing them the Memorandum or using its precise language'. Typically, Thomas did not bother to do this himself, but instead left it to Sir Edward Harding, assistant Under-Secretary of State at the Dominions Office. The latter saw Australian and New Zealand representatives the next day and gave them an *aide-memoire* to hand to their High Commissioners. The New Zealand representative remarked that Wilford was then without instructions from his government, but no doubt when they were received they would be, as in the Shanghai case, to 'cooperate as closely as possible with His Majesty's Government in the United Kingdom'. In reply, Harding assured the Dominion representatives that the British government would communicate with the Dominion governments by telegram if the situation at Geneva warranted it, and that every effort would be made to keep Bruce and Wilford informed. The *aide-memoire*, in fact, was a good précis of Simon's memorandum, although it did not reveal the contradictory aims at its end.[42] The next day a 'British group meeting' was held in Geneva, and Simon told the Commonwealth delegates that the 'Lytton Report had made it clear that there was a good deal to be said on both sides of the Sino-Japanese question' and that he favoured Chapters 1 to 8 being made the basis of a settlement. This excluded Chapters 9 and 10, which were the Lytton Commission's own 'Principles and Conditions of Settlement' and 'Considerations and suggestions to the Council'.[43] Simon, in short, was ignoring the Lytton recommendations and seeking a settlement on the more vague and less condemnatory (to Japan) background history and economics of the dispute. He was pursuing a policy of not offending Japan, rather than maintaining the justice of the case.

Meanwhile, back in London, Sir Thomas Wilford, who had noted the atmosphere of gloom over the 13th Assembly of the League, announced at a meeting with staff from the Foreign and Dominions Offices that he might ask his government for permission to support Japan if a vote were taken on the Lytton Report! One wonders what Forbes would have made of such a request.

Wilford argued that he had visited Japan, Korea and China and had studied the East, and was 'most strongly convinced that it was in the interest not only of New Zealand but of the Empire as a whole to back Japan in the present dispute with China'. Japan was the strongest military power in the Far East, and 'constituted a grave military menace to the security of Australia and New Zealand'. Moreover, Japan was chief bulwark against possibly the principal danger to the world—the spread of communism. He feared that the growth of communism in China would link that country with Russia in a formidable power bloc. This was a foretaste of Cold War ideas of the 1950s.

Sir Victor Wellesley, deputy Under-Secretary of State at the Foreign Office, did his best to moderate Wilford's alarm and make him more circumspect. Britain had enough troubles without New Zealand rocking the boat. So he pointed out to Wilford that he was ignoring the dispute in question, and asserted that Britain still desired to preserve the prestige of the League. Wilford remained unconvinced, and scornful of the League. He wanted a categorical instruction from his government to support Japan and declared that his reputation in New Zealand was such that the government would accept his views. When Wellesley said that this might embarrass Simon, Wilford retorted that Water's speech had been a direct attack on Japan and that he was in effect simply neutralising that. After a long argument Foreign Office representatives at last persuaded Wilford not to cable his government but instead to set out his views in full in a despatch, so that he could be sent instructions later if they were needed. However, the next day Wilford contacted the Dominions Office once again and argued that as it had been announced that the League Assembly was to meet eight days later, he would have to telegraph immediately for instructions. The Dominions Office officials, with some difficulty, contacted Geneva and found that the Assembly was likely to pass the matter to the Committee of Nineteen and not discuss it finally till 'early in January'. Wilford therefore agreed that C. Knowles could represent New Zealand at Geneva, and the procedure agreed at the previous meeting could stand.

This explosion by Sir Thomas Wilford is interesting. It seems to have derived from his longstanding fears for New Zealand security, faced with a powerful Japan, combined with a phobia about communism. The official New Zealand historian has remarked that suspicion of communism was a hallmark of New Zealand in international affairs. Wilford also clearly feared the findings of the Lytton Commission and the repercussions of the report in the Assembly.[44]

In fact the Lytton Report, though sympathetic to Japanese grievances in Manchuria and recognising their rights and interests in that country, had condemned the Japanese invasion and refused to accept Manchukuo's independence as genuine. It proposed a compromise settlement which would recognise Japanese interests, but provide a measure of autonomy for Manchuria under general Chinese sovereignty. As noted, however, the report had come out after the Japanese had recognised the separate state of Manchukuo and were deeply involved in military adventures on the mainland. It was therefore too late for such a compromise, and Japan immediately made it clear that it would reject the proposals. The matter was bound therefore to come before the League Assembly, and at that Assembly, if the previous one in March was anything to go by, certain of the smaller nations were likely to demand effective action against Japan—at the very least the imposition of economic sanctions.

Wilford was, from his own viewpoint, naturally concerned, and his concern was shared by Simon. The latter warned the British Cabinet on 30 November that the Manchurian question was reaching a climax, that he 'proposed to do his utmost to avoid taking a lead', but that if other nations wanted to pass a resolution unacceptable to Japan he would stress that the Lytton Report did not recommend the

League to do anything specific, but addressed most of its proposals to the two countries concerned.[45] This was a lawyer's argument. He admitted, however, that if a non-recognition motion was moved, he would have to come into the open and oppose it. The British government, and Simon, were more timorous at the end of 1932 than they had been at the end of 1931. The Shanghai crisis seems to have opened their eyes to Far Eastern realities.

Britain, Canada and Australia in the Assembly, December 1932
The League Assembly met on 6 December 1932. The British seem to have accepted that the Dominions would differ in their attitude; at any rate, there was no attempt to coordinate a policy. Dominion disagreements therefore rapidly came into the open. The Assembly had barely begun on the first afternoon when the representative of the Irish Free State, the first to speak after the Chinese and Japanese delegates, made a long speech. He praised the Lytton Report and stressed the importance of the Assembly's decision for the future of the League. Japan had employed methods of imperialist expansion, and the Assembly must agree not to recognise Manchukuo.[46] He was followed by speakers for other small nations: Czechoslovakia, Sweden, Norway and, on the morning of the 7th, by Spain and Switzerland. By the end of this, the second morning, it was becoming doubtful whether the British scheme, whereby a formal resolution passing the matter to the Committee of Nineteen, supplemented by American and Russian representatives, and not criticising Japan, was likely to succeed. Rumours began to circulate that Czechoslovakia, the Irish Free State, Spain and Switzerland were to sponsor a draft resolution which dismissed Japanese arguments, demanded the non-recognition of Manchukuo, and called on the Committee of Nineteen to settle the dispute, in cooperation with Russia and America, along the lines of the Lytton Report. Simon felt obliged to intervene, even though this ruined his strategy of letting others take the lead. After the delegate for France had stressed the complexity of the Manchurian situation, Simon spoke, and, despite his intentions, became a leading figure in the Assembly.

After praising the Lytton Commission's report, Simon stressed two features: that it brought out the complicated nature of the Manchurian problem, and that it criticised both sides in the dispute. He went on to admit that the methods of the League had not been employed. Their duty therefore was to defend the Covenant; Britain remained loyal to the League and in this respect there was no difference between the small and the great powers.[47]

This was a clever speech, for Simon, posing as a champion of League principles, still urged caution in applying them, so that at least 'one critical observer found himself "paralysed for the moment" by the flow of the argument . . . '. But Simon did not convince all who heard him. The Assembly passed over his asserted support for the Covenant and his observation that Japan had not employed the methods of the League, and noted instead his continued emphasis on conciliation, the faults of China and conditions in Manchuria. There was strong criticism of Simon in Geneva, made all the more bitter by the comment of the Japanese delegate that Simon had succeeded in saying in a short space of time what he had been trying to get across for ten days. Simon, despite his cleverness, simply appeared as a hypocritical supporter of the Japanese case, and at the end of the day on which he spoke the president announced that two draft resolutions were indeed before the Assembly.[48]

Simon desperately needed support for his views from 'smaller nations', and the obvious ones were the Dominions. Here, however, he found the division of opinion as deep as during the previous meeting of the Assembly. According to Gwendolen Carter, 'The British Commonwealth meetings during the Assembly are said to have been the scene of violent disagreements and these may have occurred over the Irish Free State's sponsorship of the resolution'.[49] No authority is cited for this remark, but it seems to be based on conversations with eyewitnesses. Moreover, since many other assessments of this author have been supported by recently available British documents, her judgment deserves consideration.

Simon was in trouble. The South African and Irish delegates would have disagreed with him, while New Zealand, as we have seen, was only represented by the High Commission official, Knowles. Perhaps, in view of the vehemence of Sir Thomas Wilford's views, this was just as well. Indeed, the British may have deliberately understated the importance of the Assembly in talking to him, so he would not think it worth his while to attend. Simon therefore turned to the representatives of Canada and Australia and 'urgently advised'[50] them to speak to the Assembly. The result was dramatic.

On 8 December the Canadian delegate, C. H. Cahan, made a long speech to the League. He opened with the remark that, owing to the distance between Geneva and Ottawa, he could not communicate with his government easily and was therefore about to express his 'more or less personal' opinions, though doubtless his government would agree with them. This qualification tended to be lost in what followed. It was not so much the ignorance revealed by many of the remarks as the strong support for the Japanese case which offended many delegates. After criticising the League Covenant and doubting whether it could be applied to China, Cahan went on to build up arguments against that country, using Chinese history since 1922. On the other side, he accepted the Japanese statement that they were not connected with the independence movement in Manchuria and denigrated the Lytton Commission and its report. He did end by remarking that if the Japanese were not willing to compromise, any further delay would be 'unfortunate',[51] but this final statement did not tally with his previous remarks and went unnoticed in the general reaction to the speech, which went from incredulity to outright hostility.

Representatives of four other minor powers then spoke before the Australian delegate, Bruce, took the floor. Bruce was a much more urbane man than Cahan, and his speech therefore did not have the passages in it that struck such a jarring note. Nevertheless, its purport was similar to that of Cahan. After making the usual pious generalisations about Australia's concern in the dispute, her friendship with both sides and support for the League of Nations—in unctuous terms—he went on to argue that the authority of the League was based on moral and not physical force. As for the Lytton Report, Bruce said that it revealed that the rights and wrongs of the case were not all on one side. He remarked that the Chinese government was not in complete control of all its territory—without the crude criticism of China in which Cahan had indulged—and that this brought new problems to which the Covenant could not apply. He urged that there therefore should be no 'censure, open or implied' of either China or Japan, since that would make reconciliation impossible, and supported Simon's speech to the Assembly stressing conciliation.[52] Bruce's studied moderation did not impress all the League delegates. Indeed, it made some of them think that Commonwealth collusion was proved.[53] In that they were not very far from the truth.

The Canadian delegate, Cahan, was a lawyer for large corporate interests and 'a figure of some importance in the government party, identified with its most conservative elements'. He had represented Canadian financial interests in hydroelectric developments in Mexico, and, according to Riddell, 'had very decided views regarding countries with weak or unstable Governments. He considered that China was one of these countries and therefore he had a great deal of personal sympathy with Japan'. Moreover, Cahan was a conservative of the old school. As one commentator says, 'even had his own predilections been different from what they were, it would have been something like impiety to take a line in high policy diverging very far from that of the British Government'. Moreover,

> Mr Cahan, and those who thought like him, had never been sympathetic with the idea of a League of Nations. To them it was an idealistic absurdity. They were of the old-fashioned school of thought, and inclined to view the Japanese adventure as the natural desire of a strong and orderly people to impose order on a weak and turbulent neighbour.

More than this, it seems that Cahan's understanding of the world around him was limited.[54]

When, in September 1932, the Canadian Institute of International Affairs had listened to a Japanese speaker defend Japan's actions, Cahan had afterwards supported his views to the American chargé d'affaires in Ottawa, arguing that the Japanese should be allowed to work out their manifest destiny in Manchuria and that it was foolish to try to interfere. The American was not impressed by Cahan, whom he regarded as a 'garrulous old man . . . inhibited by a tendency to contrariness', and whom the Cabinet would be glad to see the back of once the economic conference was over. However, the American chargé d' affaires did foresee the possibility of Cahan making 'some indiscreet comment at Geneva', though he thought that Bennett would pull him into line. He therefore suggested that perhaps the American minister in Berne have some conversations with him 'with a view to clearing his mind somewhat . . . '. Cahan adopted the same attitude when he arrived in Geneva, apparently accepting the Japanese arguments at face value and being swayed by their spokesman Matsuoka's fluent English. Riddell, the Canadian advisory officer, noted that Matsuoka was a graduate of a United States University, and was very persuasive, so that seasoned listeners began to wonder whether he was a dupe of the militarists or an accomplice. Cahan, however, 'could not, of course, be expected to have acquired the attitude of mind of some of us who had been following the dispute for more than a year, for this was his first attendance at a meeting of the Special Assembly'. Cahan, indeed, was noted in Canada for obstinately sticking to his own opinions. He told one listener that he regarded himself as much better qualified than Bennett to be Prime Minister. He was not, therefore, likely to take much advice from Riddell, whom he considered to be merely an efficient manager of the Canadian office at Geneva—good enough at keeping in touch with minor officials, but unable to influence the better-known delegates of the great powers. Cahan himself felt a little out of his depth in such august company. As he wrote much later to Mackenzie King, 'Never before in my life . . . did I realise the full measure of my personal responsibilities in the position in which I was then placed'. He had arrived at Geneva on 25 September and soon become restless. He wanted to be consulted by the British, whom he thought underestimated Canada's concern in the matter. As a result, it was very natural for Simon to turn to Cahan, especially since the British had already come to the conclusion that he agreed with them.[55]

The outcome was also caused, however, by a division of opinion within the Canadian government. Skelton, informed as late as 23 November that the Assembly was to deal with the matter, wrote in a memorandum that though Japan had made war in Manchuria and was 'as definitely the aggressor as any country can well be', no other nation would say so bluntly, especially if the burden of economic and military sanctions fell on it. He therefore considered technical means of avoiding a flat condemnation of Japan and finally sent instructions to Cahan on 2 December. According to these, the League should exhaust every possibility of conciliation, so discussion of sanctions would be out of place then. However, the government favoured the Lytton Report, stressing that Chinese and Japanese interests in Manchuria could be reconciled, and that it hoped Japan would not become hostile to the League. If Japan would compromise, the League should avoid drastic measures; but if Japan remained intransigent, the League could not ignore it, for 'further delay without any clear evidence of readiness to cooperate would be most unfortunate'.[56] Cahan incorporated this statement into the last part of his speech.

Skelton's rigid attitude to instructions for Canadian delegates at Geneva had not worked out well when Perley had made his speech to the Assembly, however, and Bennett disagreed with Skelton's attitude. He believed in allowing Canadian representatives the greatest possible flexibility. He therefore had argued like Simon that no declaration of policy could be made before the Assembly meeting and refused to make a statement to the Canadian parliament, or let its members debate the issue. Indeed, in parliament he stated that Canadian representatives should not be given detailed orders, but be free to speak according to the circumstances at the time.[57] This idea was incorporated into Skelton's instructions to Cahan, for they ended with the remark that they were made for his guidance only and the government realised that he would have to consider the speeches of the great powers, though he should keep Perley's previous statement in mind, especially 'the non-recognition of territorial changes effected by force'.

What had been clear instructions now included a fatal loophole to anyone with Cahan's sympathy for the Japanese case, emotional support for Britain and fear of what was transpiring at Geneva. For Cahan was clearly worried by the draft resolution of Czechoslovakia, Switzerland, the Irish Free State and Spain. Cahan thought that this was a prelude to the application of sanctions under Article 16, which might lead to war, and the British were able to play on these fears. As he described it later, the Lytton Commission had reported in favour of a provisional intervention in Manchuria with an international force.

> It was . . . made clear to me that any such intervention would have to be made by British naval and military forces, in which Canada would be expected to participate . . . Japan would probably declare war and . . .

the Japanese naval forces were so strong in the Pacific that in all probability the British flag would be driven from the Pacific, from Singapore to . . . Vancouver, B.C., within sixty days thereafter.[58]

Clearly Simon and his advisors had stressed the disastrous military situation in the Far East with great effect and used it to put pressure on Cahan.

Cahan therefore wrote out his speech and, brushing aside Riddell's objections, took it to Simon, with whom he was dining. The next morning he briefly showed a copy of it to Riddell. 'My hurried reading of it convinced me that there were a number of things that might better not be said. Mr Cahan, however, was not prepared to make any changes.' Indeed, he remarked to Riddell that if the government did not like it they could have his resignation and took the speech away before Riddell had finished reading it. Cahan was strengthened in his resolve because he had previously informed Skelton of his intention of showing the speech to Simon—though in such general terms that Skelton probably did not realise the significance of the move he was approving.[59] He doubtless came to regret it.

If Cahan is to be believed, Bruce too had submitted his speech to Simon beforehand. Moreover, in the previous month an Australian representative had had discussions with the Foreign Office; so Australian cooperation with Simon at the League was partly the result of their policy of integrating their External Affairs apparatus with that of Britain. However, it was also due to the fact that, in the new High Commissioner, Bruce, Australia had a representative who identified himself with British aims and leadership. As he put it in a report to Lyons, 'I had an opportunity, prior to Sir John Simon making his speech, of fully discussing with him the situation that was developing. We were both in accord as to the line which should be taken, and the type of speech which it was necessary for him to make'. Bruce apparently did not think it necessary to inform the Australian government that Simon had asked him to support him in the Assembly, or that Simon had seen the speech beforehand. He did indicate, however, in a cable, that he had intended not to speak, to avoid offending either China or Japan, but that the draft resolution of Czechoslovakia, Ireland, Spain, and Switzerland 'compelled' him to do so.[60]

In short, Commonwealth 'collusion' *had* occurred. Simon had got the Canadian and Australian representatives to support his stand. For all their fine rhetoric in favour of the 'principles' of the League, in practice they stressed conciliation, even at the price of condoning Japanese aggression, and giving no semblance of justice to China. Under no circumstances should the aggressor be offended. As one commentator remarked, Cahan 'pleaded eloquently on both sides—but only briefly and in closing on the side of the victim'.[61] Bruce gave less offence than Cahan, but the substance of his speech was the same.

Repercussions in Canada
The repercussions of the debate in the different Commonwealth countries varied. The New Zealand delegation, as we have seen, had said nothing, probably because Wilford himself was not present. He later sent a studiously moderate report on the debate to Forbes, giving no indication at all of his own opinions. His nervousness had passed, and he seems to have been satisfied with the results of the Assembly meetings. Bruce too simply reported to the Australian government without revealing the extent of his collusion with Simon. Had he done so, however, the government would probably have approved. As for Australian public opinion, the only criticism which reached the government came from the League of Nations Union, which urged support for the League, and some Trades and Labor Councils, which suspected that organisation. They seem to have been under the influence of communist ideas.[62]

The repercussions in Canada, however, were much more far reaching. Cahan's speech had disappointed those Canadians who thought that a clear moral issue was involved. The press almost unanimously criticised it and Canadian opinion seems to have swung against the Japanese. Cahan, however, at the time appeared oblivious to all this, and also to the hostile reaction of other countries especially the Chinese. Their Consul-General in Ottawa protested to the Canadian government and, according to the Secretary-General of the League, Sir Eric Drummond, they nearly imposed a boycott on British Empire goods after the speeches of Simon, Cahan and Bruce. Skelton feared that one might be imposed on Canadian goods.[63]

Even more embarrassing, however, was the damage done to Canadian–American relations. For Skelton's instructions to Cahan had been forwarded to Stimson. Why this had been done is complicated. It seems that the Canadian minister in Washington, W. D. Herridge, had been in Ottawa for the official opening of a new American legation building and expressed an interest in the matter of the instructions, since he knew the Manchurian crisis interested Stimson. Accordingly, when they were drawn up, a copy of the instructions was sent to Herridge to discuss with Stimson. This seems part of a somewhat vague move to reconcile Canadian and American attitudes to the League. Herridge read the instructions to Stimson, who warmly approved of them. Meanwhile, Cahan himself had dined with the American minister in Geneva, who had urged him, ironically enough, to take an active part in the debate.[64]

It was not surprising, therefore, that the Americans were dismayed by Cahan's speech. It seems that in Washington Stimson had been lulled by Herridge into thinking that Canada would influence Britain. Skelton therefore wrote that, had the Americans 'not known that we Canadians are simple folk unversed in the ways of diplomatic intrigue, they would have thought that we had double-crossed them'. Some did. The American minister at Berne told Riddell as he was leaving the Assembly Hall that Cahan's speech was a 'straight double-cross'. Herridge, in Washington, told a State Department official that Cahan 'had made him look like an idiot' and that the only course open to him was to resign. However, Riddell in Geneva and Lester Pearson in Ottawa managed to persuade the Americans that the speech was an aberration of Cahan and did not represent considered Canadian policy.[65] Nevertheless, 'the Cahan affair suggests that the successful execution of policy required more control from Ottawa and more unity of purpose and action among Canadian policy makers and representatives.[66]

The only praise the Canadians received, not surprisingly, came from the Japanese. Their minister in Ottawa called on Skelton, and 'warmly thanked' him. Skelton simply accepted the thanks, 'thinking we had better keep at least one friend for the time being'. According to Pearson, the Japanese minister was 'jubilant in his oriental fashion' and bowed 'excessively low to all members of the Department of External Affairs'.[67]

Skelton, however, was not pleased. He was in a difficult position, since Bennett was in London, and—under the influence of the British and Cahan himself—did not seem to realise the significance of the latter's remarks. He enquired from Riddell what had happened and what parts of Cahan's speech had been influenced by Sir John Simon and then wrote to Riddell: 'the useful custom of consultation between Commonwealth delegates at League Assemblies can hardly be continued if it takes the form of submission "on approval" of the views of the Canadian Government to the British Secretary of State for Foreign Affairs'.[68] He went on to restate his attitude to the position of Canadian representatives abroad. 'Canadian delegates to . . . international conferences . . . are in a purely representative capacity . . . [T]he views they express will be inevitably ascribed to their Government and should, therefore, be confined to the presentation of the policies which have commended themselves to the Government.' Skelton continued by systematically criticising Cahan's speech, using phrases like 'a gratuitous and unhelpful addition to the instructions' and words such as 'mischievous' and 'dangerous'. He was equally incensed by Cahan's misjudgment of the situation and his quotation, at the end of his speech, from the instructions sent by the Canadian government purely for his guidance.

Bennett's first reaction on returning from London, when informed of Herridge's troubles, was simply that 'Cahan made a good speech'. Early in January, however, Herridge stayed with Bennett and at the same time Skelton had 'the most serious discussion he ever had with the Prime Minister, and . . . convinced him of the seriousness of the situation'. Skelton's arguments were doubtless helped by the possibility that the reports of Cahan's speech might provoke a debate in the Canadian parliament, an eventuality which Bennett had avoided till then. Accordingly Skelton informed Riddell on 7 January 1933 that the Prime Minister was 'much disturbed' by Cahan's speech, but that the government could hardly repudiate Cahan, and would merely have to try to smooth matters over if a discussion in parliament resulted.

The debate in the Canadian parliament occurred on 30 January, when Bennett argued that by reading the whole speech, not just parts taken out of context, they would see that the criticisms of it were unwarranted. 'As a whole' it did not depart from either his instructions or the principles which Bennett had laid before the House. This was not a sound argument, but it was the only one open to Bennett. Cahan made a more lengthy defence of his speech the following May, when he gave a detailed account of the history of the dispute, in Manchuria and the League, backed by long quotations from *The Times* and the *New York Times*. It is doubtful whether his listeners received much enlightenment from it. After rambling and inconsequential remarks on both sides of the House the issue lapsed.[69] It was hardly an example of the successful working of parliament.

Meanwhile, the League Assembly had passed the Lytton Report to the Committee of Nineteen, as Simon gloomily informed the British Cabinet. The committee would want to pass judgement, 'and after judgement comes execution, which would bring up the alarming subject of sanctions and Article 16'. Simon and the British, indeed, were determined that sanctions should not be applied, or, if they were, that the British government should dissociate itself from the proposal. They were very lukewarm even about non-recognition.[70]

They need not have feared, for procedural quibbles were still open to them—and to the Japanese. The Committee of Nineteen began by holding conversations with the representatives of both China and Japan to try to get them to come to a settlement. The Japanese reaction was hostile. They objected to the inclusion of the United States and Russia on the committee and insisted on the maintenance and recognition of Manchukuo, refusing to consider the Lytton Report's suggestion of an autonomous Manchuria under the general sovereignty of China. By 14 February the Committee of Nineteen decided it had exhausted conciliation and drew up its report to the Assembly.

Despite all the evidence that conciliation had failed, its report still suggested that a 'Negotiations Committee' should be set up to assist

China and Japan in their dispute. Members of the League and signatories of the Nine Power Treaty were to be invited to nominate representatives.

This immediately raised the issue of Dominion participation. Simon pointed out to the Secretary-General, Drummond, that some of the Dominions had signed the Nine Power Treaty separately, and might wish to be represented on the new Committee. His motives in this matter are not clear. They may have been an awareness of the prickliness of the constitutional situation, or they may have been a desire to get Canadian and Australian support on the Committee. Simon was informed, however, that the Committee of Nineteen did not intend to include representatives of both Britain *and* the Dominions on the Negotiations Committee. Indeed, there was likely to be strong opposition to the inclusion of Canada or Australia owing to the attitude of their representatives during the previous Assembly debate. However, the matter was referred to the High Commissioners of Canada, New Zealand and Australia.[71]

The latter two declined to appoint a representative. Bruce, indeed, did his best to dissuade his government from interest in the Negotiations Committee and suggested that the British representative hold a 'watching brief' for the Australian government and provide the 'fullest consultation' in London. He also appears to have been worried by one phrase in the resolution of the Committee of Nineteen, which suggested or implied sanctions.

The Canadian government, on the other hand, insisted on being represented. Skelton, in London at the time, argued strongly against Canadian membership, but Bennett accepted instead the advice of the acting Under-Secretary of State for External Affairs, Norman Robertson, who, with the Canadian Chief of General Staff, felt that Canada should cooperate with the League, since a refusal would seem like an 'evasion of responsibility'. Moreover, Canada could balance the 'doctrinaire interests of some European countries'. Robertson and Bennett probably also wished to prove that Canada was a good League member after Cahan's speech in the previous Assembly.[72]

Drummond, the Secretary-General of the League, was concerned at the possible reaction to Canada's offer. He therefore suggested that it should stress its special interests in the Far East and relations with China and Japan, rather than the Nine Power Treaty, since that would involve inviting all the Dominions. Skelton, who disliked being involved at all, asked whether the Committee of Nineteen had the power to discriminate between signatories to the Nine Power Treaty. Bennett overrode his objections, however, and after some discussion Drummond agreed to get the Committee of Nineteen to invite all the Dominions which had signed the Nine Power Treaty, on the understanding that only Canada would accept.[73]

Skelton and Bennett were in complete agreement, however, that Canada should make amends by a sound speech at the next Assembly of the League. The man chosen to give this was Riddell, despite some criticism of him over the Cahan affair.

Skelton kept in close touch with developments through Riddell, who asked for, and received, a text of the statement to be made to the Assembly. He gave this on 24 February 1933, keeping word for word to the text sent to him. The statement stressed the Canadian government's desire for a peaceful settlement, its acceptance of the Lytton recommendations and support for the Committee of Nineteen. It therefore urged the adoption of the committee's report. This was repeated, verbatim, to the Canadian House of Commons on the same day and strongly approved of by the leaders of the other parties. Riddell thought it was 'well received' by the Assembly, and he was thanked by the United States' observer and the Chinese representative. A more impartial report by a Dominions Office representative, however, was that it was too 'early, perhaps, to erase the impression of Cahan's last speech'.[74]

The Canadian government, however, was committed by this policy to a more active participation in League affairs than perhaps it desired. For the League Assembly unanimously voted in favour of the Committee of Nineteen Report and set up an 'Advisory Committee' on Far Eastern affairs. Since Canada had insisted on inclusion in the Negotiations Committee, it was given a seat on the new body. This was none too welcome, and neither was the note from the Secretary-General the following June that since Canada was on the Advisory Committee which had drawn up a note on the non-recognition of Manchukuo he assumed the government would effectively adopt that policy.[75]

Australian reservations

The Australian government had managed to avoid such involvement, or indeed firm support for the League. It had declined membership of the Negotiations Committee and it was only on Canadian initiative and with British pressure that it decided to apply for a seat on the League Council. It seemed concerned by the cost of maintaining a representative at Geneva. The British, however, were more concerned that the Commonwealth seat on the Council be maintained. The Australian government was worried by the turn events had taken. The loss of confidence in the principles of the Covenant and the Pact of Paris was noted in the Department of External Affairs, the question of continued Japanese control over Pacific Mandate islands was raised in federal parliament, while the White

Australia policy loomed in the background to the crisis, being raised by Japanese demands for outlets for emigration.[76] But more serious by far was the government's fear that sanctions would be applied. This question was bound to be raised once Japan had refused to accept the Lytton Report or to cooperate with the League. Bruce discussed the matter with the Australian government at the end of January. At that stage, he claimed, he had had no indication of British policy—which throws an interesting light on 'imperial consultation'. He felt that there were 'objections to moral sanctions that were condemnatory' yet 'Material sanctions under Article 16 cannot be accepted'.[77] He seems therefore to have ruled out *any* action against Japan, even moral condemnation.

His attitude was completely accepted by the Australian government. For Latham immediately drew up a reply: 'We agree that economic sanctions should not be applied or even considered by the Commonwealth Government. No objection to Lytton Report so far as it finds facts.' He went on to suggest a committee of League members and that Japan and China should be invited to send representatives. This steadfast refusal to face the fact that Japan was totally determined to have her own way, and would ignore the suggestions of every committee the League might care to set up, was based primarily on fear of consequences. For Latham went on: 'We are anxious not to adopt at any stage any attitude which might commit us to any participation in military etc. action on account of a quarrel between China and Japan in respect to Manchuria.' He ended with an exact parallel to the British attitude: 'This should be guiding principle while endeavouring to maintain League principles as far as possible.' The Australian government, no more than the British, accepted that these aims were mutually exclusive, and that attempting to follow them only resulted in 'newspeak' and lack of action.

This remained, however, the attitude of the Australian government. Accordingly, a telegram to Bruce at the end of February remarked that 'economic sanctions, whether applied by League under Article 16 or by China as economic boycott . . . are in truth applications of force in all but technical sense'. And in reply to a parliamentary question, Latham declared: 'It would be neither practicable nor in the interests of Australia or of the cause of peace for the . . . Government to attempt to take any action in the matter other than the action already taken in supporting efforts towards conciliation.'[78]

For this reason the government was very unhappy about the non-recognition policy. It received the recommendations of the Advisory Committee on that subject on 14 June 1933, but delayed over a month before enquiring what the British reply to this would be. It was informed, a month later again, that the British government would apply the regulations.[79] External Affairs circulated the various departments informing them of the policy, but Latham seemed very unwilling to apply it. On 13 September he noted the difficulties involved and wanted Bruce to enquire about the attitude of the United States and Russia, and how many other states had complied. When Bruce informed him that the 21 states represented on the committee had apparently accepted the recommendation, but most others had postponed action, the Australian government deferred replying to the League's letter. It continued to do so in 1933 and the story dragged on into 1934, for the government was very reluctant to follow the policy of non-recognition.

Instead, it concentrated its efforts on curtailing League expenditure, rather than upholding its prestige. Lyons' comments in federal parliament have already been noted, and on 27 February 1933, he sent a long, strongly worded letter to the British, urging that attempts to reduce League expenditure should be renewed. In July he wrote to Bruce on the matter. A member of the usually parsimonious British Treasury commented that expenditure should only be reduced if it were 'without detriment to its [i.e. the League's] objectives', but as a result of Australian prompting an informal conference was held in July 1933 between representatives of the Dominions and India. The Treasury sent a letter to Australia House on 3 August, remarking that a direct assault on League finances for the second year running might be bad tactics and, moreover, 'the general policy of His Majesty's Government is support for the League, and we cannot take action looking to large scale reduction of League activities which would be inconsistent with that policy'.[80]

It is difficult to avoid the conclusion that the Australian government was only a half-hearted supporter of the League.

Likewise, in New Zealand, Forbes still managed to avoid any discussion of the crisis as late as 28 February 1933. When the Labour opposition leader suggested a motion approving the attitude of the League and asking Japan to accept its decision, Forbes replied that while the government deplored the position that had developed, no useful purpose would be served by discussing the matter, which was still under consideration by the world body.[81]

The end of the affair
Japan gave notice of withdrawal from the League on 27 March 1933—though it would require two years under the Covenant to be effective—and the Manchurian crisis died away.

Public opinion within the Commonwealth reacted to the final

failure of the League on the issue in a variety of ways. Intellectuals were divided in their response. There was a Commonwealth Relations conference in Toronto in September 1933. Some cynicism was expressed by a New Zealand delegate, who thought the aspirations of the League were akin to the Ten Commandments; an Australian talked about falling back for security on the British Commonwealth; while a Canadian thought his country would turn to America and isolationism. The discussion was very general, though members pointed to the failure of the League to solve the crisis on generally recognised principles, and blamed the absence of major powers. They failed to suggest any practical changes to the machinery of the League, however, and the Canadian members were divided on the future use of Article 16.[82]

Canadian intellectuals, indeed, seemed somewhat confused. At the First Study Conference of the Canadian Institute of International Affairs in Montreal in mid-1934, after deciding that the League was a disguised form of the balance of power, they went on to discuss neutrality and painted a picture of civil war in Canada if it joined Britain in another European war. They concluded however, that the only way to avoid this, and the break-up of the Commonwealth, was to develop the system of collective security through the League. The implications of this seemed to escape delegates. Although they thought that an Act should be passed enabling the Canadian government to impose sanctions without debate in parliament, they also decided that until a collective system that was worth defending was created, 'there is no conceivable war in sight in which it will be to Canada's interest to take part'. The contradictions in this policy were not noted. The basic ideas behind the attitude of Canadian intellectuals, however, was probably that later called 'economic appeasement', as was revealed by Escott Reid in the same year.[83]

In the Canadian parliament, Senator McRae argued that at all costs Canada should avoid involvement in any future war, and suggested that Canada then had an opportunity to withdraw from the League 'with honour'. This provoked a rambling debate in the Canadian House of Commons on 12 February 1934. Members who spoke wished to force Bennett to adopt a more independent line on Commonwealth matters and to debate foreign policy more fully. As J. S. Woodsworth remarked, 'It is true that we may ask a question of the minister, to which generally speaking, we do not receive any very illuminating answer'. The same statement could have been made equally truthfully in the Australian and New Zealand parliaments. Bennett resisted the idea of referring Canadian foreign policy to a committee.

On 21 March 1934, however, a resolution was tabled in the Canadian Senate that Canada should withdraw from the League. This caused some embarrassment to Bennett, since the German press reported that Canada would indeed withdraw. Bennett flatly denied this. The debate finally began on 17 April and continued on eleven separate days thereafter until 31 May. A large number of speakers held forth at length on Canadian foreign policy, noting the failure to restrain Japan in Manchuria, but almost none supported the resolution and it was finally defeated without a formal vote being taken.[84]

As for Australia, the *Round Table* in December 1933 noted that though Australians had never regarded the League as an essential element in world security, nevertheless it had lulled their fears of possible enemies and made them think of an international community for peace. Its failure to act effectively during the Manchurian crisis, moreover, had reminded them that the major nations around the Pacific were outside the international organisation. As a result, Australian security seemed diminished, while Japan's rulers seemed intent on promoting their own interests by any means at their disposal. Perhaps Manchuria would occupy Japan's energies for years to come, but if not, trade relations and the White Australia policy might provoke a desire for the sparsely occupied parts of Australia. 'In Australia, neither Government nor people can be expected to feel indifferent to the spectacle of even a distant country in the Pacific growing so powerful for war . . .' Fear of Japan and a new war did increase somewhat as a result of the crisis. The left-wing anti-war movement grew slightly stronger. In April 1933, 750 delegates attended a peace rally in Sydney,[85] although this was probably not representative of public feeling. Most of those who thought about international affairs turned their attention to strengthening Australian defence, as will be shown in the next chapter.

In New Zealand the opposition, provoked by Sir Thomas Wilford's extremely vague report on the 14th Assembly of the League of Nations, at last forced a debate on foreign policy. Nash accused the Forbes government of never really considering the League, but simply paying its dues. Even the Minister for Customs admitted that when he had attended the Institute of International Affairs conference at Toronto in 1933 he had been struck by Canadian support for the League, whereas Wilford had admitted to him in London the previous year that he had difficulty in finding what New Zealand opinion was. This was not calculated to placate the Labour Party, which apparently attended the debate in force, while government members were few. As a result, the discussion was dominated by the opposition, one of whom remarked: 'It is left to the Prime Minister to understand the international monetary system and these other matters, and we all know what that means, because we have heard the Prime Minister in this House so often, and we know that all he could give to us could be put on a twopenny stamp.' The Labour leader,

J. Savage, remarked that New Zealand might get a rude awakening some day, and demanded that the government take an intelligent interest in the League and make a definite statement to the House. 'I wonder what the Government has in its collective mind in connection with this matter'—a query that the historian can only echo.

The Labour members returned to the attack in September 1934, Savage suggesting that the expenses of the delegates to Geneva were so small as to suggest that they had walked there. Other speakers attacked the government's constant support for British policy. Wilford's cryptic report—cryptic partly to hide his reservations about the usefulness of the League and his support for Japan—had provoked this. Forbes intervened to defend the government's record and was criticised by the opposition. Rattled, he made a second short speech.[86] This was part of the decline of Forbes' administration before his defeat at the polls. The new government would adopt an attitude to the League and foreign policy very different from that of Forbes.

The Commonwealth, the League and Dominion influence on Britain
The attitude of the British and Commonwealth governments clearly varied. For example, British aims during the Manchurian crisis had been mixed. The Foreign Office in 1933 had thought that they were twofold.

> First, to play a loyal part as a member of the League of Nations in contributing to the settlement of the dispute by conciliation and, when this was found to be impossible, to a verdict which, by doing justice to the merits of the case, would preserve the moral position of the League, and, secondly, to avoid incurring the antagonism of either China or Japan.[87]

The British government never admitted, even to itself, that these aims might be contradictory or impossible to fulfill. Indeed, the Foreign Office added on that occasion, 'These objects may be said to have been achieved'—an extremely doubtful judgment.

Dominion governments, too, were much divided. As Carter says,

> In general, the division tended to follow geographical position, those parts of the Commonwealth with Far Eastern interests, Great Britain, Australia and New Zealand, pursuing a cautious policy, the Irish Free State and South Africa supporting a strong stand by the League of Nations while Canada balanced between them.[88]

This is not quite accurate. As we have seen, Canada had Far Eastern interests and New Zealand was quiescent rather than cautious, but clearly geographical position and economic interests did determine to a large extent the attitude of the various Dominions.

This was true of other members of the League too. As one cynic remarked, 'it must be said of the case of the Small Powers that their moral fervour and determination to carry out the Covenant to the letter varied noticeably in proportion to their geographical proximity to the scene of action'.[89]

Apart from those factors, the policies of the various governments were affected by the attitudes of the men who governed in each. The Australian government, of all the Dominions, was least happy with the League and put least faith in it. Hughes may have shocked some commentators by the bluntness of his language, but his attitude was shared by many in power. Not only was the Australian government determined not to risk economic sanctions or the threat of war to support the League, it was also very touchy about League infringements on national sovereignty. Sir George Pearce, the leader of the Australian delegation to the League Assembly in 1927, had warned it against involving the League in fresh subjects, which, though possibly important, 'were of purely domestic concern, with which self-respecting nations would not tolerate interference even from the League of Nations'. And in 1933 Bruce noted this attitude in the British government in a message to his own, and implied approval.[90]

In contrast, Canada had publicly moved towards support for the League, in reaction to the fiasco of Cahan's speech. The main proponent of this appears to have been Prime Minister Bennett himself, who had overruled Skelton on the matter of the Negotiations Committee and became willing to adopt a less isolationist policy. In fact he became increasingly involved in the League, attending the World Economic Conference in London in 1933 and heading the Canadian delegation to the League Assembly in 1934. He used ratification of League treaties in 1935 to begin a program of social reform and in the same year came to support the idea of comprehensive and effective sanctions against any aggressor. Bennett had thus gradually taken over the control of foreign policy from Skelton and reversed his policies.[91] The effect would be seen in the next crisis, in Abyssinia.

The New Zealand government, on the other hand, was too preoccupied with its own affairs to pay much attention to the Manchurian crisis, apart from idly deploring it. As in Canada, however, the crisis had repercussions on later policies. In New Zealand it stirred the Labour opposition to support the League and this led them— later—to oppose appeasement.

The question remains as to how far the Dominions influenced British policy during the crisis. Carter indeed asserts:

> If any of the Dominions were particularly influential on British policy during the dispute, it was Australia. Mainly this was because of the

similarity of concern over a potential Japanese attack on British possessions in the Far East. In this regard the Australian reaction probably strengthened the British resolve to avoid any action which might lead to a breach . . .

As we have seen, however, although the Australian government totally agreed with British policy—except that one suspects it might have preferred Britain not to have been involved with the League at all—it did little to initiate moves. It, or at least Bruce who was on the spot, was a loyal supporter of Britain, and Bruce formed a useful and suave seconder to Simon in the crucial League debates. But that was all. The Australian government sent very few cables on policy to the British government and those that were sent supported Britain's position. Indeed, Carter continues by remarking, 'though had Australia been eager for positive action, it is very doubtful whether it would have changed British policy in any way'.[92]

This is the crux of the matter. The British government decided its policy and then persuaded the Dominions to accept it, or used their support as an additional argument for the policy it had determined on. This was suggested in a note by Riddell to a British Commonwealth meeting at Geneva. He gave an account of a long speech by Simon on British policy, and a shorter one by MacDonald, but no record of any discussion by the Commonwealth delegates. Cahan indeed had complained that British officials at Geneva 'appeared to assume that Canada could have no special interest in the proceedings, and that they were entitled, without conference or discussion, to the invariable support of the Dominion delegates upon all matters under discussion'. They rather nonchalantly assumed this attitude, but, 'as a matter of fact, they were really afraid that in some way their influence at the League might be weakened by the Canadian delegation taking an independent attitude'.[93] He added that in a private conversation Simon 'seemed rather surprised when I mildly suggested that Canada, in view of our geographical situation and increasing trade relations with both China and Japan, had special interest in the adjustment of the Sino–Japanese problem'. Some New Zealanders too, by 1934, had become tired of their government's policy of constant support for Britain. Peter Fraser, later to become Prime Minister, remarked: 'It was not satisfactory . . . to see the representative of the Dominion, instead of expressing New Zealand's opinion, simply re-echoing the opinion of whatever Government—whether Conservative or Labour—that happened to be in office in Great Britain.'[94]

This did not stop the British using the Dominions as a reason for supporting policies they had decided on anyway. Thus Thomas continued to use Dominion opinion as a reason for opposing sanctions. There is a long contradictory and rambling memorandum on the matter in the Dominions Office files dated January 1933. This cited Dominion opinion, as did Thomas to the full Cabinet meeting in May of the same year.[95] But, despite Thomas' use of their opinions, the Dominions were a pretext, not a reason, for British policy. As Thorne says,

> Throughout the crisis, both Foreign and Dominions Office files, together with Cabinet conclusions, show that, while the Dominions were kept informed of Britain's general policy, they contributed almost nothing in the way of advice or even demands for discussion at government level. They *existed* as a defence responsibility, that was all.

And as for Thomas' memorandum of March 1932, this 'single major summary of Commonwealth opinion . . . derived from a British initiative . . . simply to reinforce a decision that had already been taken on other grounds'.

It was not only, however, that the Dominions 'were being informed rather than consulted', as Thorne says, but that the British *were capable of censoring the information they provided the Dominions*. The Foreign Office decided in 1933 to vet the copies of telegrams which the Australian 'liaison officer' in London would see, to remove those 'which reflect a divergence of interest, or might cause a difference of opinion, between H.M.Gs. [sic] in the U.K. and the Commonwealth'.[96] So much for the Australian government's faith in the value of that appointment in gathering inside information from the British ministries! Moreover, as the Australian reference to the Nine Power Treaty revealed, when British information provoked an undesired response, Dominion opinion was hastily dampened down.

All this meant, however, that the British government decided 'Commonwealth foreign policy' and the Dominions agreed or not after the important decisions had been made. Imperial policy, as F.T.A. Ashton-Gwatkin, the first secretary at the Foreign Office, noted, was drifting. Australia sold wool and wheat to China and Japan, and yet had a White Australia policy; New Zealand was not yet concerned with the Far East; while Canada was closer to the policy of the United States than that of Britain. He suggested an interdepartmental Committee on the Far East. It was vetoed by the Foreign Office, which feared for its primacy. The rift in the Commonwealth between the Irish and South Africans on one side, the Australians and New Zealanders on the other, and Canada in the middle, continued into 1934.[97] It did not augur well for the development of a coherent and united Commonwealth foreign policy.

Commonwealth intellectuals, as we have seen, were little help. Those who attended the Fifth Biennial Conference of the Institute of Pacific Relations, held at Banff in August 1933, were confused by the Manchurian crisis. They skirted round the political and military problems and dealt instead with 'International Economic Conflict in the Pacific Area'. This was understandable, since the British government, pressed by Lancashire interests, had taken action against Japan's textile trade with India and the African colonies. A minor trade war developed in 1933 and 1934,[98] which did nothing to improve Anglo–Japanese relations.

Nevertheless, the intellectuals were unwise to ignore other factors such as the reappearance of imperialistic nationalism. For the rise of the future Axis powers, seeking to change the peace settlement of 1919–20 by aggression, posed immense problems for the divided Commonwealth. Differences of opinion had in the past been papered over by reference to support for the principles of the League of Nations, but as Watt says, 'this position could only last while the League itself functioned as an instrument to maintain peace without any major effort being actually called for from its signatories'.[99] After the Manchurian affair, the League itself might need the backing of sanctions or armed force in any future crisis. This immediately raised in an acute form questions of policy: whether the Dominions and Britain would support the League in that way; and of defensive power: whether the British Commonwealth, seeing the writing on the wall, could rearm and strengthen its strategic and military position in the Far East. It is to the problems of military security, therefore, that the following chapters will turn.

4 The writing on the wall: problems of defence

> *The whole of our territory in the Far East, as well as the coastline of India and the Dominions and our vast trade and shipping, lies open to attack . . . First priority should [therefore] be given to requirements in the Far East. . . . We cannot ignore the Writing on the Wall.*
> CHIEFS OF STAFF SUB-COMMITTEE, ANNUAL REVIEW FOR 1932,
> PRO CID 1082-B CAB 4/21.

When the Manchurian crisis began in September 1931 the British Cabinet did not immediately realise its military implications, and there were no great heart-searchings within the service departments or the CID. As Thorne remarks, 'A diplomatic dilemma, not a military danger, was how the affair was perceived in this period'.[1] The reason for this was partly a smugness born of the past history of the British Empire—it never occurred to British politicians that their power and possessions in the East were seriously threatened—and partly a preoccupation with the disarmament conference, which was soon to be convened.

The disarmament conference, Geneva 1932

This conference deeply affected the British government, so that, although the weaknesses of the armed services had been made 'abundantly clear' at a three-party conference in 1931, Cabinet ministers did not seriously consider rearmament. They were unwilling to take any action which might prejudice the success of the conference. It must be admitted, however, that their support for disarmament came from a variety of motives. A major factor was idealism—pacifism and the desire to avoid another war such as the last. This desire was reinforced by concern for public opinion. For example, in October 1932 Simon reported to the Cabinet that there was a danger that the disarmament conference would fail, and a large body of public opinion thought that the British government should give a lead to the nations. MacDonald reported that he had received several deputations, and that the time had come not only to follow the experts but also to take public opinion into account. This attitude continued, so that although the three ministers of the armed services were to urge the government in April 1934 to educate the people in foreign affairs and the need for moderate rearmament, the Cabinet was extremely reluctant to do so and Chamberlain in particular continued to cite public opinion as a major argument against rearmament. Chamberlain's main motive, however, was probably that other major factor in support for disarmament, the desire for economies in government expenditure as an answer to the depression.[2]

As for Commonwealth opinion, the British government was aware of a need to keep the Dominions informed, but tended to do so when it wanted their support, as in its opposition to the proposals put forward on poison gas.[3] The interests and policies of the Dominions, however, did not always coincide with those of Britain or each other.

For example, they strongly objected to Britain involving them in Europe; they were divided on budgetary disarmament and also on the proposal to abolish naval and military air forces and control civil aviation. Britain was concerned by the threat to London posed by the new bombers and tried to impose her views on the Dominions. For example, the CID paper, 'Imperial Defence as Affecting New Zealand', March 1932, remarked: 'London is the terminus of many of the most important of the Empire's lines of communication. The bombing of the vital centre would be a catastrophe which no Dominion could view without dismay.' Canada, on the other hand, wanted to use large planes to counter forest fires and develop the outback. Its government felt so strongly on the subject that its delegate spoke to the disarmament conference in February 1933—a most unusual step for one of the Dominions. Meanwhile, Australia wanted to merge the RAAF with the Australian army to save money.[4]

The Dominions were also a problem to the British in naval disarmament. Those who aimed for more independence in foreign affairs, such as Canada and the Irish Free State, wanted separate tonnage limits on their own navies, which conflicted with United States policy, while Australia and New Zealand were concerned with British naval weakness in the Pacific and opposed further unilateral British disarmament.[5]

As it happened, the disarmament conference was to fail. Simon had indeed been pessimistic before it opened, partly because of the rise of Nazism in Germany and the problem of French security. Any failure, however, was bound to concern the Dominions, since it would involve them in defence expenditure and also perhaps in warfare in Europe. They expressed this concern at a meeting in June 1932. Latham of Australia went further. He sent a letter to the president of the disarmament conference, Arthur Henderson, and suggested that governments might be more willing to sign an agreement if they only bound themselves for ten years. He reported this to his own government and Lyons sent a long letter to Simon. Lyons, indeed, took a much more detailed interest in disarmament than he did in the Manchurian crisis and Latham gave a long and somewhat schoolmasterish speech on the disarmament conference to the House of Representatives. For Latham too felt the need for some sort of agreement.[6]

The Dominions, however, were not only worried at the possible breakdown of the conference, they were also concerned that they should be consulted by the British—especially in any desperate plans to make it a success. In June 1932 the New Zealand government complained about the short notice it had been given of the air proposals, so that it could not study them properly, and in July it commented on the inadequacy of the information with which it had been provided. Nevertheless, the British Cabinet in the beginning of November decided to make simultaneous statements on the matter in Geneva and the House of Commons, without informing the Dominions first.[7] The Australian government was caused 'considerable embarrassment' by this procedure, and opposed some of the proposals. Lyons wrote and complained, and Thomas telegraphed an apology, implying that it was the exigencies of parliament that provoked the British government into releasing its proposals—a dubious excuse. He also telegraphed the British representative in Australia, and discussions occurred between the Foreign and Dominions Offices and Bruce in London. Hardly had the British soothed the Australian government, than a telegram arrived from New Zealand, also commenting on the lack of consultation, as well as doubting the policy:

> On this occasion . . . as on previous occasions, they feel that with the information available here and at this distance, it is not possible for them to make any comment of value on details of policy which they observe has now been definitely adopted by the United Kingdom Government. Nevertheless . . . recent events in the international sphere have not diminished a certain scepticism which they feel as to the value of further international undertakings to refrain from the furthering by force of arms of national policies.[8]

The Foreign and Dominions Offices concerted a reply and agreed that the Admiralty should report on developments to the Dominions Office, which should then communicate with the Dominions. Despite these good intentions, Canada still had to cable for information in January 1933. Fresh efforts were made in March and December of that year to keep the Dominions informed,[9] but the British government did not seem to do so naturally, without Dominion pressure. Despite its frequent remarks about consultation, it usually discussed matters with the Dominions when it wanted their support. Otherwise it forgot them, or informed them of moves only after lengthy debate with other European nations.

Britain's military weakness

If the British were poor in consulting the Dominions in the matter of disarmament, they were naturally worse in discussing the vital military weakness of their Empire/Commonwealth. For early apathy towards the military implications of the Manchurian incident ended abruptly in January 1932, when the Japanese struck at Shanghai. The British realised, with something like panic, that they were almost totally defenceless in the Far East.

On 8 February 1932 the Deputy Chiefs of Staff Subcommittee reported that if Japan became hostile the first priority would be to get the British naval forces out of Shanghai, for an encounter with the Japanese 'would mean inviting a disaster of the first magnitude'. They agreed that Hong Kong in its undefended state was a gift to the Japanese, and blamed the Ten Year Rule. After looking round desperately for help—men from India and planes from French Indo-China, perhaps the deterrence of the American fleet, as well as 'assistance from Australia and New Zealand'—they admitted that it would take the British fleet 38 days to get to Singapore and another ten to arrive at Hong Kong. From their discussion it was obvious that the British forces in the Pacific were in a pitiful state, outgunned, hopelessly outnumbered and with little hope of help from England.[10]

Then two reports, which discussed the grim situation in detail, came out almost simultaneously. On 22 February, the Deputy Chiefs of Staff, in 'The Situation in the Far East', began by admitting that any further defence spending was contrary to the 1930 imperial conference decision, but thought that proposals to strengthen Singapore and Hong Kong—whose defences were hopelessly inadequate—would be welcomed in Australia and New Zealand. They noted the speed of Japanese moves in Shanghai, where an international crisis had blown up in a fortnight. If Japan turned suddenly hostile again, British ships would be trapped there, and would be lucky if they had sufficient warning to enable them 'to disappear into the blue'. They went on to discuss possible help from Australia and New Zealand, but noticed how much those two countries had disarmed and how outdated their equipment was. Time would be needed to get help from them, and their public opinion in the opening stages of any war would be likely to demand their own protection. At best, in the long run, Australia and New Zealand might agree to provide part of the peacetime garrisons of Hong Kong or Singapore.[11]

The next day, 23 February, the annual review of the Chiefs of Staff for 1932 came out. This incorporated a full-scale attack on the whole concept of the Ten Year Rule, with its effect on British power in the Far East, where the position was 'about as bad as it could be'. Indeed, as the quotation at the beginning of this chapter reveals, they considered the whole of the Far East was open to attack and it should therefore be given priority in defence spending. Taken together, the two reports revealed that British weakness in the area was not only due to the small forces stationed there, but to the undefended state of British bases, especially Singapore. It alone was far enough from Japan to be defendable, yet, as we saw in chapter 1, successive British governments had economised on the base, even though it was essential for any British fleet to operate in the Pacific. As the First Lord of the Admiralty pointed out in July 1932, apart from the floating dock, they had at Singapore little more than 'a hole in the earth'. He went on to remark that those countries in the area who had 'contributed so largely towards the cost of the base' were dissatisfied with the situation, 'although it is doubtful if they realise as yet how incomplete is the provision for the dock'.[12]

The immediate problem was to persuade the British Cabinet that a start had to be made with rearmament. The Chiefs of Staff and their deputies therefore demanded an end to the Ten Year Rule and urgent reinforcement of the Far East. Their remarks came at a bad time, however. MacDonald and those who felt like him were preoccupied with the disarmament conference, and the need—if anything—to *reduce* armaments. To such politicians, armed forces existed in peacetime either for imperial policing or as defensive precautions against war. It never occurred to them that they might also be used as instruments of diplomacy, such as a deterrent against further aggression. Instead, to begin large-scale rearmament seemed to be equivalent to deciding to take the road to war. Supporting this opposition to rearmament were the hard-headed businessmen in the Cabinet, in particular Neville Chamberlain, who were concerned with the depression and convinced of the absolute necessity for keeping government expenditure to a minimum.

Accordingly, on 11 March 1932 Chamberlain requested that a Treasury note be printed in the CID papers. This, after remarking on fears about the Far East, argued that to deter Japan Britain would have had to have launched major operations in the Far East. Yet it was 'no more in a position financially and economically to engage in a major war in the Far East than . . . [it was] militarily'. It then defended the Ten Year Rule and ended by remarking that the future of the country depended on the maintenance of sound finances, and that the British people were anxious to avoid a heavy expenditure on armaments. 'What has to be considered, therefore, is one set of risks balanced against the other, and the Treasury submit that at the present time financial risks are greater than any other that we can estimate'.[13] This action by Chamberlain and the Treasury revealed very clearly their determination to control military expenditure, unfortunately just at the time when the Japanese army dominated the civilian government. In Britain, in contrast, the Treasury submission, with its typical appeals to the need for economy and a supposed public opinion, was inserted into the CID papers, where Chamberlain could appeal to it in his continuing opposition to rearmament.

The main opponents of Chamberlain in the various Cabinet committees were the Admiralty and Sir Maurice Hankey. Hankey's father had run a sheep station in South Australia for a time, his mother was Australian, and his wife came from South Africa. His early career was as an officer in the marines, and he had served in flagships in the Mediterranean, before going into the naval intelligence department of the Admiralty. During the First World War Hankey had worked closely on Lloyd George's War Cabinet secretariat with Lord Milner, and had become firm friends with some of Milner's circle, including Lionel Curtis, Phillip Kerr and Geoffrey Dawson. Hankey was thus closely connected with both the navy and the 'imperial federation' school in Britain. Since he was secretary of the CID and the Cabinet, as well as numerous other governmental committees, he could push his views extensively. Roskill notes his use, for example, of the Deputy Chiefs of Staff Committee on the Far East, and Watt stresses his weight in the counsels of the government. But in fact Hankey could always be overborne by determined or totally slothful politicians. As he admitted, his business was to assist the government, 'irrespective whether at the bottom of my heart I agree with [its] policy or not'. He had met his match in Chamberlain.[14]

On 23 March 1932 the Cabinet, on the advice of the CID, cancelled the Ten Year Rule, and the Prime Ministers of Canada, Australia, New Zealand and South Africa were so informed.[15] Little activity, however, followed. The two themes, economic recovery and disarmament, clearly dominated government thinking. For example, the Cabinet, when cancelling the Ten Year Rule, added that 'this must not be taken to justify an expanding expenditure by the Defence Services without regard to the very serious financial and economic situation that still obtains'. And it passed the matter over to—of all bodies—the Ministerial Committee on the disarmament conference. For the British politicians were preoccupied with disarmament, not rearmament, and once the urgency of the Shanghai crisis was over, the weak position of British forces and possessions in the Far East could be ignored. Thus Cabinet's first reaction, when it discussed the report of the service chiefs on the needs of the Singapore base in October 1932, was to wonder whether the proposals did not infringe the armaments truce then in process. The Cabinet therefore agreed to continue the construction of the Singapore base, but only as long as there was no increase in its armaments till after the truce ended, and 'the proposals of the Defence Departments were subject to approval in detail by the Treasury'.[16] There was no sense of urgency, and the stranglehold of the Treasury remained.

What provoked a change was not events in the East, where the crisis was becoming less acute, but the situation in Germany, where Hitler and the Nazis gained great electoral strength in 1932 and ultimately the government itself on 30 January 1933. In England, therefore, Hankey turned his attention to Europe, and thought that if the disarmament conference failed the situation would be very serious indeed. By midsummer 1933 Liddell Hart was writing articles on Germany's armament and military plans.[17]

The service chiefs, however, still had to defend the Far East; and they were not happy. On 28 February 1933 the Chiefs of Staff noted that the army thought Hong Kong could only hold out against a Japanese attack for 21 days, while the navy estimated that it would take 38 days for the main fleet to reach even Singapore, which was still not secure or defendable. It was not surprising that the First Sea Lord, Sir Ernie Chatfield, remarked that 'the whole bases of our war policy were . . . built up on sand'.[18] The next month the Chiefs of Staff re-examined 'The Situation in the Far East', and were more specific. After remarking that the naval base at Singapore was the pivot of Britain's strategic position there, they warned that until it was provided with adequate defences it was liable to capture or destruction before the British main fleet could arrive from European waters, that its recapture would be a major operation, and that Hong Kong would be in danger, while British trade and territory in the Far East, including India, Australia and New Zealand, would be 'exposed to depredation'. Hankey therefore tried to persuade MacDonald that it was time that the government took the defence of Singapore seriously, for its loss 'would be a calamity of the first magnitude'.[19]

The waiting dominoes: Canada, New Zealand and Australia
British weakness was only aggravated by the corresponding weakness of the Dominions, who, as was pointed out in chapter 1, had disarmed to the point of danger as a result of the depression. The most striking example was Canada. There, the defence forces were run down to such an extent that they were almost nonexistent. Yet in May 1933 the Bennett government decided to lop $3 673 023 off the already depleted defence expenditure,[20] and the Chief of General Staff, Major General A. G. L. McNaughton, suggested the virtual disbandment of the Canadian navy, reliance being placed instead on aerial defence. It was only the strong and intelligent opposition of the Chief of Naval Staff, Rear Admiral W. Hose, that saved the Cana-

dian navy, after a major showdown with the Treasury Board. Even so, naval estimates were cut further. At that stage Canadian naval forces on the Pacific coast comprised two destroyers and a minesweeper.[21]

Nor did the air force flourish, despite McNaughton's patronage. In 1931 civil aviation estimates were cut and savage economies imposed. Any expenditure, however slight, came before the Chief of General Staff, including such lowly items as dishwashing machines, toasters and bread-slicers! Nor did the advent of the Manchurian crisis affect government thinking. Money for civil and military aviation was reduced from $5 232 000 in 1931 to $1 750 000 for 1932. All 79 non-permanent air officers were discharged, causing a furore, since 50 of them, together with 200 airmen, offered their services to China. This made the fate of the Canadian air force front-page news and led to criticism in the Canadian parliament. In the event, none of those offering their services went to China, and five airmen who had previously gone were stranded and had to be helped to return. The Bennett government, however, was determined on even further economies, and ignored the desperate pleas of McNaughton and the senior air officer. Instead, it cut the 1933 vote to $1 405 000, which by 1934 reduced the hours of service flying to zero. Indeed, the expenditure 'was the lowest in the history of the air force since the earliest days of the Air Board'. In March 1934 McNaughton reported that there was only one modern service aeroplane in Canada, and even that was on loan from the RAF. By then, however, the air force had become so weak that even the economy-ridden Bennett government recognised the fact. In March 1934 it raised the vote to $1 850 000, and so began the slow revival of the Canadian air force.

As for the militia, this had never been popular with Canadian governments. In 1931 expenditure was barely sufficient to allow city regiments to train at their local barracks for four or five days a year, without pay. The government even slowed down the production of ammunition, and by May 1933 the Treasury Board 'by ruthless pruning' had cut the money provided for the militia to $1 994 000 and for the permanent army to $4 910 000, 'a low point for the century'.

All this was occurring during the time when the British government had revoked the Ten Year Rule and the German government was rearming. But, according to Eayrs,

> the increased tempo of military activity abroad had little effect upon the military affairs of the Dominion. The Prime Minister remained indifferent to the dilapidated condition of the country's defence forces, and took no interest in the activities of the Department of National Defence with the exception of its unemployment relief camps and the construction of new barracks in and about his home town of Calgary.

Indeed he adds: 'During 1933–1934, the armed forces of Canada reached the nadir of their neglect.'[22]

The only reason that Canada could afford to do this was because successive governments believed that they were safe under United States protection, and far from any sources of trouble. Even the crises in the Far East did not affect them sufficiently to make them change their mind. There was, indeed, a tendency for other Dominions to hope for protection from the United States. In 1933 Hughes' erstwhile advisor remarked that American and Australian interests were bound up in the Pacific, and that American and Australian fleets could cooperate with advantage; and in 1934 Hankey reported that there was anxiety in all the Dominions for firm ties to be built up with America.[23] Nevertheless, the Canadians naturally were most closely concerned with America, and felt themselves protected by her.

New Zealand on the other hand, isolated in the South Pacific, placed its faith partly on the British navy and partly on distance from trouble spots. It was, however, more aware of danger than Canada. One New Zealand historian remarks that the government was in fact most concerned by the renewal of Japanese expansion.[24] It is true that it spent small sums on defence, but, like Britain and the other Dominions, it was preoccupied by the depression. Nevertheless, in May 1932 Prime Minister Forbes announced that his government would not accept the recommendation of the National Expenditure Commission and hand the New Zealand naval vessels back to Britain, or make any reduction in the annual contributions to Singapore. He still believed that 'the base was vital to the welfare of New Zealand'. The next month in Britain Sir Thomas Wilford challenged the conclusion of the Oversea Defence Committee that Japanese estates overlooking Singapore harbour and the Straits were no danger to it. The committee's investigation, indeed, had been provoked by Wilford in 1930.[25]

Moreover, New Zealand defence expenditure, on all three services, reached its nadir earlier than Canada, in 1931–32. The estimates for 1932–33 showed a slight rise, but still fell far short of the urgent demands of the service chiefs. As in Britain and Australia, there was therefore in New Zealand a clash between the three services over the allocation of the meagre amounts of money available. The Chief of General Staff, Major General W. L. H. Sinclair Burgess, wanted a New Zealand branch of the Committee of Imperial Defence formed, against considerable opposition from the navy (who feared that a 'Ministry of Defence' was in the wind and that their own funds would be reduced). Sinclair Burgess, however, was determined that the politicians should recognise New Zealand's military weakness. In May 1933 he declared that her defences were well below CID requirements, pointed out that the Royal Navy was then unable to guarantee New Zealand's protection and argued that the government should choose between economic recovery and military preparedness. This provoked the government, after further information had been provided by Burgess, into appointing a committee of five senior officers to study New Zealand's defences. The committee reported in August 1933 and emphasised the dependence of New Zealand on the British main fleet reaching Singapore. It painted a gloomy picture of the country's defences and demanded a modest six-year rearmament program.[26]

The New Zealand government accepted the general principles of the report, although, as the estimates for 1933 had already been approved, the main increase in defence expenditure was delayed till the 1934–35 fiscal year. However, it had decided to establish a New Zealand section of the CID, and this was begun immediately. The first meeting took place on 15 November 1933.

Little explanation for these moves was given, either to parliament or people. Forbes said that the CID had been formed, not as the result of any crisis, but simply as part of a long-term plan to improve New Zealand defences. J. G. Cobbe, the Minister for Defence, said in 1934, however, that the increase in defence expenditure was due to the change in world conditions. Perhaps the government wished to be diplomatic until the Singapore base was completed, as one historian has suggested, but it was more likely the result of an ingrained habit to tell as little as possible to avoid criticism. And the increase in expenditure was very small indeed. If one exaggerates Forbes' concern with New Zealand security, it becomes very difficult to account for his attitude at the 1935 Prime Ministers' meetings in London. Nevertheless, it is interesting that the government pegged naval expenditure and increased that on the air force.[27]

The greatest weakness remained, however, the lack of cooperation between New Zealand and Australia. Sinclair Burgess, in his report of August 1933, had recommended that the New Zealand government give preference to Australia in the purchase of munitions, since they would be more available during any Pacific war than British arms. Soon afterwards, in October 1933, the Australian Prime Minister, Lyons, wrote to Forbes suggesting closer defence cooperation. He suggested that New Zealand use Australian facilities for training its personnel, the dockyards in Sydney for fitting its cruisers, and Australian armament factories for certain naval weapons and small arms ammunition. He also suggested combined naval exercises. The latter did indeed take place in January 1934, but the New Zealand government made no great effort to accept the other offers, even after the Australian Minister for Defence, Senator Pearce, travelled with Hankey to Wellington in 1934 to repeat them.[28]

This is hardly surprising, for the Australian offer must not be taken at its face value. The 'cooperation' of which Lyons talked turned out to be somewhat one-sided. New Zealand would have had to pay handsomely for all the services of which it availed itself, and it is difficult not to see the move as simply a veiled attempt to produce sales for the Australian armaments factories. Lyons indeed apologised for appearing like a salesman in his letter. One shrewd contemporary remarked: 'it seems that Australia wants orders in peace to assist in keeping the factories going and to provide for expansion, whereas it would suit New Zealand better to obtain her peace reserves from Home [i.e. Britain] and to rely on Australia for the further supplies required during the war.'[29] This was typical of the clash of interests between the two countries, and made any cooperation between them minimal. For example, they did not exchange information and defence decisions with one another directly, but passed information back to Britain, who might then forward it to the other nation. The New Zealand authorities, for example, only learnt about a major statement by Senator Pearce on defence policy from the British CID, and the decisions of the New Zealand Chiefs of Staff went to London but not to Canberra. The secretary of the New Zealand Council of Defence noted in 1938: 'The situation is really absurd, in that we are each hearing of the other's activities per medium of CID papers.'[30]

Moreover, the strategic interests of the two countries differed. Both were interested in Singapore and the Dutch East Indies, but Australia was more concerned with the Indian Ocean and the Suez canal, while New Zealand looked to the Pacific Islands and the Panama canal. Cooperation therefore was limited to the occasional combined naval exercises and the exchange of technical information. It was not until the Pacific Defence conference of April 1939 that any attempt was made to coordinate the defence preparations of the two countries. Even then the Australian government was reluctant to send representatives to the conference, thinking that London was the place to discuss defence, not Wellington, and equally reluctant to discuss general policy with New Zealand, or to grant New Zealand a liaison officer in Canberra.[31] It is difficult to avoid the conclusion that the Australian government regarded New Zealand as of peripheral interest, except as a possible market for Australian equipment and ammunition, while at the same time it excluded New Zealand primary produce from Australia.

The attitude of the two Dominions is the more surprising, in that both had received intimation of British weakness in the Far East. On 7 February 1933 Thomas had sent a circular announcing the meagre naval building program for that year,[32] and on 26 April the Admiralty sent a memorandum on naval dispositions in a Far Eastern emergency to their navy offices. This was quite blunt. It quoted the Chiefs of Staff report on the situation in the Far East, including the danger of the capture of Singapore and the threat to the coasts of Australia and New Zealand, already cited, and remarked, 'The present strategical position . . '. is fundamentally unsound'. In an emergency, therefore, the Admiralty had decided that the first priority was to defend Singapore, even if that meant abandoning Hong Kong.[33] If the secretaries of the navy boards in Wellington and Melbourne had passed this note to their political masters, the latter should have realised the seriousness of the situation. There is, however, no evidence that they did so.

The Australian situation was grim. By early 1932, as a result of the depression and the policies of the previous government, the country was virtually defenceless. Or, as Hankey put it, 'in 1931 . . . it may be said that Australian military defence preparations were in a worse state than they had ever been since the Great War'.[34] The new United Australia Party government began a series of discussions on defence, but unfortunately, instead of completely reassessing the problem, simply reaffirmed on 12 February 1932 the traditional policy of reliance on British imperial naval defence. It probably did this from a mixture of ideological and practical motives—conservative support for the 'mother country', Britain, combined with a desire not to spend too much money or hard thought on a specifically Australian defence policy. Accordingly, unlike New Zealand, it decided to stress the navy, maintaining the Australian force at a level which could be regarded—though the British might disagree—as a fair contribution to imperial defence. Economies would be made on the other two forces. It would organise the army merely as a defence against raids, while hopefully providing a nucleus for an expeditionary division in an emergency. It at first toyed, as we have seen, with abolishing a separate air force altogether, merging the pilots and planes with the army. That idea was squashed, but the tiny air force had no independent role and was merely to cooperate with the other two services. In March 1932, therefore, the Military Board proposed reducing the strength of the army, although Senator Pearce postponed any changes till the result of the disarmament conference was known.[35]

The Australian government's decision was soon communicated to the British. Latham, the Minister for External Affairs, was in England during part of 1932 to attend the disarmament conference and so was able to discuss Australian defence with the British authorities. He apparently saw them first in April, when he informed them of the decision the Australian Cabinet had just made. The next month he approached Hankey, secretary of the CID, for advice on the most effective way to spend what money the Australian government was willing to devote to defence.[36]

As a result, Latham had a meeting with the British Chiefs of Staff on 2 June 1932. He stressed the difficulty of apportioning funds between the three services in Australia. The army postulated an invasion by the Japanese, which Latham ruled out unless the Empire were defeated in war. The logistical problems the Japanese would have to face in launching an invasion over such a distance were too great, and in any case Japan was so involved on the mainland of Asia in Manchuria that the risk of her invading Australia for many years was small. Moreover, the Australian government assumed that the British would send a fleet to Singapore in any emergency. The government had therefore decided to organise its defence as against raids, and also wished to have an expeditionary division to integrate with a possible overseas imperial force. Latham ended, therefore, by repeating Australia's concern for the Singapore base.[37]

The British Chiefs of Staff were not altogether happy with Latham's ideas, at least in so far as they seemed to accept very little defence expenditure. They were worried by the poor state of Australia's forces, especially the navy; and they asked bluntly for Australian troops to garrison Singapore, a request to which Latham avoided giving a direct answer. Indeed, he managed to turn them off these dangerous topics to a discussion of the disarmament conference. The minutes reveal Latham as an astute politician, as capable as the British of directing military leaders away from troublesome realities. Whether they reveal him as a statesman with foresight in military affairs is another question.

The result of his meeting with the CID was the British Chiefs of Staff Report, CID 372-C, 'The Defence of Australia', August 1932. This began with a review of the world situation, mentioned British weaknesses, and then turned to general principles of imperial defence. There was nothing new in them, however. They were simply whole sections of the CID paper 358-C (on the defence of New Zealand) reprinted verbatim. They stressed the extent of the British Empire and its dependence on sea communications, with the corollary, accepted in the 1923 imperial conference, that each part was responsible for its own defence while the general command of the sea rested with Britain. There followed a somewhat vague lecture on naval strategy and the effects of a 'one-power' standard on the British fleet, which meant that the local areas of the Empire might *have* to defend themselves before that fleet arrived in their waters. As for air power, they assumed this would be more important in Europe and over England than for the more outlying Dominions—a challengeable assumption.

The Chiefs of Staff finally turned from these generalisations to the problem in hand—Australia's needs. Australian security, they said, rested on three things: the protection of imperial sea communications; sufficient force for local defence; and imperial forces to defeat the enemy. The whole Empire was involved in the first and last of these: Australia could provide the second.

They then stressed the need for each Dominion to maintain its naval expenditure and urged the Australian government to keep two cruisers in full commission and two in reserve, to start replacing the obsolete *Brisbane* and to consider taking and maintaining some British destroyers. They admitted that imperial naval defence in the Far East presupposed a base at Singapore.

> *Provided that the British Fleet arrives in time and finds a properly equipped base at Singapore, Australia has nothing to fear* beyond sporadic attack. If, for any reason, the main Fleet is unable to reach Singapore or if the base is captured or seriously damaged by naval or air bombardments before its arrival, then Australian interests become exposed to attack on a considerable scale. [Emphasis original]

As if this were not enough, they went on to add, 'Singapore, then, is the pivot of Imperial Defence in the Far East . . .'. The British Admiralty may here have been trying to drop a strong hint to the Australian government. Australian support would have been useful in the Admiralty's case for more money.

However, presupposing that Singapore was secure and that a fleet would be sent to it, the Chiefs of Staff plumped for their traditional policy, that Australia's defence need only be organised to counter raids by cruisers or armed merchant vessels and submarines, or planes carried on them. Therefore, after technical advice on the defence of ports, in which they emphasised the heavy gun rather than air power, the Chiefs of Staff suggested that the Australian government organise its military forces to provide garrisons for defended ports within Australia and reinforcements for garrisons in the Far East. As for air power, they simply dwelt on the danger to London and urged the Australian government to send pilots to Britain in any crisis.[38]

Clearly, Latham had gone to the Chiefs of Staff with the imperial defence system in mind. He had not worked out an alternative or formulated basic criticisms of the system. It was not surprising, therefore, that the result was firm support for British imperial naval defence. The British Chiefs of Staff, helped by Latham's arguments, were supporting his government's predilections for relying on the British navy.

There were, however, many weaknesses in their analysis. To begin with, the language of the report was vague and hid by generalisations the fact that the British navy had been so weakened by government economies that it was unable to fulfill its role of imperial defence. In the same way, the report glossed over the unlikeliness of the fleet going to Singapore in an emergency. The British were torn between the desire to educate the distant colonials in the facts of life, and the fear that if they did so too effectively, by showing how important Singapore was to them, how undefended it was and how unsupported it was likely to be, they might provoke a strenuous reaction.[39] Moreover, the British Chiefs of Staff disagreed among themselves, as we have seen. When Bruce approached them again in September 1933, the air staff thought that the money spent on new ships would be better spent on planes. The Admiralty, needless to say, disagreed.[40]

As a result of this, the report did not really answer the Australian question—how to apportion the money available for defence. Bruce pointed this out to the CID, tactfully, in November 1932, but was much more scathing in letters to Pearce: 'it is obviously impossible to ever get the Chiefs of Staff to deal with the particular point Latham put to them.' No one would let down his opposite number in Australia. It was therefore probably better to get the report dropped from the agenda and instead to deal with each service chief separately. Indeed, the Chiefs of Staff, in the beginning of their report, had remarked that it was beyond their province to answer such a question, and MacDonald himself disclaimed any responsibility on the part of the British government. It was a technical report only—though this did not stop the British government sending copies of it to New Zealand, Canada and South Africa.[41]

Neither the British politicians nor the military had really faced Australia's defence needs, but instead had left her building a fortress on sand. This was, however, no excuse for the Australian government. It had many hints of the situation, apart from 372-C, from the Chiefs of Staff report on 'The Situation in the Far East' to the Dominions Office circular on the British naval building program for 1933 and the Admiralty memorandum on naval dispositions, previously mentioned. Moreover, Latham himself received a much more blunt warning. At a meeting of the CID on 9 June 1932 he naively enquired whether the work on Singapore would proceed 'immediately' or be connected with the disarmament conference. He was promptly snubbed by MacDonald, who pointed out that there was *nothing* in the current estimates for Singapore, while the Secretary of State for War pointed out that it might be three years before the 15" (426mm) guns were installed. Simon however tried to soften the blow, and Latham accepted his explanation. He did not fight for a greater sense of urgency in the British Cabinet.[42] Nor, indeed, was there much urgency in Australia. The defence estimates for 1932–33, brought down in November 1932, were the lowest for twenty years.

The staff of the navy was much reduced, though the expenses of this and the other forces were much the same as the previous year. Pearce, indeed, was strongly criticised in the Australian parliament by a member of his own party for the poor provision for defence, especially air defence, as compared with the stress on it in Canada. Pearce pleaded lack of money, the disarmament conference and the government's hope for a review of imperial defence. He admitted that Britain bore an unfair share of the burden, but thought that Australia paid more than other Dominions, even though their seaborne trade was greater.[43]

The greatest action the government took in the defence of Australia in 1932 was the long overdue beginning of the development of Darwin. Even so, progress was painfully slow, and there was no sense of urgency.[44] Pearce on 8 February 1933 admitted that the defence estimates had been so reduced that scarcely a skeleton force for normal protection had been left. He argued, however, that the financial situation was such that Australia could do no more, and added that the government was reconsidering Australian defence and was being advised by Bruce in London. The government therefore only agreed to a slight increase in defence expenditure, from £3 084 447 to £4 246 016. For the navy, the ships in commission remained the same, though there was a slight increase in naval personnel. The army also slightly increased in numbers, while the air force remained the same. Any improvement was minimal.[45]

The government was equally reluctant to spend money on new ships for the navy, despite its stress on naval defence. It requested the loan of four destroyers from Britain in March 1933, and also wanted Britain to crew them as far as Singapore. Discussions over the replacement of HMAS *Brisbane* went from January 1933 onwards between Bruce and the Admiralty. The Australian government wanted Britain to provide four new cruisers, which Australia would man for twenty years. The British government, understandably, was reluctant to meet the whole cost of building the cruisers itself, especially as the Admiralty feared that the Australians might want them tied to Australian waters in any international crisis. Nevertheless, the Admiralty's loan of the destroyers—and also a flotilla leader—was necessary to restore the balance of the Australian naval force, which, as constituted, was unable to operate effectively.[46]

It was hardly surprising, therefore, that Australian newspapers began to demand a more active defence policy, especially after Japanese naval manoeuvres in the Pacific. Indeed, the British representative in Australia reported that there was a growing nervousness about Japan in the country,[47] while the *Round Table* for December 1933 commented that Japan might be occupied in Asia for years to come, but that this might not last, and neither the Australian government nor people could remain indifferent to her growing capacity for war.

It was during this period that the possibilities of air defence began to be discussed at length. The size of the country and the speed and flexibility of aeroplanes made them particularly attractive to Australians, as to Canadians. It was not until late 1933, however, that it was suggested that planes would be cheaper than ships. The Labor Party opposition took up the argument, and in November its deputy leader, F. M. Forde, expressed a preference for air defence in the debates in federal parliament.[48]

The government, however, was still concerned with economies, and its response to this public pressure was to attempt to argue that all was well. On 25 July 1933 Senator Pearce made a speech which was turned into a small pamphlet and even became CID paper 392-C. It was, however, a poor speech, for it tried to hide under verbose language the tiny amounts the government was spending ('a considerable sum of money is being set aside this year'), appealed to the wisdom of the British authorities ('the best naval, military and air experts in the world') and ended with a plea that the government knew best and its critics did not know all the facts.[49] That the Cabinet's reaction to criticism was not fresh thought but a public-relations exercise, can be seen in a questionnaire it circulated to all government departments in late 1933. In this it stipulated that each department's statement 'should be designed to show the benefits that accrue from the Government's administration'. The army authorities found some difficulty in meeting this demand.[50]

Commonwealth at loggerheads: the possible sale of arms to China
Australian government economies forced its Defence Department to consider all sorts of schemes to maintain efficiency. Perhaps the most unusual was its reaction to a Chinese appeal for arms. Approaches had first been made in October 1931, but the then Scullin Labor government declined to supply arms, in view of the chaotic conditions in China and the threat of war with Japan.[51] The new United Australia Party under Lyons, however, thought differently. The Defence Department was anxious to get rid of stocks of obsolete cadet rifles and deteriorating ammunition, and persuaded the government to send a cable to Britain, asking its views. The British government did its best to discourage the Australians; it replied that though there were difficulties in preventing private arms sales to Japan, the supply of government arms 'would be incompatible with the duty of a neutral'. The Shanghai crisis was then causing concern,

but once it had blown over, the temptation to get out of economic difficulties by selling arms was too great. In August 1932, after eliciting the fact that the British government had ended its embargo on the sale of government arms, Senator Pearce gave the go-ahead to his department. This was a mistake, for the Defence Department was inclined to regard itself as the premier department in Australia and to act independently of the others. Through the assistant minister to the Treasury, Senator Massey Greene, it came into contact with shipping interests in Sydney, who had connections in Shanghai. A flurry of activity occurred, an inventory of stocks was taken and samples provided. At this stage, however, other motives intruded. The Australian small-arms factory at Lithgow near Sydney was in serious trouble. Staff were being dismissed and the plant systematically closed down. Pearce and Massey Greene had been responsible during 1919–22 for extending munitions production in Australia and were therefore interested in the fate of the factory. The idea was put forward to sell stocks of current rifles and to use the money from their sale to keep the factory going. This at least would prevent trainee operatives from drifting away, and keep a factory in being for any crisis. The Defence Committee therefore agreed with the suggestion.

Though militarily sound, however, the plans of the Defence Department had political ramifications. They involved Australia's neutrality, her attitude to the dispute between China and Japan, and her relations with Britain. Keith Officer in the Department of External Affairs noted that the British might reimpose an embargo, but he, Latham and Lyons apparently did not realise how deeply the Defence Department was involved in negotiating an arms sale. This was not surprising, since that department went out of its way to maintain strict secrecy, but it was unfortunate, since—as Officer had foreseen—the British government was moving in the direction of another arms embargo.

In Britain, pressure was building up on the MacDonald government from League supporters, the TUC, the Labour Party and the press to act effectively in support of the League. Simon's equivocations had roused public feeling, especially his speech in December 1932. The final straw was Japanese action in Jehol in January 1933, which resulted in the League Assembly proposing to ban the sale of arms to Japan. As it happened, in Britain, alone of all the arms-exporting nations, the government had statutory control over the arms trade, since under the Arms Export Prohibition Order of 1931 all arms sales had to be licensed by Whitehall. The government therefore had the power to make a gesture on this matter which would gain the support of the pacifists, League supporters and those on the left wing who bitterly opposed armaments. It would be the more striking in that Britain did enjoy a reasonable arms trade with both China and Japan.[52] More important, however, an embargo on the sale of arms might forestall what the British government feared most, the suggestion that general economic sanctions be applied to Japan.

Simon first raised the issue on 18 February, but the Cabinet and its committees were deeply divided. Morally, there was a strong case for an embargo on Japan alone, but the consequences were too frightening. An embargo on both sides seemed an absurdity, but the pacifists wanted action of some sort. Simon sat on the fence; the service chiefs and Hankey bitterly opposed the whole idea; MacDonald and Baldwin were jaded; and the main proponent turned out to be Neville Chamberlain. It was decided to impose a temporary embargo while sounding out other countries. Thomas, the Dominions secretary, who supported the embargo, did not mention the Dominions once during the lengthy debates. He probably did not know of the Australian cables on arms exports, since he rarely read Dominion cables himself, and the matter was so secret that he probably did not inform the officers of his department of the debate. They therefore could not warn him.[53]

The Cabinet dithered; Simon changed his mind; and finally, on 24 February, Thomas at last got off a telegram to the Dominions. It stressed the urgent need for international agreement, but carefully refrained from informing them that the Cabinet had decided to take unilateral action itself. The Australian government, in its reply, was equally cautious, agreeing that every effort should be made to obtain an international policy, but that they were not prepared 'to bind themselves in any other manner'. This arrived in Britain at 9.15 on the morning of 27 February, the day the Cabinet was to reconvene, and the Dominions Office sent a copy to the Foreign Office stamped 'Important'. It does not seem to have reached Thomas, however, for the Dominions were once again not mentioned in the debate which followed. Chamberlain and his supporters won the day and an embargo was placed on the export of arms to both combatants immediately, without time limit. From the British minutes it appears that the main motive for this strange decision was the desire to appear favourable to the League without actually offending Japan. Australian sources, however, suggest another motive. Bruce informed Latham that the Leader of the Opposition, Lansbury, had given notice in the House of Commons of a move on 27 February to reduce the vote of the Foreign Office, to force the government to provide a complete statement on the League and the situation in the Far East. According to Bruce, it was this parliamentary pressure which forced the government's hands. It was such an unexpected and hasty decision that the government did not even inform the Under-

Secretary of State for Foreign Affairs, Anthony Eden, who was in Geneva handling the embargo question in the South American dispute. Eden, who opposed the embargo, also had the humiliation of being forced to admit to the Japanese ambassador that he did not know anything about the decision.[54]

If this was so, it is not surprising that the British government did not keep the Dominions informed, let alone 'consult' them. The decision had all the signs of panic and political expediency. There is little excuse for Thomas, however. As Dominions secretary it was his duty to study any relevant files and to realise that some of the Dominions, and Australia in particular, might be concerned. It was here that the idleness and incapacity of Thomas wrecked the organisation which was supposed to establish Dominion harmony. The result was unforgivable. The Cabinet presumably made its decision before 1 pm on 27 February; Simon made his statement to the House at 4.50 pm on the same day; but it was not until 6.53 pm that the Dominions Office finally sent a circular to the Dominions. This circular, because of time differences and delays caused by coding and decoding, did not arrive in Australia till late on 28 February, by which time the Australian Minister for External Affairs, J.G. Latham, had read of the British decision in his morning newspaper.

A wrathful telegram went to Bruce on 2 March. The Australian government, to avoid embarrassing Britain, had informed her of the Chinese request to buy arms. It had been informed of the lifting of the previous embargo, and the next correspondence was the cryptic message of 24 February. Then came the sudden British action. Latham cabled: 'We do not regard this as real consultation or as giving any consideration to joint interests.' Moreover, he went on to enquire if any other commodities were to be banned.

> Stoppage of Australian trade in metals etc would be disastrous to our community. Has any consideration been given to these matters? Is there any information as to possible treatment of these or other articles as contraband? Does Great Britain propose to acquiese in such treatment if threatened? We have heard nothing from Admiralty or War Office or Air Ministry . . . Is Eastern conflict regarded as purely local dispute not necessitating any preparations against any contingencies?

The British representative in Canberra also reported to the Dominions Office the concern of the Australian government.[55] Bruce in London saw Simon, who wrote an apology, in which he argued that pressure of time compelled an immediate announcement. This was not, strictly speaking, true, for had Simon thought of consulting the Dominions when he first raised the issue on 18 February, he would certainly have had time to do so. His final remark, that he hoped there had been no embarrassment caused, was a suitable ending for a defence of this muddled and ill-considered policy.

The embargo was finally abandoned by the British government on 13 April 1933, but the Australian government's embarrassments continued. Latham was faced with three questions in federal parliament, which fortunately were vague enough to be parried. More serious, however, were the Defence Department's continuing attempts to sell arms abroad. It ceased while the British arms embargo was in operation, but recommenced immediately afterwards. It was injudicious enough to sell a small number of rifles to an entrepreneur who then sailed for the Far East, posing as the representative of the Australian government. When enquiries began to come in, Prime Minister Lyons personally intervened and instructed the Investigation Branch of the Attorney-General's Department to find out what was happening. Their report was not reassuring. The government had the humiliating task of sending cables to British authorities in Peking and Hong Kong and the Japanese Consul-General in Sydney, disclaiming responsibility. Even Bruce in London was involved. The result was a clear warning from External Affairs to the Defence Department that it should not meddle in political matters and should consult when they were likely to be involved, and the categorical decision *not* to sell arms abroad. This, however, placed the burden of supporting the small-arms factory back on the government. It was for this reason that Lyons wrote to New Zealand in 1933 offering Australian facilities.

In its concern for a native small-arms industry the Australian government was very different from the Canadian, which ignored the urgent recommendations of its Chief of General Staff and did little or nothing before 1939.[56] In the matter of arms sales to China, too, there is an interesting comparison between Canada and Australia. In 1900, during the Boxer rebellion, the then Canadian government had passed an Order in Council prohibiting the export of arms, ammunition and military and naval stores to China. This Order in Council had never been rescinded. Since then, the Dominions Office had kept the Canadian government informed of the state of the China arms embargo, trading regulations, etc. The Chinese indeed had appealed to Canada for arms, before the Manchurian crisis broke out, in July 1931, and once the crisis did occur they requested to be allowed to buy a Canadian fighter plane, army clothing, equipment and rifles. On 29 October 1931 Skelton passed a memorandum to Bennett, recommending that the Order in Council be rescinded immediately, since if there were open war between China and Japan they should not, as neutrals, refuse arms to one side only. The point was taken by the Justice Department, which noted that the original Order in Council had been intended to prevent arms reaching Chinese insurgents, and was not applicable to the governments of China and Japan if they were at war. Nevertheless, it seemed improper to allow the export of arms to one member of the League in a dispute with another. The Canadian government therefore applied to Britain for advice in January 1932, and received the reply that strict impartiality might necessitate an embargo on both countries, but such a move would favour Japan, since she could manufacture her own arms. The British government therefore doubted the desirability of trying to prevent the flow of arms to China. This was sound advice that the British should have later followed themselves. Bennett, however, chose to ignore the British conclusion, and instead of lifting the ban on the export of arms to China thought of extending it to all oriental countries.[57]

Nothing seems to have been done, however, until the British embargo on the sale of arms to China in February 1933 brought the matter forcibly back to the Canadian government's attention. McNaughton strongly criticised the British move, as helping Japan and being out of sympathy with the recommendations of the Committee of Nineteen. He thought the British were not moved by moral considerations, but simply feared involvement and sanctions. Bennett, however, was inclined to support the British, since he had previously considered an embargo on all Eastern countries and had always opposed the trade in arms. He told parliament on 1 March that an Order in Council was being prepared. When he received a cable from Marler in Tokyo, warning against a nickel embargo and especially an action against Japan alone, he cabled back that the government 'had', by an Order in Council, rescinded the 1900 proclamation and established an embargo on the export of arms to all countries, but only on armaments.[58] This seemed to answer Marler's objections, but in fact Bennett was being premature.

He was subjected to increasing and steady pressure against any such action. On 2 March the Canadian minister in the United States telephoned and urged that they should make no decision till they had his cable. When his message arrived, it informed the government of the unfavourable response in the United States, where the British move was regarded as a declaration of neutrality. The Chief of General Staff also urged that they should do nothing quickly, should restrict any embargo to military armaments in the narrowest sense, and above all should keep the peace between Britain and the United States. The next day Herridge sent another long account of the hostile American reactions and the limited powers of the president, and urged his government to take no immediate action. The following day another long message arrived from an obviously worried Marler in Tokyo. Japan would regard any sanctions as an act of war, and would probably be provoked into taking further action against China. Canada should preserve, therefore, the 'disinterested position' it had attained. On the same day the General Staff sent another long memorandum listing all the arguments against 'this extremely individualistic and embarrasing move on the part of the

British Government', and urging that Canada should do nothing to exacerbate a dangerous situation and should not act on the export of arms.[59]

Faced with the united opposition of his ministers in Tokyo and Washington and the General Staff, Bennett gave way. McNaughton, indeed, was insistent that Canada should take no action. Seeing the impotence of the country militarily, this was not surprising. Therefore, on 9 March Bennett cabled the High Commissioner in London that no action would be taken on the arms embargo. He remarked that the embargo order of 1900 could not be rescinded without appearing to favour China. The government had therefore decided to do nothing. The High Commissioner was reminded of the need for close cooperation between Britain and the United States, and was told to impress on other Commonwealth representatives at the disarmament conference the need to concert any action.[60]

When the Chinese asked in March and April to be allowed to buy munitions, they were refused, though they were permitted to buy clothing. Even a long report from the Canadian legation in Tokyo on 'the very considerable Japanese armaments industry' did not move the Canadian government to end the 1900 prohibition of arms exports to China. The Canadians might criticise Britain for wishing to avoid involvement in the dispute, but they themselves were content to leave China at a grave disadvantage, rather than take any action which might bring Japanese disapproval on themselves. Bennett seems to have salved his conscience by getting Riddell to propose, at the disarmament conference in June, a motion for the abolition of all private armaments manufactures. This took the British by surprise—so much for Canadian stress on concerted action by the members of the Commonwealth. The British High Commissioner in Canada noted dourly that it had no armament firms on whose orders the prosperity of a steel industry depended.[61]

British, Canadian and Australian reactions to the embargo on the sale of arms to China were not very impressive. None were concerned that the victim of aggression was being further disadvantaged or that the culprit was being helped. The Australian government, at least, was aware of the need to maintain an armaments industry, but did not succeed in doing much about it.

Australian defence: confused policies and the appeal to Britain
The most serious weakness in the Australian government's defence policy had been its failure to face the implications of its own strategy. It had decided to place its reliance on British naval strength; but that required an effective naval base, properly defended, at Singapore. Hints had been coming through to Australia that the British navy and

its base were dangerously weak. Bruce certainly realised this in London, and Latham, as his comments there showed, also had at least a glimmering of insight. If the government had really believed its defence policy, it should have done its utmost, even in the straightened financial situation of the time, to increase its naval expenditure and to strengthen Singapore. Yet it not only declined to provide any funds to assist the British in building the base, it also failed to develop its armed forces so that they could move to defend the base in an emergency. Moreover, joint plans were not developed with the British defence planners. The government rejected a British request to provide a garrison for Singapore, even though that might have given some Australians an insight into the weaknesses and needs of the base. Nor did it create the nucleus of an expeditionary force that might move to Singapore in an emergency. Instead, it allowed the army to spend its defence vote, not on equipment for the proposed expeditionary force, but on fixed gun defences. This was partly a failure by the politicians to discipline the army and make it follow policy: they also, however, lacked a clear policy of their own. For example, when in July 1934, the British suggested that RAAF units could exercise with the RAF based at Singapore, there was no Australian response. This negative attitude continued. At the 1937 imperial conference Parkhill was to refuse to consider giving priority in RAAF development to those squadrons which would be capable of contributing to Singapore's defence. Instead, priority would be given to Australian defence, even though the base at Singapore was supposed to make that unnecessary.[62] It seems, therefore, that the government did not fully believe its own propaganda about linking Australian defence with imperial defence. Perhaps it simply tried to back the defence horse both ways—it hoped that Britain would defend Australia on the seas and so save the Australian authorities unnecessary money and thought; on the other hand, supplied with rumours of British weakness, it kept some of its puny forces in reserve in case of emergency. By adopting this ambiguous policy, it in the end got the worst of both worlds.

The official reliance on British naval power, moreover, raised two problems: whether the Australian government was right in assuming that Britain could or would come to its aid in time of crisis; and whether it was right, accordingly, in reducing the strength of the Australian army. The CID report, 'The Defence of Australia', therefore, in January 1933 provoked a fresh round in the long dispute between the Australian army and navy. The naval authorities, as could be expected, strongly supported the paper, arguing that there was 'no sound reason' why the British main fleet would not travel to and operate in the Pacific Ocean. The naval staff must have realised how debateable their optimism was. They did not go unchallenged, however. The army remarked: 'it is not merely doubtful, but certain that for some years the British Main Fleet will not be able to operate in the Western Pacific, because the base at Singapore will not be ready.' Moreover, 'if ever' it were finished, trouble in Europe or the Near East might make the British unwilling to send their fleet so far away.

A member of the Staff Corps, J.D. Lavarack (who was later to be made Chief of General Staff) even wrote an article in the British *Army Quarterly* in January 1933 playing down imperial naval defence and stressing the need for an army.

The Australian army authorities prepared a critique of the CID paper and handed it to Pearce on 26 January 1933. They seized on its provisos that if a British fleet arrived in time and found a base at Singapore that was properly equipped and defended, then Australia need only fear sporadic attack. They then analysed three CID papers, 'The Defence of Australia', 'The Defence of Australian Ports' and 'The Defence of New Zealand', to show that those assumptions were invalid. Singapore was not properly finished or equipped and there was no guarantee that a British fleet would be sent to it. British governments had postponed or cancelled action in the past on Singapore and probably would again. They then quoted from the Treasury note that the financial risk was more important than the military one, and commented: 'The detachment of this . . . is admirable, from the British point of view, but what for Britain is merely the acceptance of a risk means for Australia the facing of imminent disaster. Australia, with her various interests, is a part of the stake, and is therefore not in a position to take a detached view of the question.'[63] They therefore strongly urged that the Australian government take no action on the CID recommendations until the Singapore base and defences were complete, and either a fleet was stationed at it or guarantees were received from the British government that they would send a fleet in an emergency.

The Australian army authorities undoubtedly had vested interests at stake that prompted them to analyse the CID report so carefully, but it is difficult to fault their logic and foresight. On 5 March 1933 the Chief of General Staff, Major General J.H. Bruche, made a stinging attack on the optimism of the Australian Defence Committee and used the British Chiefs of Staff annual review to back up his arguments. On 29 March he produced a revised and enlarged version of the army critique of that CID paper and added, in an appendix, that as a contribution to solving the problem set in the terms of reference—the apportionment of money between the three services—'the report seems to be of very doubtful value'.

The argument in Australia between the three services, all fighting for their prestige and a share of the meagre funds available, turned on the future intentions and reliability of the British. Would they complete the naval base at Singapore and would they send a fleet there in an emergency? As Major General Bruche remarked in his paper, 'This has always been, and remains, the only point at issue between the services in Australia'.[64]

The Australian government, faced with continuing disagreement between its service chiefs, decided to appeal to Britain to complete the base at Singapore and so make imperial naval defence, as assumed in the CID papers sent to Australia, a reality. This involved Australia's representative, Bruce, in the arguments within the British CID and Cabinet. On 6 April he sat with the CID to discuss the Chiefs of Staff report on the situation in the Far East. At this meeting he made an impassioned plea for action, stressing the importance of Singapore to Australia. It seems that he had been informed of the debate in the Defence Committee, for he added that unless the Singapore base could be made stronger the Australian government might have to consider larger land and air forces, which they could only do by reducing naval expenditure and leaving Britain to pay for a larger proportion of the imperial navy. He concluded that, to Australians, the situation in the Far East seemed the more dangerous and the defences of Singapore ought therefore to be completed as quickly as possible. His argument, however, was simply brushed aside by MacDonald, who remarked that the question was primarily one of finance—'It must clearly be understood that there would be no big extension of expenditure, because this would be out of the question'. After this example of logic the British Prime Minister left the meeting![65]

The debate had only begun, however. In mid-1933 the British Chief of Naval Staff was still pessimistic, and in September the Cabinet was warned of American and Japanese naval contruction. Chamberlain still appeared anxious about the cost. The First Sea Lord was therefore determined that the Chiefs of Staff annual review for 1933 would reveal the real weakness of the navy. When the review came out in October it certainly painted a grim picture. The Chiefs of Staff noted that although tension had relaxed in the Far East, Japan had set up Manchukuo and left the League. The area was still therefore a potential danger zone. A second danger area had now developed, however, in Europe, where, under Hitler and the Nazis, Germany was 'once more manifestly becoming a public menace'. War in Europe would provide Britain with many problems, for she could no longer remain supreme in European waters and still send a fleet to the Far East, where Singapore remained completely vulnerable. War both on the continent *and* the Far East simultaneously would strain Britain's resources—by then seriously deficient—to the limit. They still maintained their old priority of the Far East, followed by Europe and then India, but appealed to the full CID to state its views.[66]

Armed with this document, Bruce had a long meeting with the Chiefs of Staff on 3 November and discussed the whole organisation of the defence forces in Australia and the CID paper on that subject. It may signify the importance of the matter, or the divergence of views among those concerned, that no minutes of this meeting were kept—a most unusual circumstance in this period. However, the repercussions of the meeting were soon seen.

When the CID met on 9 November to discuss the Chiefs of Staff Report, Chamberlain objected to a cut-and-dried set of priorities and remarked that Europe might soon become a greater danger zone than the Far East, a point to which he continually returned in the debates which followed. His motive, however, was most unlikely to have been the European situation itself. More probably he was preoccupied with the economy, and orthodox financial methods to improve it, and wished to avoid expenditure which he regarded as unnecessary, because it was to defend places so far away. Moreover, Britain herself could be protected much more cheaply by the air force and a small army than with the navy, whose ships were expensive enough in themselves, but also needed even more expensive bases built for them. The dangers of Europe therefore became one of his battery of arguments, along with the appeal to public opinion, the need for an accomodation with Japan, and the more straightforward economic argument. At this CID meeting, indeed, Chamberlain assured the First Lord of the Admiralty that Japan had no ambitions outside China, 'certainly nothing in the direction of Australasia'. At that stage, however, Bruce intervened and argued strongly that the Far East was the outstanding danger. As he put it, 'It was difficult to see what could prevent Japan obtaining a complete mastery of the Pacific if she chose to go to war between now and the time that Singapore was completed'. He realised the difficulty of finance, but appealed for concentration on the Far East. Bruce's speech provoked a discussion of the ways to coordinate defence expenditure and establish a system of priorities. Finally, it was agreed that a committee should be set up, consisting of the Chiefs of Staff, representatives of the Treasury, the Foreign Office and Hankey. In this way the 'Defence Requirements Committee' was born.[67]

This committee sprang from the concern of the Chiefs of Staff and Bruce over British weakness in the Far East. They had therefore opposed the Chancellor of the Exchequer, Chamberlain. It would be naive, however, to assume that, by the creation of the committee, the Chiefs of Staff and Bruce had won a victory. It is a time-honoured move of politicians to pass matters over to a committee, which they hope either to dominate, or at least use to prevent or delay unpleasant action. It is perhaps significant that this committee was suggested by Hailsham, who, as Secretary of State for War, was more concerned with the army and Europe than the navy and the Far East, and in the preceding debate had said that Japan would be fully occupied by China. Moreover, the composition of the committee is significant. The representative of the Treasury on it was Sir Warren Fisher, and that of the Foreign Office was Sir Robert Vansittart. These two men, according to Watt, were ' . . . obsessed, not to put too fine a point on it, with the peril to Britain represented by Germany'.[68] Fisher had succeeded in getting himself, as permanent under-secretary of the Treasury, recognised as head of the Civil Service. His great influence was reinforced by Chamberlain's dominance in the Cabinet. Neither he nor Vansittart would be sympathetic to the demands of the navy in the Far East. Indeed, this was seen at its third meeting in December 1933, when Vansittart insisted that the main danger was not Japan but Germany. Britain had not the resources to fight both at once, so should finish the defences of Singapore and then concentrate on Europe.[69]

The fundamental question, however, was whether the new committee could inject a sense of urgency into the members of the British government and so stimulate serious rearmament, which would affect Britain's position throughout the world. The answer to this even more important question was to be seen in 1934.

5 Armaments or diplomacy: *the search for security*

> ... an ultimate policy of accomodation and friendship with Japan, and an immediate and provisional policy of 'showing a tooth' for the purpose of recovering the standing which we have sacrificed of recent years.
> DEFENCE REQUIREMENTS COMMITTEE 1934
> C.P. 64(34) PRO CAB 24/247.

By the beginning of 1934, the governments of Britain and the Dominions had recognised the weakness into which the Empire/Commonwealth had drifted. They were still undecided, however, on what action they should take. The service chiefs, and a few other leaders, stressed the need for rearmament, but most politicians, in both Britain and the Commonwealth, disliked the idea of this intensely. They thought it would be unpopular with their electorates, they feared it would lead to more international tension and even war, and, most importantly, they thought that it would impose an impossible burden on their people and retard economic recovery. They had no sympathy with the idea which Keynes had begun to put forward, and Hitler's Germany was to prove, that government spending was the way out of the depression, by providing work and so creating new economic growth. Instead, government leaders in Britain and the Dominions were liable to turn to diplomacy, in an effort to avoid the need to rearm. This was seen very clearly in 1934.

The Singapore conference and its aftermath

Defense needs were aired once again at a conference held at Singapore from 23 to 27 January 1934, the successor of conferences held in 1921 and 1924. At this one, representatives of Australia and New Zealand met the commander-in-chief of the China station and staff officers of the British air and sea forces in the East Indies, India and the area. In theory, it was a technical conference, to arrange for operations in an emergency, before the main British fleet arrived.

The conference turned, however, into an exercise in putting pressure on British politicians. The members present stressed the weakness of Singapore. One, for example, suggested that since they lacked any mines with which to block the channel, they might instead simply put up warning notices of minefields, and thereby perhaps induce the Japanese to be cautious! Another, from the air force, remarked that the Japanese had four carriers operating 152 aircraft, whereas the Singapore garrison merely had a squadron of four flying boats with which to protect the oil storage tanks, which stood in full view with 762 037 tonnes of fuel oil in them, the dockyard itself, and 77 699 square km of ocean. The military chiefs pointed out, once again, that Singapore could not hold out till relief came, and its loss would prove serious in any war. Therefore, 'unless the Government felt that they could ignore such a risk, they should take immediate steps to provide security for Singapore'.[1] They suggested that a battle cruiser squadron should be sent out, and the existing fleet in the Pacific be strengthened by replacing its old ships and increasing numbers.

The conference report laid great stress on New Zealand opinion, foreseeing serious consequences if the New Zealand people found they were contributing to a scheme that might never be finished. Clearly, the British naval and air authorities thought the presence at the conference of Australian and New Zealand representatives was a good opportunity to press their own government to put in hand urgent work. How effective these complaints from 16 000 km away might be remained to be seen, but the commodore commanding the New Zealand Station, Rear Admiral Burges Watson, bluntly wrote to the New Zealand government that his presence there had been a waste of time and money, since the British commanders had been in close consultation for months and the Dominion representatives could add little. 'Australia and New Zealand, therefore, formed a sort of Greek chorus, chanting "Yes, we agree" in unison, and appended their signatures.'[2] He thought that though the final draft would be a useful weapon in the hands of the Admiralty, New Zealand had paid heavily for his signature to be included on it.

Burges Watson's assumption that the Singapore conference report was not New Zealand's direct business is surprising, given the expressed and continuing concern in that country about British naval weakness in the Far East and the Singapore base. There was much publicity given by the press in the opening months of 1934 to the matter, and Burges Watson's silence on his return 'strengthened the suspicion that the present situation is critical'. The New Zealand High Commissioner in London, at that time Sir James Parr—Sir Thomas Wilford having retired—intervened in a debate in the CID on the air defence of Singapore and remarked that it was 'of great interest to New Zealand'. Concern was indeed revealed by remarks in the New Zealand parliament in July and September. As we have seen, the government had decided to rearm but had postponed expenditure increases till the 1934 fiscal year, merely instituting its own branch of the CID in 1933. The following year, however, defence expenditure for the first time exceeded that of 1930–31.[3]

In Australia also the British representative noted a new defence awareness by the end of 1933. By March 1934 the Defence Committee thought that war might come in the next two years, and F. G. Shedden, the secretary of the Defence Department, wrote a 28-page appreciation of the international situation, the growth of Nazi arrogance in Germany and Japan's military strength. He suspected that if Britain were involved in Europe, Japan would strike again in the Far East. At the end of the year Hankey was writing to correspondents in Britain that there was an exaggerated fear of war in Australia. 'Everyone seems to have the wind up about Japan.'[4]

The Australian government reacted in a variety of ways to the public criticism of its earlier defence economies and the growing concern over Japanese strength. To start with, it at last began to face the need for increased expenditure. The turning point came in 1934, when a 'Three Years Programme' was instituted, 'to make good the severe cuts during the depression'. Even so it was a slow start—the government later prided itself that all the funds allocated to defence had been provided from revenue. During the next three years it spent an average of just over £7.5 million on defence each year. The increase was not dramatic, but a beginning had been made. Even more significantly, the government maintained its priorities: the navy continued to have first call on funds, followed by the army, with the air force a very poor third.[5]

The Australian government, like the British, disapproved of defence expenditure at a time of economic hardship and tried to avoid it by spending a little more on its diplomatic services instead. Previously, in June 1932, it had discouraged a Japanese move to appoint a minister to Australia, akin to their minister in Ottawa. It did not wish to follow the Canadian model, preferring to remain linked to the British Foreign Office. That, however, did not preclude Australia providing herself with her own sources of information about an area of the world that was of particular interest to her. Moreover, the independence of the Defence Department over the matter of armaments, and the embarrassment it had caused, perhaps spurred the government to upgrade its Sub-Department of External Affairs to correlate and control all dealings with foreign governments. On 18 April 1934 it therefore announced that an assistant secretary had been appointed to the Prime Minister's Department, to deal solely with External Affairs.[6] It may be significant that the man chosen, Major W.R. Hodgson, came from the Defence Department. He could the more easily liaise with it.

The cautious strengthening of the 'Department' of External Affairs did not satisfy Australian intellectuals. They were beginning to demand the appointment of ministers to Canada, New Zealand, the United States and Japan. They argued that though the Manchurian incident had involved Japan on the mainland of Asia, and led her away from Australia, she might yet turn back to expansion in the Pacific. The Australian government needed to watch events. The intellectuals, in particular Dr A.C.V. Melbourne of Queensland, combined with the pressure of the economic and military situation to provoke the Australian government into taking a totally uncharacteristic diplomatic initiative—the sending of a mission, led by the Minister for External Affairs, Sir John Latham, to the Far East.

The Australian Eastern mission: Sir John Latham, March–June 1934

The motives for the mission were mixed. Trade played a large part, since the depression had made this subject important. In April 1932 the Japanese had suggested a commercial treaty between Australia and Japan, but the Australian government had been unwilling to act until the Ottawa conference had ended. Thereafter it continued postponing action. In September 1932, after a visit to China and Japan, H.W. Gepp, a consultant on development to the government, had produced a 'Report on trade between Australia and the Far East', in which he recommended a six to nine month visit to the Far East by a special Australian envoy, and that 'commercial counsellors' should be attached to British diplomatic posts in Tokyo and Shanghai. About the same time Melbourne, in a survey for the University of Queensland, recommended the cancellation of tariffs, a trade agreement between Australia and Japan, and the appointment of an economic mission by the government. The Cabinet, however, in that month postponed once again any decision on trade representatives in the Far East. A conference of interested parties was held in Sydney in February 1933, but the general feeling was against the appointment of trade commissioners and official government help. Melbourne, however, continued his campaign, writing to the Minister for Commerce in May. In July, Latham was provoked by a letter from an Australian traveller, who pointed out that the Canadian government had representation in Japan. Latham wrote to Lyons suggesting once again that trade commissioners be attached to British offices. Accordingly, the Trade Commissioners Act was passed in December 1933, granting the government the necessary powers.[7]

In 1934, however, the government still insisted, both publicly and privately, that trade was not its main motive in sending the Latham mission. This was to be expected, for trade was a divisive subject, especially after the Ottawa Agreement. Moves to bypass that agreement would lead to protests from Britain, while close public adherence to it would offend Japan. Moreover, government supporters were divided between manufacturers, who wanted high tariffs to save them from Japanese competition, and farmers, who wanted low tariffs to keep their costs down so that they could take advantage of the Japanese market for their primary produce. Both parties feared government regulation of trade as 'socialism', and their State representatives also feared giving the federal government more power. The British were themselves involved in tortuous negotiations with Japanese interests over cotton and rayon, negotiations which broke down in March 1934. Lancashire industrialists requested that the Australian mission be cancelled. The British government demurred, but informed the Australians of the situation. In such a minefield, the Australian government did well to walk warily. Indeed, its future was at stake. An election was to be held in 1934, and a successful overseas mission could improve the government's standing against the Country Party, which was urging more trade with the East. Latham was concerned that such demands did not threaten the Ottawa agreements—hence the argument, so often advanced by government spokesmen, that friendship did not depend on reciprocal trade.[8]

Finally, the motive discussed at the beginning of this chapter was also present. The Manchurian and Shanghai crises had revealed the weakness of Britain in the Far East, and the Australian government had been urged to rearm. Perhaps it could avoid that unpleasant need by a diplomatic move. If, at the same time, trade with Japan could stimulate Australia's flagging economy, so much the better.

Considerations of trade, international peace and disarmament therefore all coincided. This was reflected in the somewhat confused statement which Lyons gave to the press on 2 December 1933. A Melbourne newspaper had breached the government's secrecy and printed a report on 1 December that the Australian Cabinet was considering a diplomatic mission to the Far East. The story was picked up by the London *Times* and thoroughly embarrassed the government, which had not yet either made up its own mind or received the British and foreign governments' approval. It now found itself flooded with suggestions—such as that the famous Australian aviator Sir Charles Kingsford Smith should fly his plane, or one by the Graziers' Federal Council that a representative of the pastoral industry should accompany the mission—offers of help and applications for posts. All these, needless to say, the government rejected.[9]

The mixture of aims was also apparent when Latham returned to Australia on conclusion of the mission, in the long and secret reports to the government on trade between Australia and Japan, on the appointment of trade commissioners, on Australian wool in the East, and on the international diplomatic and strategic situation,[10] and also in the wording of the official report on the mission to the Australian parliament. In the latter he remarked:

Australia . . . has a special relation to the Far East. The continent of Australia is actually in the geographical area often described as 'the East'. The risks attendant upon any disturbance of the peace or actual outbreak of war in that region are of the greatest moment to our people. Our trade relations with Eastern countries are most important to our welfare. Accordingly, the maintenance of friendly relations between Australia and our neighbours and, more generally, the maintenance of peace in the East, should be the major objectives of Australian policy.[11]

The connection between trade and friendly relations could not have been put more clearly.

One other motive remains—it is possible that Latham was already considering his retirement from politics. The honour of leading Australia's first diplomatic mission may have been given to him by his fellow Cabinet members out of regard for his long service and for surrendering the chance to be Prime Minister when the United Australia Party first came to office.

Be that as it may, Latham threw himself into planning his mission with enthusiasm. A telegram went to Bruce on 13 December, asking for advice on the organisation of the trip, and this too stressed international goodwill, 'to offset the idea that friendship depends upon equivalence of volumes of trade'. The British government had no objection, but thought that China should definitely be visited if Japan was. The fact that the Australian government even considered ignoring China reveals where it thought its interests lay, and some critics did indeed suggest that the government was favouring Japan. Melbourne, who had offered his services to Latham on the assumption that the latter was organising a trade mission, also stressed the need to visit China for an equal length of time as Japan.[12]

Latham was meticulous in his planning. He appealed to the secretary of the Department of External Affairs for information on the countries he was to visit, Australian legislation affecting them, British diplomatic representation in them and the personnel, policies and League involvements of the different governments. He and Lyons then contacted the Australian press and asked editors not to refer to the mission as a trade mission, or as one to Japan, or to sneer at it as a 'ministerial joy ride'. Not content with this, Latham got the Australian liaison officer in London to approach the British and arrange for a question to be asked in the House of Commons, enabling Anthony Eden to announce that the British government was happy to help organise the mission and had confidence in it. Latham did the same thing after the mission, getting another question asked, to enable Simon to remark on its value.[13] These attempts to influence Australian press and public opinion in favour of the mission helped Latham and also the British, who were anxious that Japan should not see a rift between Australia and Britain and take advantage of it in the cotton negotiations. Moreover, some clarification was needed, for confusion existed in Britain, Australia and Japan (where Marler thought that Latham's mission presaged a trade agreement while the Japanese feared increased tariffs).[14]

The 'Australian Eastern Mission' finally set out on 17 March 1934. Latham took his wife and daughter, a secretary, assistant secretary and stenographer, a representative of the Department of Trade and Customs, and, from the Intelligence section of the Attorney-General's Department, 'Mr' (actually Major) Longfield Lloyd, thinly disguised as an 'advisor'.[15] With them went two press representatives, Frank Murray for the Sydney *Sun* and F.M. Cutlack of the *Sydney Morning Herald*. The group visited the Netherlands East Indies (for ten days), Malaya (three days), French Indo-China (three days), Hong Kong (two days), China (twelve days), Japan (twelve days) and the Philippines (two days). When sailing time was added, the mission was away from Australia for nearly three months. It was a major undertaking, and the first of its kind for the Australian government.

Because of his senior position in that government, Latham was able to meet Premiers, Governors, the Japanese Emperor and members of the British diplomatic corps. He, or other members of the mission, also had discussions with commercial and industrial men; and he made many public appearances and spoke frankly with officials.

Nevertheless, how clear a picture he got of the countries he visited remains doubtful. In the East Indies, for example, he spent his time with the Dutch colonial officials and planters. One commentator remarked:

> Contact with the indigenous population was ceremonial rather than substantive. On 5 April, for example, Latham was received by the Sultan of Djokjakarta in a manner reminiscent of the Arabian Nights. The Australian representative rode to the reception in the Sultan's red and gold coach, along roads lined by the Sultan's army. The army was clothed in a variety of European uniforms one hundred and fifty years old. In the courtyard of the Sultan's palace eight girls performed a two hour long dance illustrative of Hindu legend. By the time this ended, at 10.30 p.m., the unappreciative Australian contingent was both bored and uncomfortable. Electric lights had added to tropic heat and they "had sweated all the starch from their shirts".

Likewise in Shanghai Latham spent his time with the British and Australian community, even attending an Anzac Day service and ball. What he saw of China itself did not impress him. As he later wrote,

> the masses of the people are pitiably poor and . . . life and property are generally unsafe. The simplest illustration of this is found in the fact that

throughout China all the railway stations are, even in remote country districts, guarded by soldiers and generally surrounded by barbed wire. . . The Chinese appear to have a great instinct for politics but little instinct for government. They can write wise books and enunciate fine principles, but they do not appear to be expert in the actual tasks of governing a country.[16]

He did, however, have discussions with senior Chinese officials while in Nanking and Canton, though not Generalissimo Chiang K'ai-shek.

The visit to Japan was more impressive. Latham was welcomed there, partly because, as the *Japan Times* reminded its readers, the Australian and New Zealand governments had shown restraint when the League had condemned Japan for the Manchurian incident.[17] The fact that Latham was a senior member of the Cabinet also pleased the Japanese.

Much of his time, of course, was spent on ceremony, such as luncheons, dinners, audiences with the Emperor, the Empress and the Prime Minister. Much of it was also spent as a tourist. 'It was, after all, as one hostile labour newspaper in Australia disgustedly recorded, cherry blossom time. He visited the old Imperial Palace at Kyoto, inspected a famous lacquer factory and spent a week-end in a mountain resort at Nikko with a British embassy official in tow.'[18] The most substantial part of Latham's visit, however, was a conversation of one and a half hours with the Japanese Foreign Minister, Mr Hirota. Hirota was a diplomat of long standing, having worked in England and Russia before becoming Foreign Minister. Latham was therefore dealing with a skilled and experienced man.[19]

He began by stressing Australia's connection with the British Empire and rejecting Hirota's suggestion for diplomatic representation between Australia and Japan. He argued that 'happily' there was no need for such diplomatic intercourse. His motive was probably the cost. The British chargé d'affaires—Sir Francis Lindley having retired and the new ambassador Sir Robert Clive not having arrived—had impressed on Latham 'the outward and visible evidence of the expensiveness of the Canadian establishment'. The British diplomatic service was anxious that Canadian independence was not copied by other Dominions.[20]

On the dangerous matter of Australian tariffs, Latham denied discrimination against Japan—there was one tariff for British goods and another for all other countries. He agreed, however, to expedite trade negotiations. Egged on by the British chargé d'affaires Latham then, 'with the utmost confidence', remarked that there was fear and suspicion of Japan, since other countries were not sure what her policy would be. Hirota, naturally, denied that Japan had any aggressive intentions and blamed the League for encouraging China and so forcing Japan to take action in Manchuria—a somewhat dubious argument that Latham did not challenge. Latham, however, did request that Hirota make a public announcement that Japan would not fortify her island mandates, though he added that he thought Japan should be allowed to keep them even after she had finally left the League. Hirota agreed, gave the declaration which Latham sought about the mandates and then denied that Japan had any designs on the Netherlands East Indies. Latham happily accepted Hirota's assurances.

In all of this there was a certain deviousness on the Japanese part and naivety on Latham's. Latham said that he 'might be excused as a mere barbarian from the South for saying things which would give offence if said by a professional diplomatist'. Accordingly, he even went so far as to remark that if the Japanese attempted to land an army in Australia, they would find they had a very lively hornets' nest on their hands![21] The British Foreign Office also thought that Latham might be useful in broaching subjects which it felt were delicate, but that he underestimated the difficulty of satisfying all sides, including China. 'It will be interesting to see what formula Mr. Latham produces to save the faces of Japan and the League of Nations—not to mention China.'[22]

Strong support for the League, however, had never been a noticeable trait of Latham. Nor was it of the members of his mission. One agreed with a British correspondent that Manchuria was a natural outlet for Japan and told him that Australia had always regretted the termination of the Anglo–Japanese Alliance. The correspondent was also told that the Australians were in full sympathy with the Japanese view of their right to the mandated islands.[23]

It does seem that Latham's support for Japan and bias against China was only confirmed by his Far Eastern tour. He was a conservative lawyer, with a strong distaste for anarchy—which he thought only encouraged communism—combined with a loyalty to the British Empire and a feeling of white superiority. Accordingly, the chaos of China, the apparent lack of Western commercial and industrial development, the Chinese boycotts of foreign goods and the presence of communism in the country roused his white, Western, conservative and commercial prejudices. He wrote:

> It appears to be universally admitted even by the most enthusiastic supporters of what is described as the Chinese Republic that the conditions of the people are more wretched and hopeless than they were in the last days of the Empire . . . China is in pieces today, and it may be in fragments to-morrow. It is, I suggest, desirable to frame a policy covering this contingency.

He may well also have been influenced by Cutlack's pro-Japanese views. Certainly some of his speeches in China were patronising (and embarassing to read) and at a dinner in Canton he complained to the chairman of the provincial government and the Marshall that British trading interests were being seriously prejudiced.[24]

Japan, on the other hand, was an example of a nation that had modernised, accepted Western ways, and was under a 'strong' government. Latham was bound to approve of this, even if he feared the consequences for Australia. Moreover, he found he was warmly welcomed there. The British resident in Canberra, E. T. Crutchley, wondered if Latham in Japan 'had not had a little wool pulled over his eyes. He is not a man of the world exactly and I should not be a bit surprised if some of his judgements were a little biased by the enthusiasm of his reception'. This assessment is supported by Latham's official report to the Australian parliament. His description of his arrival in Shanghai contrasts with his glowing account of his reception in Japan. 'It is almost impossible to exaggerate in attempting to describe the cordiality of the reception.'[25]

As far as Japan was concerned, indeed, Latham's visit was a resounding success. Perhaps spurred on by his sympathy for the country, Latham dealt good-humouredly with the Japanese pressmen, made a perfect speech (translated) to the nation over Japanese radio and left with much goodwill. Both the British chargé d'affaires and the Canadian Kirkwood agreed that the visit was a success, and would help Australian–Japanese friendship. The British, however, were also relieved that Marler was away sick at the time, so that they were unchallenged in claiming diplomatic precedence during Latham's visit.[26]

Other reactions to Latham's mission were mixed, however. In Australia, the tour was well reported in the Sydney newspapers, which was not surprising since both journalists who travelled with Latham came from Sydney. It is odd that Latham did not realise the weakness of this arrangement, for as a result the mission was reported less in Melbourne and hardly at all in Brisbane. Most of the articles while the tour was in progress were merely factual reports, though some comment, disapproving of extended diplomatic ties abroad, was expressed. The *Sydney Morning Herald* published a series of thirteen articles and a conclusion by Cutlack between 6 and 21 August. Their pro-Japanese bias raised a storm of protest in Australia, from the Chinese Consul-General, the League of Nations Union and others, and even a complaint from the British Legation in Peking, which thought them a 'deplorable piece of anti-Chinese propaganda . . . libellous in parts'—though Latham still thought them 'fair'. Meanwhile, the *Daily Telegraph* printed a series of lurid articles highlighting Chinese poverty and drug addiction, which forced Lyons to intervene and get a conciliatory article published. It was not a very savoury incident, and did not speak well for the judgment of Latham or the reporters he had taken on his 'goodwill tour'.[27]

Latham did, however, make a major speech to the Australian parliament, in which he argued Australia's special interest in the Far East.

> It is the Far East to Europe, to the old centres of civilisation, but we must realise that it is the 'Near East' to Australia: . . . it is important . . . to develop and improve our relations with our near neighbours, whose fortunes are so important to us, not only in economic matters, but also in relation to the vital issues of peace and war.[28]

Latham went on to argue that friendly relations should not depend simply on trade balances and that there was need for understanding between Australia and the East.

He backed the speech up with the five lengthy reports already mentioned: one for general consumption, three referring to trade, and a 'Highly Confidential' one dealing with the military and diplomatic situation. The general report elaborated his statement to parliament and gave an account of his journey, stressing the Chinese parts, although all the speeches printed in the appendix had been given in Japan.

As for trade, Latham recommended that trade commissioners should be appointed in the Dutch East Indies, China and Japan. He thought that Japan was being pressed in a hostile direction by business interests. He foresaw possible action by Japan against Australian trade unless some trade agreement was made. He urged government action, either to develop Australian–Japanese trade, or to prepare for hostile Japanese reaction.[29]

The result, however, was disappointing. The Japanese expected the Australians to send a trade commissioner immediately, and, if a Canadian report is accurate, had even put into their estimates for the next financial year the cost of setting up a 'High Commissioner's office' in Canberra.[30] They therefore tried to prod the Australians into action, sending three negotiators in December 1934 for trade talks in Melbourne and a 'Pacific Economic Inspection Party' and a naval training squadron in April 1935. Plans were made for a visit by Mr K. Debuchi, a senior Japanese minister, in September. As one historian comments:

> Never before indeed had Australia been the recipient of so much overseas attention. She found it embarassing rather than stimulating. Ironically, the Japanese demands, especially on immigration, frightened and outraged the Australian government. They had never thought out what they could offer the Japanese commercially, and they could not placate Japan without offending British economic interests, which were more important.

Some even thought that 'it was a thousand pities that Sir John Latham ever went to the East, since the visit had brought about this deluge of "good-will" in return'.[31] The government, however, pressed on. It finally appointed trade commissioners to Shanghai, Tokyo and Batavia in 1935, and an exhibition of Japanese manufactures was set up in Melbourne. The trend to better relationships with Japan was to be reversed, however, by the Trade Diversion Policy of 1936, when Australia, at the instigation of Lancashire cotton interests backed by the British government, placed prohibitive tariffs on Japanese textile imports into Australia. If Latham's intentions, therefore, had been to improve trading relationships between Australia and Japan, he did not succeed.[32]

Latham's other interest was discussed in his 'Highly Confidential' report to the government on the international situation. In this, he mentioned fears of a Japanese attack in the Dutch East Indies, where oil supplies important to any Japanese war effort were located, and dwelt at length on the chaotic conditions in China, arguing that Japan at least gave some security to people in Manchuria. He urged 'firm and unhesitating action in maintenance and defence of existing rights (or even "privileges") in China'. As for Japan, he had a great admiration for her culture and efficiency. He repeated Japanese arguments about the Manchurian affair, and asserted that the policy of non-recognition would not work. He wanted a formula that would enable both the League and Japan to save face, and simply dismissed the objection that this would not satisfy the Chinese. Despite noting the power of the army and navy in Japan, and the bellicose statements of some Japanese leaders, he asserted that nevertheless Japan did not desire further adventures in China, but merely trade. He thought that the greatest danger of war lay between Japan and Russia, but that Australia could and should stay out of involvement in it. He adhered to his old opinion that an invasion of Australia, because of the problems posed by distance and logistics, would be too difficult for Japan. In any case, her ambitions were on the mainland of Asia.[33]

This report, which was a mixture of shrewd insights and miscalculations, was not, of course, made public, so Australians were left with the rather vague and confused reactions of the press. As for Britain, Foreign Office officials were not greatly impressed. They thought Latham had misjudged China and disagreed with his assessment of the Manchurian problem. In this they may have been right, but they also disregarded him in his all too sound warnings about Singapore. Latham had visited it early in his mission and was most concerned. In his report to Lyons he noted the weaknesses of the base, and later contacted the Dominions Office, reporting on the lack of fighter planes and urging that the British should concentrate on finishing one major item rather than part-finishing many. He received no reply from the Dominions Office, and when he approached the Admiralty he received 'a polite snub'.[34] He did not influence thinking in Britain on the Far East or its problems. Perhaps this was due to the weakness of Thomas, who failed to bring the matter to the Cabinet's attention; on the other hand, despite talk of an 'Imperial Foreign Policy' and 'consultation' the British assumed that they had the superior knowledge and expertise, against which no Dominion representative's opinion was worth serious consideration. They therefore made no attempt to use Latham's mission to provoke a wider reassessment of imperial strategy or policy. 'Imperial' foreign policy remained in fact *British* foreign policy.

Nor did they publicise Latham's mission throughout the other Dominions of the Commonwealth, even though the Foreign Office was thankful for Latham's public loyalty to Britain, regarding it as 'an impressive demonstration of imperial solidarity'. For the despatches from the chargé d'affaires in Tokyo, though praising Latham, also included references to ticklish points of trade and the status of Dominion representation abroad. As a result, the British decided not to circulate the despatches to the Dominions, nor to show them to the Australian liaison officer in London. Latham did not receive a reply or commentary on his report—a discourtesy which naturally enough disappointed him.[35]

Finally, Latham put his report before the Australian parliament, and made his speech on international affairs, just before that parliament was dissolved. There was no opportunity to discuss the report or Latham's statements during the remainder of the parliamentary session and he did not seek re-election. It was all most curious. The first Australian diplomatic mission, begun for ambiguous reasons, ended on a note almost of anticlimax. The knowledge and expertise that Latham had gained would seem to have been wasted in the 1930s, though he continued to advise Lyons indirectly on international affairs and was to become Australia's first minister to Japan in August 1940.

It is odd that the British ignored the Latham mission so completely, since while it was being planned and taking place they were themselves discussing defence expenditure for the Far East and, in a desultory fashion, possible ways of coming to an understanding with Japan. For a rapprochement with that country was an obvious answer to British military and naval weakness in the East. In October 1932 the Chief of Imperial General Staff, Sir George Milne, had remarked that a friendly Japan was essential, and in August 1933 the new CIGS, Field Marshall Sir Archibald Montgomery-Massingberd, bitterly criticised the ending of the Anglo–Japanese Alliance. This was a theme that Chamberlain took up in October 1933, when he asked Simon whether anything could be done to improve relations with Japan.[36]

The matter came to a head in 1934, for in that year decisions had to be made about the Washington and London Naval disarmament treaties. The British government was desperately keen to see them renewed, or replaced by something else, such as a non-aggression pact, preferably with guarantees for China. For such a pact would lift from Britain the burden of arming to fight Japan—a burden that appalled the British Treasury.

Yet no one in the British government apparently thought of using Latham to make specific enquiries of the Japanese. There were probably a variety of reasons for this. Apart from the points already noted—the weakness of Thomas and the British government's dominance in 'imperial' foreign policy—there was the fact that the Latham mission was being planned in December 1933, before the British were ready seriously to discuss an agreement with Japan. It took the findings of the Defence Requirements Committee and its demand for massive defence expenditure to goad the British into action.

Britain: the defence requirements debate begins
In January 1934 Sir Warren Fisher, the Treasury representative on the Defence Requirements Committee, circulated a paper arguing for an ultimate policy of accommodation and friendship with Japan (combined with an immediate policy of 'showing a tooth') and assuming that Germany was the ultimate British enemy. This policy was adopted by the committee in its report, which came out commendably quickly on 28 February.[37]

The Admiralty, indeed, seems to have decided that, rather than fight Fisher in the committee, it would be better to put their needs before the Cabinet in the committee on the forthcoming naval conference. Even so, the recommendations of the Defence Requirements Committee involved an expenditure of £85 million in a five-year program and spurred Chamberlain to seek some means of escape. He was doubtless also moved by the memorandum produced by the Admiralty in March, which argued that the Washington agreements had been unsound, and that with the rise of Japan a two-power standard was needed for the navy.[38]

Chamberlain needed allies and found one in the Foreign Office, which early in 1934 produced a volume of thirteen memoranda which assessed Britain's relations with Japan, economic, military and political developments in the area, and the position of China. Vansittart argued that Britain should keep her aims flexible, neither antagonising Japan nor allowing herself to be made the spearhead of opposition to her, but also cultivating Chinese goodwill.[39] It was not only Latham who had illusions.

Trotter has remarked that the survey ignored naval questions and this failing invalidated its conclusions.[40] For example, on defence Vansittart wrote: 'it is assumed that we shall proceed unostentatiously with the defensive plans already drawn up.' As the War Office testily remarked, 'Ostentation does not appear to be in question' and it was 'altogether too optimistic' to assume that friendship with China would not involve Britain in embarrassing commitments, or offend Japan. The memoranda and Vansittart's comments on them, however, revealed that the Foreign Office too was opposing the more urgent claims of the Admiralty and opting instead for a policy of appeasing Japan.[41]

This policy was likely to appeal to members of the Cabinet, for the immediate reaction of the politicians was to try to win Japanese friendship rather than spend money on rearmament. This being so, Commonwealth opinion could be used as an argument. MacDonald had raised the question of Dominion attitudes to the ending of the Anglo–Japanese Alliance, and this provoked Thomas into circulating a report. Commonwealth opinion was also raised in Cabinet discussions and by Simon in a memorandum. The Dominions Office suggested a pact to include Canada, Australia and New Zealand as well as Britain and Japan.[42] No one, however, suggested that they should actually contact the Dominions afresh—they might have changed their minds in the meantime! Nor did anyone pretend that Commonwealth opinion was a major factor in the decision. The motives of the Cabinet were clearly pacifism combined with a view of British interests, especially reluctance or inability to provide money for rearmament.

The attack on the Defence Requirements Committee report, therefore, was led by Chamberlain. 'He saw no point in the effort and expense of "showing a tooth" when ultimately the olive branch would be extended.'[43] Therefore in Cabinet on 14 March he urged that they should end the naval agreement, to show that Britain was not lining up with America, and instead sign a non-aggression pact with Japan. On 16 March Simon produced one of his usual double-sided reports, giving the pros and cons of a non-aggression pact. On the whole he thought the disadvantages predominated, and suggested that the idea should be kept in reserve, pending the naval negotiations. The linking of the non-aggression pact with the naval talks was an attractive idea to the British and was to recur. On 19 March, however, Chamberlain suggested that they could go slowly in rearming, an opinion which appealed to Cabinet members.[44]

Instead of discussing the Defence Requirements Committee report, therefore, the Cabinet continued its search for an understanding with Japan. Chamberlain, in the Ministerial Committee on the Naval Treaty, suggested that spheres of commercial interest could be arranged. He ignored China's interests and her national feeling. However, the Japanese demand on 18 April revealed that they wanted not shared commercial rights but predominance in China. The situation was therefore embarrassing for Chamberlain—the Japanese were appearing intransigent in the Far East while the disarmament conference appeared about to break down. Yet on 17 April Chamberlain's third budget had given tax concessions and restored pay cuts to the British, which reduced the amount of money available for defence. The government, moreover, had argued that it was leading the country out of the depression; it could hardly therefore start an economy drive designed to finance rearmament, especially given the pacifism current at the time.

On 30 April, therefore, when the Cabinet did discuss the Defence Requirements Committee report, MacDonald used procedural excuses to delay action, talked of the disarmament conference and of bringing the opposition into the debate, and remarked, 'These proposals are not going to be popular'. On 2 May the Cabinet referred the matter to the Ministerial Committee on Disarmament, despite Hankey's very reasonable plea that such a move would be 'inappropriate'.[45]

For this, being a committee of politicians, gave even greater scope to their reluctance to rearm. The very next day, in discussing the Defence Requirements report, Chamberlain stressed the need to get back to good relations with Japan, before letting the Germans know they would concentrate their forces in Europe. A series of divisions, however, were developing within the British government; some wanted moderate rearmament in the Far East while others wished to appease Japan; and some stressed the danger of Japan while others feared Germany more. Nor did it escape their notice that the two powers might unite. 'The possibility of our being menaced in the Far East at a time when we might be faced with a dangerous situation in Europe is one that we ought to do our utmost to avoid.'[46] Wandering between the various camps were the pacifists and those who opposed rearmament, the service chiefs, whose interests varied (the army looked to Europe while the navy stressed imperial commitments in the Far East), and lastly the men of the Treasury, led by Chamberlain.

Chamberlain's attack was two-pronged. He wanted to appease Japan, so reducing the pressure on Britain in the East, and at the same time he argued that the main danger was Germany. This last argument was partly the result of his narrow vision and partly a desire for economy. An air force was cheaper than a navy, especially if expensive naval bases had to be built abroad. Thus, while no immediate moves were made to come to an understanding with Japan, Chamberlain was still determined to reduce defence expenditure if possible. Therefore, although he agreed to a five-year program, he insisted that the period might have to be extended. A rambling discussion continued at later meetings, and on 15 May Chamberlain agreed that the air force should be strengthened in Britain, for the public would accept that, 'but he did not think that arguments to increase air forces at such places as Penang would carry very much conviction'.[47] This was an example of his habit, seen at the time of Munich, of dismissing places that were 'far away'.

The full implications of his attitude became painfully clear on 20 June 1934, when he submitted a note on the Defence Requirements Committee report. (Having notes on reports placed in minutes of committee meetings was becoming another habit of his.) This particular note made another appeal to public opinion and went on to argue that the British government should concentrate therefore on measures to defend its own islands—measures which involved spending money on the army and the air force and reducing naval expenditure. They had, 'if only out of good faith to the Dominions', to complete Singapore, but they should 'contemplate its use as a base for submarines and other light craft, and we must postpone the idea of sending out to it a fleet of capital ships capable of containing the Japanese Fleet or meeting it in battle'.[48]

This note illustrated exactly the point the Australian Chief of General Staff had made—that Australia could not rely on either the ability or the intentions of the British government. However, the policy was not yet decided. Chamberlain's attitude provoked bitter protests from his opponents, led by Hankey. Their attitude was summed up by the General Staff, which wrote that Chamberlain's ideas meant 'placing our possessions, our Dominions and our great trade interests in Eastern waters at the mercy of Japan'. The Empire would collapse with far more certainty than could result from any air attack by Germany on Britain. And it was the Empire, as Chatfield was to point out to Fisher, that gave Britain its great voice in the world. Without it, Britain would become nothing but 'an insignificant island in the North Sea'.[49]

The next day Hankey sent a thirteen-page memorandum to the Prime Minister. He argued not against the amount of money that Chamberlain had allocated but his priorities. He dismissed Chamberlain's appeal to public opinion and gave a detailed analysis of the rise and consequences of Japanese power in the Far East, followed by a history of imperial conferences since 1923, with their stress on the base at Singapore. The Dominions, therefore, ought to be informed if any change in policy were decided, since British forces had been starved of funds for years. They could manage Navy Weeks, Tattoos and Air Displays, but could not sustain a major war. 'We have but a facade of Imperial Defence. The whole structure is unsound . . .'[50]

Hankey's was a well-reasoned and comprehensive paper, but one cannot help wondering if it was not too long. Few members of the government bureaucracy would have had the patience to read it through.[51]

Hankey was, as could be expected, strongly supported by the Dominions Office. They quoted Bruce at the CID meetings and argued that Chamberlain was proposing to exclude from consideration those deficiencies that were of the most vital concern to certain of the Dominions. They then repeated Hankey's point that the Dominions had been encouraged to build their defences around a British fleet going to Singapore, and it would be difficult to convince them that circumstances then made it unnecessary, especially as most Dominions were increasing their defence expenditure. They might draw the conclusion that Britain was abandoning the Empire for Europe and would certainly feel that their interests were betrayed 'if anything like the policy outlined in Mr Chamberlain's memorandum is approved'.[52]

When the Ministerial Committee on Disarmament met on 25 June the Dominions Office stress on the Commonwealth was seized on by the Admiralty. The First Lord pointed out that Chamberlain's new policy—of sending only light craft and submarines to Singapore—completely altered imperial defence policy. 'He did not see how it would be possible to tell the Dominions, in fact, that they would have to shift for themselves.' Thomas, on this issue, seems to have been affected by his permanent officials, for he repeated the arguments the DO had put forward and added that 'we could not expect that the Dominions, and especially Australia and New Zealand, would agree with this . . . because it would be quite impossible to convince the Dominions that there was no danger from Japan'. The debate, however, was desultory, with various people wavering or changing sides. Only Chamberlain remained firm, stressing financial difficulties, doubting Japan's hostile intentions, and hinting that the Dominions should not be told of any decision. The debate continued a second day, with Chamberlain and the Chiefs of Staff still at loggerheads. As a result, at a *third* meeting on 2 July, it was decided to take the decision on air defences first.[53]

This in fact was a victory for Chamberlain, since the air proposal could be passed, and then the army budget, while continuing debate on the navy meant that Chamberlain's desire to cut back expenditure would take effect. This became apparent on 24 July, when Chamberlain reduced the naval estimates from £21.7 million to £13 million.

There was possibly a final meeting of the Ministerial Committee on 27 July. At any rate, its draft report was circulated to the Cabinet on that date. If the meeting was held, no minutes have survived, either because it was a hurriedly called and informal meeting, or, what is equally probable, because the dispute between Chamberlain and his opponents became so blunt that it was thought better to have no minutes taken.[54]

In its report, the Ministerial Committee stressed the need to avoid the hostility of Japan, acknowledged Britain's weakness in the Far East and naval deficiencies, adding that Australia and New Zealand were especially concerned. Nevertheless, it proposed to reduce naval estimates by postponing the date of 'full readiness' from 1938 to 1940 and argued that no long-term naval program could be set up before the result of the international naval conference was known. Therefore, they should operate for one year at a time. Even this was further than many of the Cabinet wanted to go, for the Cabinet itself, when it finally discussed the ministerial report and made its decisions on defence requirements on 31 July, postponed the year of readiness still further from 1940 to 1942.[55]

Chamberlain had won—as he himself claimed.[56] His control over the allocation of money and the half-hearted acceptance of the need for rearmament by the other members of the Cabinet meant that the final remarks, with their echoes of 'newspeak', followed quite naturally. A decision on a long-range naval program was postponed, and even in those matters where rearmament was decided upon there was a striking disparity between the dire warnings in the report of imperial weakness in the Far East ('Thus the whole of our Imperial Defence arrangements in the Far East are thoroughly unsatisfactory') and the small amounts actually allocated to defence. For example, the first schedule of the report reduced the previous recommendation of seven squadrons of planes to be sent to the Far East to one!

Moreover, Chamberlain insisted that his view of financial caution be expressed throughout the report and repeated in the full Cabinet. The programs were tentative only, and were subject to annual review. Chamberlain warned his colleagues that he did not bind himself or his successors to find the additional money, either within five years, or in the particular years to which they were allotted. Roskill thinks that the reasons for this decision were that MacDonald was a sick man and did not want rearmament, while Baldwin was worried by the air threat and did not want the unpopularity of rearmament.[57]

The politicians' reluctance to rearm was revealed by their procrastination. The Defence Requirements Committee had produced its report within four months, but the Cabinet had waited two further months before discussing it and then passing it on to the Ministerial Committee, which then took a further two months to bring in the emasculated version. The delay, as the official historian points out,[58] was due to the fact that the government was preoccupied with the closing stages of the disarmament conference, and a last-minute effort to find some form of agreement. Moreover, further delays resulted. July—the month of the Cabinet decision—was much too late to do anything that year. Discussion on the 1935 budget would begin about October; the next budget would not come into effect until July 1935. In the meantime, the Cabinet turned to the possibility of an understanding with Japan. It was only when that had clearly failed that the Defence Requirements Committee was revived—also in July 1935.

Appeasing Japan

As we have seen, the British had made no serious overtures to Japan, but simply mentioned the possibility of an agreement with her in the course of defence debates. The daydream of a rapprochement was revived at the opportune time, when the Cabinet had just turned down naval rearmament, by a message on 5 July from Sir Robert Clive, the newly appointed British ambassador in Tokyo, describing a conversation he had had with Hirota. It appears that Latham was not the only westerner to be impressed by the smooth-talking Japanese Minister for Foreign Affairs. On this occasion Hirota declared that Japan was ready to sign non-aggression pacts with Britain and the United States. In August, Simon reacted to this with an entirely unwarranted optimism—for the 'moderates' in Japan were no longer effective. The Far Eastern Department of the Foreign Office showed a more realistic attitude, arguing that it would simply aid Japan, but they were overruled when Chamberlain threw himself energetically into advocating a naval agreement and non-aggression pact. In early September, therefore, the Foreign Office reassessed the matter, but remained unconvinced. A non-aggression pact might encourage Japan to attack Russia, which would in turn remove a restraint on German action in Europe. In any case no pact safeguarding China was possible. Simon therefore replied to Chamberlain on 7 September that a non-aggression pact was liable to give Japan a free hand in the Far East and should be investigated in detail before any decision on it be made. On 25 September, however, Simon changed his mind and argued in Cabinet that a pact would be of inestimable value to Britain. He was, of course, supported by Chamberlain, largely, it appears, because a pact with Japan would enable the Treasury to reduce naval expenditure. He could not resist adding, however, that such a pact would suit the Dominions.

Accordingly, the British ambassador had a long conversation with Hirota and asked him what he had in mind by the suggestion of a non-aggression pact. Hirota's reply showed that he viewed the pact as a means of keeping on friendly terms with Britain even though the naval conference failed. The British, on the other hand, regarded a non-aggression pact as part of a naval treaty, and an encouragement to Japan to sign one. The two governments therefore clearly had different aims in mind when discussing the idea.

In early October the Foreign Office produced a number of memoranda which revealed all too clearly the difficulties ahead, and finally listed a series of considerations to be kept in mind—that the proposed pact should not hamper a naval agreement or alter the naval ratios with Japan; that Britain, Japan and the United States should be involved, preferably with Australia and New Zealand being parties; that the Nine and Four power Treaties should be reaffirmed; and that confidential assurances should be obtained from Japan about her China policy. This list was meant to warn off the British politicians, and would have made the negotiations with the Japanese very tricky.[59]

Nevertheless, Simon saw the Japanese ambassador to London on 8 October and asked for further clarification of Hirota's ideas, and on 16 October he and Chamberlain produced a joint memorandum for the Cabinet. This again stressed the Empire as a reason for coming to terms with Japan.

> ... if we had to enter upon ... a struggle with a hostile, instead of a friendly Japan in the East; if we had to contemplate the division of our forces so as to protect our Far Eastern interests while prosecuting a war in Europe; then not only would India, Hong Kong and Australasia be in dire peril, but we ourselves would stand in far greater danger of destruction by a fully armed and organised Germany.[60]

The memorandum therefore assumed that India, Australia and New Zealand would 'warmly approve such a course' and remarked that Bennett while in London had expressed a wish 'to see Anglo–Japanese relations on the best footing'. There was clearly a mixture of motives here. Simon and Chamberlain's prime aim was the safety of Britain, or, as the memorandum put it, 'the safety, first, of this country, and then of the British Empire'. But the interests of the Empire and Britain coincided, as did that of economy in defence expenditure. As Chamberlain confided in his diary on 9 October, 'The result would be an instantaneous easing of the Australasian position, a new security in the East and possibly a better atmosphere in economic relations with the Japs'.[61] This was not to say, however, that either Simon or Chamberlain were willing to consult the Dominions beforehand or listen to their opinions. They had decided on their policy and found the interests of the Dominions a useful argument to support it. Canadian opinion, for example, tended to be suspicious of an alliance between Japan and Britain, similar to the Anglo–Japanese alliance of 1904, since that would offend the United States. Hints of this reached the Foreign Office from discussions in Chatham House.[62]

The Dominions Office seemed aware of possible trouble, for it reminded the Admiralty and the Foreign Office that the Dominions would be especially interested in any naval conversations with Japan. This resulted in a meeting of Dominion representatives, Thomas and the Chief of Naval Staff on 13 November. At this, however, Bruce and Smuts stressed the need for a strong navy, Bruce arguing that Britain had to build 'to keep her naval position within recognisable distance of the present position', and G. H. Ferguson of Canada thought that Japan intended to win dominance in the East. These were not the sort of arguments that Chamberlain wanted to hear. He intended to cut back on naval expenditure rather than increase it. The Cabinet was informed that 'at the end the Dominion representatives had expressed full agreement with British policy', but this is hardly the impression given by the minutes. As it was, those minutes were apparently not circulated to the Dominions. Canadian concern was revealed on 23 November, when the Canadian acting High Commissioner asked for more information, since Canada was particularly interested in naval conversations with Japan 'in view of their bearing on the Pacific problem and relations with the United States of America'. The Australian government too telegraphed for more information. As a result, on 8 December Dominion representatives attended a further meeting, at which Simon himself was present. He promised to provide them with full information and consult them before any agreement was signed. He then informed the Cabinet that 'no difficulties with the Dominions need be apprehended'.[63] It seems as if Simon and Chamberlain, by appealing to Dominion opinion, had roused debate and concern that they did not desire and had with difficulty dampened down.

This, indeed, was typical of their attitude. Their joint memorandum of 16 October had noted the difficulties raised by the Foreign Office, but discounted them and adopted an optimistic tone The memorandum, therefore, 'was by no means the thorough survey which Simon had suggested to Chamberlain would be necessary before a decision could be taken. The cabinet was presented with the best possible case for a pact, based on apologetics rather than well-grounded calculations'. It was not, therefore, the result of Dominion influence—a point that Ann Trotter makes at length[64]— that the proposed pact with Japan fell through. The British government was saved from a blunder—or worse—by the intransigence of the Japanese. For on 19 November the latter at last disclosed that the idea of a non-aggression pact was to be considered separately from the naval talks and dismissed the British suggestion of a 'gentleman's agreement'. Nevertheless, the British Cabinet agreed with Simon that it would be 'disastrous' if negotiations broke down. A further meeting with the Japanese ambassador on 21 November, however, produced no result. For the Japanese Cabinet had decided as early as 7 September to withdraw from the Washington Treaty and to reject the ratio system of naval agreements. They gave formal notice of this at the end of December. Accordingly after December 1936 no general naval agreements would be in existence, unless another could be negotiated in the meantime, and the need was more urgent, since Japan had more than doubled her naval expenditure between 1930 and 1935.[65]

The British, therefore, continued their search for an agreement. The Japanese hinted that they might be willing to negotiate in 1935, and the British government therefore made arrangements for naval conversations with France, Italy and Germany. The Cabinet discussed relations with Japan in January 1935 and set up a committee on them in February. By the time the naval conference opened in December 1935, however, they had few hopes that she would negotiate. In fact, Japan withdrew from the conference in January the following year, once again making suggestions for a non-aggression pact. The British, however, were by then more wary. Meanwhile, Chamberlain had sent to the Far East a mission headed by the government's chief economic advisor, Sir Frederick Leith Ross. He was supposed not only to advise the Chinese on currency reform, but also to reconcile China and Japan. This was clearly a diplomatic as well as an economic mission and the Treasury once again impinged on Foreign Office ground. The mission, needless to say, was a failure.[66]

The attempt to come to an understanding with Japan was a forerunner in many ways of the later efforts to appease Italy and Germany. Britain started from the same position of military weakness and tried to avoid its consequences by coming to agreements with possible aggressors. The strategic implications of the agreements were ignored every time. This is not surprising, since the person primarily responsible for all the attempts was the same man—Neville Chamberlain. With Japan, as with Germany, he allowed himself to be fooled by conciliatory talk and hints that certain people in the governing circles were moderate, while in fact aggressive policies were being pursued.

Chamberlain's motives in attempting to conciliate Japan were probably mixed, but prime among them was the desire to save money. Defence against Japan would need a strong navy and naval bases in the Far East, whereas at a time of government stringency the easiest way to save money and yet secure the defence of Britain was to stress air power and reduce naval expenditure. This may have been the best set of priorities from the British viewpoint, but it ignored the interests of the Dominions in the South Pacific—Australia and New Zealand. For Chamberlain was in effect reducing naval expenditure and strength in that region *before* any agreement with Japan had been made. If no agreement was forthcoming, those Dominions would be left undefended.

Moreover, the British Cabinet could hardly expect to gain a non-aggression treaty with the Japanese, while at the same time they were engaged in what was virtually a trade war with them. For in April 1934 at Simla a new commercial agreement between the Indian and Japanese governments had been signed, which gave British textiles a 30 per cent tariff margin over Japanese and linked Japanese textile exports to India to the amount of Indian raw cotton it purchased. Next month, restrictive quotas were placed on Japanese cotton and rayon textiles throughout the British Empire. This policy continued: in 1935 the Egyptian government terminated the Japan–Egypt commercial agreement and imposed a 40 per cent surtax on Japanese goods; and in 1936 the Australian government, following British requests, imposed its trade diversion policy. Nowhere in the discussions over a non-aggression treaty with Japan did Chamberlain or any other Cabinet minister suggest that trade concessions might be made to encourage the Japanese to come to an agreement, or apparently realise that British trade policy might be one reason for Japanese aggression. The British, instead, appeared totally self-righteous.

Finally, the decisions on defence made by the British Cabinet in 1934 were of immense significance for the security and future of the British Commonwealth. It seems little exaggeration to say that the course of events from 1935–1939 was largely determined by them. The question therefore arises how far the component parts of the Commonwealth—the Dominions—were informed of the decisions, let alone *consulted* during the debate. To this important matter, therefore, attention must now be turned.

6 The Collapse of consultation

> ... *at some future date it would be necessary to inform the Dominions as to the Naval proposals . . . in which they take a particular interest. The time was not yet ripe, however, for any information to be given.*
>
> MINISTERIAL COMMITTEE ON DEFENCE REQUIREMENTS,
> 24 JULY 1934 PRO CAB 16/110

Defence decisions hidden from the Dominions
As we have seen, the language of the Balfour Report in the matter of consultation had been idealistic and generous. The practice of the British government since then, however, had fallen short of its ideal, and was more deficient the more vital the decision that was being made.

Reducing expenditure on Far Eastern defences was a logical step for a British government to take, but the honourable course would have been to have informed Australia and New Zealand completely, so that they realised the situation and could then do whatever seemed best to them. Yet the British government was an imperial power and was reluctant either to admit to itself, or to tell the Dominions, that its imperial days were over. It therefore continued to use the rhetoric of imperialism to hide the fact of its weakness, so that Australia and New Zealand were left trusting in a non-existent security.

All this was revealed very clearly by the history of British consultation with the Dominions during the time of its great defence requirements debate. As we have seen, the Dominions were useful and were cited extensively in the arguments of all sides over foreign-policy postures in the Far East. Nevertheless, they did not really loom large in British thinking, certainly in defence matters. For example, the papers prepared for the Chiefs of Staff when they made their annual review for 1933 had very few references to the Dominions in them. This may have been the fault of the Dominions Office, but the fact remains. Sir Francis Lindley, home in England and discussing Japanese aspirations, said that the latter had no territorial ambitions outside Asia, 'and the fears of California and British Columbia are groundless'. It did not seem to occur to him that Australia and New Zealand were even more afraid of Japan. Finally, the part the Dominions played in Foreign Office thinking was also miniscule. In the 88 pages of memoranda on the situation in the Far East, prepared by the Foreign Office in March 1934, the Dominions were mentioned only once, and that in a minor way.[1]

As 1934 progressed and the arguments raged to and fro, the various committees were warned that sooner or later the Dominions would have to be informed of the decisions. The matter was first raised in Cabinet on 25 April and Thomas on 10 May brought it to the notice of the Ministerial Committee of the disarmament conference. These warnings were not heeded. In the early discussions the question was always deferred, and as Chamberlain's attitude became clearer there appeared a desire to hide from the Dominions the way the debate was going. For example, the interim report of the Ministerial Committee remarked on 16 May that, pending a final report and a Cabinet decision, 'it would be advisable to abstain from forwarding the Report . . . even through the most confidential channel, to the Dominions'.[2]

This did not stop MacDonald, as if being completely open, telling Dominion representatives at the CID meeting on 31 May that a comprehensive survey of defence was being made and that he thought it only right that the Dominions should be informed of this. It was not so much MacDonald's hypocrisy, when he implied that the British were willing to give the Dominions advance warning (whereas the Defence Requirements Committee had been set up six and a half months previously) as the blatant lie in the assurance he gave them that 'before any big decisions were made, they would be called into consultation'. For if anything was certain, it was that the British would make their own decisions on defence matters, and only inform the Dominions—if at all—afterwards. There would be no prior consultation.[3]

The British politicians' attitude to the Dominions, indeed, only hardened with the passage of time. Thus Hankey saw the Dominion High Commissioners on 16 July and informed them of the British air defence proposals. He assured them that 'if the announcement which was shortly to be made concerned the danger from Europe, that did not mean in any way that the situation in the Far East had been neglected'. Even on the figures he gave them, this seemed untrue. Over the next five years three squadrons were to go to Singapore and one to the Far East generally, whereas the British Home Defence squadrons were to be raised, not to 56, but to seventy-five. The Dominion representatives asked what was being done apart from Britain, as well they might. According to Roskill, Hankey had considered sending the defence requirements papers to the Dominions, except Canada, where a vague set of phrases would do, but MacDonald endorsed his memorandum 'Cabinet papers, but not for circulation'. And on 24 July the Ministerial Committee on Defence Requirements agreed that although it would be necessary to tell the Dominions of the naval proposals at some future date, 'the time was not yet ripe'. Significantly, this was despite MacDonald's promise to

Dominion representatives in the CID on 31 May and also a correspondence between the British government and Lyons in Australia, in which the British promised full communication with him and the other Dominion Prime Ministers before decisions were taken.[4]

The decision not to inform the Dominions of the lack of any naval rearmament caused Hankey some embarrassment. He pointed out in a letter to Baldwin that he had been invited to visit Australia and New Zealand to advise them on naval defence and he felt he could hardly go if there was a doubt whether the British would send a fleet to Singapore in an emergency. On the other hand, it would be difficult at that late hour to find a convincing excuse for cancelling his visit. He therefore requested from the Cabinet a definite decision that he could proceed on the assumption that in a major emergency the British fleet would be sent to the Far East. At Baldwin's suggestion Hankey had a long conversation with Chamberlain. He presented him with an *aide-memoire* that, with the object of enabling a fleet to proceed to Singapore, the British would complete the first stage of the port's defences by 1938, set up fuelling stations, and make good the deficiencies of the navy 'as financial conditions permit'. Chamberlain declined to authorise even this ambiguous and misleading wording and referred Hankey back to Baldwin, simply saying that if Baldwin agreed to it, he would not oppose it.[5]

When the Cabinet discussed the Ministerial Committee's report on 31 July, the president of the Board of Trade remarked that 'it would be inadvisable to communicate the Report to the Prime Ministers of the Dominions, who were especially interested in the Navy, and who might form the impression that Naval requirements were being overlooked'. Hankey argued that the Dominions should be told what was happening, and probably also be provided with the DRC report and the report of the Ministerial Committee on it. However the Cabinet 'felt that it would be liable to cause misunderstanding to send the Report now about to be approved, for the reason that it did not deal with the Navy, in which the Dominions were principally interested'. The Cabinet therefore, although it accepted Hankey's suggestion that he should take the report with him, added a proviso about the need for secrecy of Cabinet discussions, and concluded that 'the communication of the Report to the Prime Ministers of the Dominions should be postponed until decisions have been taken as to the Naval Deficiency Programme'. As it was likely to be a long time before those decisions were made, that meant that the Dominions would remain uninformed for a long time—and British expenditure on the Far East would likewise be postponed indefinitely. The Cabinet meeting ended, perhaps most suitably, with Baldwin appealing to his colleagues that 'it was vitally important that no leakage should occur in this very secret matter'. Accordingly, Hankey gave way and suggested that the report be circulated to the members of the CID, but not the Dominion representatives, and later discussed at a meeting of the CID at which those members were absent.[6]

Hankey's Commonwealth Tour
For the time being the Cabinet could postpone officially informing the Dominions of the DRC report, despite references to it in other papers that the Dominions saw, because of Hankey's forthcoming visit to Dominion capitals.[7]

The idea of this tour had come from an Australian initiative in December 1933. The centennial celebrations of the State of Victoria were to be held in 1934 and the federal government, plagued with the dispute in Australia between the army and the navy which involved criticism of defence policy, saw the occasion as an opportunity to invite, not only the Duke of Gloucester as the figurehead of the celebrations, but also the senior officers of each of the defence services. Having failed to get much help in the CID paper 'The Defence of Australia', the government was, in effect, considering bringing out the British Chiefs of Staff to discuss matters with them on the spot. The British government did not like the idea: too many cats could have been let out of the bag. It therefore refused to allow the Chiefs of Staff to visit Australia, and added that any other officers could attend in a private capacity only.

After this rebuff, Casey, who since his stay in London had been in correspondence with Hankey and who was then Commonwealth Treasurer, suggested in Cabinet that Hankey should be invited. The latter was equally well known to Latham and Pearce, so there would be support for Casey's suggestion. In the end, the government invited both Hankey and Thomas. The latter declined to go, another indication, perhaps, of his unsuitability as Dominions secretary. Hankey, however, was delighted. He said he had been working for the Empire for years, and now he could go and 'see the lands of which I had thought so much'. He added in a letter to Buckingham Palace that 'I feel it would open my horizon to get away from the Office for once and see something of the Empire'. He began to read books on the subject supplied by the Dominions Office library.[8]

Once suggested, the concept of the tour grew. To start with, his wife still had relatives in South Africa, and Hankey suggested that he call there on the way to Australia to enable her to see them. They then intended to return by way of Ceylon. In July, however, the New Zealand government invited Hankey to call there, after seeing Australia. It seems possible that Hankey himself had provoked this invitation, in reaction to a correspondent's account of lack of coordination in New Zealand defence. Finally, the decision to make it a round-world cruise and call on Canada was a last-minute one. The Dominions Office organised it after Hankey had left for South Africa.[9]

For, once his tour had been approved, what had originally been a private visit to South Africa and a more politically oriented one to Australia came to be used by all parties for their own ends. The Cabinet used it to solve the problem of how to inform the Dominions that it had postponed any decision on naval rearmament without letting them suspect that expenditure on the navy and support for Singapore were both unlikely. This was a tricky thing to put in a letter, but Hankey could be trusted, in informal conversations, to gloss over dangerous points. Accordingly, the Cabinet decided that Hankey should take copies of the report with him on his trip to the Dominions and should make a statement to the Prime Ministers about the general results of the inquiry, 'bearing in mind the discussion at the Cabinet and more especially the extreme importance of secrecy'.[10] How clear an indication of British policy the Dominions would receive can be gauged from that wording. At the same time, Hankey had to sidestep a suggestion by Pirow in South Africa that Britain should cooperate in 'defence and police' activities in Southern Africa. The British were worried lest they be drawn into South Africa's racial repression and allow South Africa to extend her rule over the three protectorates of Bechuanaland, Basutoland and Swaziland. This was a ticklish issue, and questions had been asked in the British House of Commons on the subject. Thomas had repeated promises that the British government would respect the wishes of the natives.[11] Once again, therefore, personal conversations between the South Africans and Hankey, who knew the British view, were less dangerous than written correspondence.

On the other hand, Hankey himself was willing to use Commonwealth opinion to support his stand in the British Cabinet for a strong navy. Before he left for the Dominions he got Baldwin to initial his *aide-memoire*, and while on the trip he reported to him the argument in Australia between the army and the naval authorities, adding—in case Baldwin failed to draw the moral—that any British admission that they could not 'assert . . . sea power in the Pacific in a war emergency . . . would be absolutely shattering. No greater blow could be dealt to the unity of the Empire'. The need for a common policy of imperial defence based on an adequate navy had been put, according to Hankey, 'with extraordinary brilliance' by a young Australian civil servant [Casey?] and he trusted Baldwin would not allow the Cabinet to overlook the 'Empire aspects of naval defence'.[12] Hankey then reported to MacDonald that Smuts of South Africa had declared that if Singapore fell, South Africa would be in the front line and he hoped that 'the strength of the navy would be maintained as the shield of the whole Empire'. In a letter to the First Sea Lord, however, Hankey admitted that he, not Smuts, had made the statement about the fall of Singapore. Moreover, Hankey apparently went further, suggesting to Smuts that he speak publicly about the importance of the navy when he visited England, and also writing to the First Sea Lord to suggest that he should see Smuts when he arrived. Hankey seems to have been orchestrating the whole affair! Smuts was in fact active during his stay in England and made an important speech at a dinner arranged by the Royal Institute of International Affairs. One historian comments:

> If General Smuts was a participant in what has been described as 'the back stage battle' against any move towards an Anglo-Japanese rapprochement, it seems most likely that his initiative in November was inspired by Hankey and had as an important dimension the aim of resisting cuts in naval expenditure or any change in imperial naval policy.[13]

Many motives, therefore, were involved in Hankey's tour. They did not, however, stop Hankey and the government protesting mightily, when the newspapers broke the story, that it was purely a private holiday, in no way connected with politics or imperial defence. A rather coy public statement was concocted: 'As Sir Maurice Hankey laughingly remarked to an enquiring friend. "I am going to Australia as a guest of the Commonwealth Government. Naturally I shall meet members of the Government and all sorts of people. I shall talk to them on anything they like to talk about."' A statement to that effect was given to the House of Commons on 13 November and Hankey himself assured Hertzog that his visit was not a 'mission' but a purely private visit.[14] Rumours of course were to be expected, seeing that Hankey, the secretary of the CID and Cabinet, was visiting so many Dominions. The British government was probably not so much worried about British public opinion as that of South Africa and Canada, where suspicions were held that the British were about to drag them into imperialist wars again. The Australian government, seeing the state of opinion in the country and its strategic situation, could afford to be, and was, much more open.[15] The stream of British excuses and half-truths was undignified, however, and said much for the disunity of sentiment and interests of the various Dominions.

In South Africa, therefore, Hankey was careful to counter the impression of General Hertzog that Britain was embarking on an armaments race or becoming committed once again to the continent of Europe. Hertzog indeed, while accepting Hankey's assurances, stressed the need for Britain to avoid commitments unless they were absolutely essential to her security. It was hardly the atmosphere or level of discussion that Hankey would enjoy. He was on more happy ground with Smuts, but had to tread warily with Pirow, especially when the subject of cooperation in defence was raised. He suggested that air cooperation was probably the safest. Hankey spent some time visiting his wife's relations and much looking at the various defence installations, on which he sent a fifteen-page report back to his government. He seems to have managed nicely to talk himself out of dangerous situations when the protectorates and British naval policy were mentioned.[16]

In Australia, Hankey was treading on a different sort of thin ice. There, the problem was not fear of British involvement in Europe as fear of British non-involvement in the Pacific. The argument between the army and navy was still raging, and the government had not won over its critics in the army. The situation, therefore, required all Hankey's diplomacy. He had been warned of this as early as April, when Air Commodore Williams presented him with a memorandum on the need to reorganise Australian defence. The bombardment of memoranda continued throughout the rest of the year before Hankey left England. He was warned of the language he should use in Australia, and by the Admiralty of plans to upgrade the Australian army. The Naval Board in Melbourne had taken a leaf from the Air Staff's book and got in touch with their British counterparts, using them to support their arguments. The Admiralty pointed out that there were limited funds available and argued that they should be spent on warships. In the midst of these notes, Hankey received a long letter from Senator Pearce, then Minister for Defence, with a mass of papers on the interservice rivalry attached. It was hardly surprising, therefore, that Hankey came to the conclusion that this was by 'far the most difficult matter on which my opinion was asked' and that 'I . . . began to think that I had stuck my nose into a wasp's nest'.[17]

On arrival in Perth, in early October, Hankey had three long conversations with Pearce, who seems to have somewhat 'jumped the gun' on his colleagues. Pearce hoped that Hankey would settle the interservice dispute; he also suggested that a permanent military force, or, as he called it, a 'Brigade of Guards', be established. In doing so, he revealed the anti-communist phobia of the Lyons government, citing riots in Kalgoorlie and 'the Lang episode in New South Wales'. He thought of using the 'guards' to put down civil disturbances, though he also suggested that they could be used as a garrison for Singapore. Hankey however saw through that argument and suggested that the use of the 'guards' for internal security was what appealed 'to Ministers, who declare that there was a communist plot to get power by force during the Lang troubles'.[18] Their anti-communist neurosis is not very impressive.

Hankey arrived in Melbourne to find, to his chagrin, that there had been a change in Cabinet membership. Pearce had become the Minister for External Affairs and the new Minister for Defence was R. A. Parkhill. Hankey was not very happy, either with the need to begin discussions all over again or with the new man. He suspected that Parkhill might try to run Defence, as he had the Post Office, by long-distance telephone. Nor did he think very highly of Shepherd, the secretary of the Defence Department. He was also bothered by the long and numerous ceremonies he had to attend in conjunction with the Melbourne centennial celebrations, and complained that it was difficult to get work done without spending long hours into the night.[19]

Hankey toured the defences of Fremantle, Adelaide, Sydney, Brisbane and Newcastle and the government munitions factories, made a statement on British Cabinet defence policy to Lyons, Pearce and Parkhill (and a 'much diluted' one to the Labor and Country Party leaders, Scullin and Earle Page), and saw the Defence Committee. By that time, however, that body had itself decided to support the navy and reduce the size of the Australian army. On 9 October it had stated:

> If the ability of the Main British Fleet to move East of Suez in any circumstances and the availability of the Naval Base at Singapore are accepted, then there can be no criticism of the estimates of the scale of attack given by the Chief of Naval Staff . . . In these circumstances the Committee consider the correct policy is to reduce the organisation of the Army to the scale recommended in 1932 . . .

Hankey himself suspected that some of the younger staff officers with War Office training were responsible, though he admitted that he was never told the details. At any rate, it made Hankey's job easier, for he then simply supported the Defence Committee and was saved the necessity of arguing its case closely. Hankey's statement to it was simply incorporated into a revised and lengthened recommendation to the Minister for Defence.[20]

Hankey, however, was very worried by the state of Australian defence forces. He produced a typically long report on 'Higher Organisation for Defence in Australia' and another 'On Certain Aspects of Australian Defence'. In the first he suggested that the Council of Defence, which had not met since 1929, be revived, along the lines of the CID in Britain. It should therefore include the Prime Minister, the Treasurer (if that office was not held by the Prime Minister too), the Minister for Defence, the Minister for External Affairs, and the three service chiefs. He saw the Defence Committee as similar to the Chiefs of Staff in Britain. In the second report, Hankey went into great detail—even to the way CID documents should be kept safe. He was, however, less than completely frank with the Australians. He gave an account of the discussion on defence in the British government, but used the Defence Requirements Committee report and the CID paper 372-C, 'The Defence of Australia', without indicating that the naval program of the DRC report had come under serious attack in England. Moreover he carefully used ambiguous wording, for example remarking that the decision of the British government to continue the naval base at Singapore, improve other bases and build up British forces, 'go a long way to provide the condition of a base at Singapore which was insisted on so strongly' in CID 372-C. We have seen, however, how much the British government had decided to 'build up' its forces in the Far East. Hankey wanted the Australian expenditure on the navy maintained and argued that since only sporadic raids were to be feared the militia could be reduced in size to seven brigades and two divisions, a total peace establishment of 35 000 men. He wanted it, and the air force, to be so organised that they could provide garrisons at bases throughout the Middle and Far East.[21]

In his report Hankey admitted the arguments against reducing the Australian army, especially those which stressed the delays in building Singapore and the doubt whether a British fleet would come to it in an emergency, especially if there were trouble in Europe. He had the nerve, however, to assert that these doubts had been removed by the recent British decision to fortify Singapore. Britain had a great stake in the Far East, as well as an attachment to Australia and New Zealand.

The impression given by these half-truths was strengthened by what was very nearly a direct lie. He went so far as to say:

> Even in the very extreme case of simultaneous trouble in Europe and the Far East without our having allies . . . the ratio of naval strength in capital ships . . . is sufficient to enable a numerically superior battle fleet to be sent to the Far East and yet leave a small margin of strength in both theatres, though, admittedly, such a situation would strain the Empire's resources as severely as did the events of the Great War, and must be avoided by all possible means, diplomatic and otherwise.

Hankey must have known from his conversations with the British Admiralty that such naval strength barely existed, even on paper; his attendance at the Ministerial Committee on the defence requirements report must have convinced him that the British government was exceedingly unlikely to send a fleet to the Far East in any such emergency. That was exactly the gist of Chamberlain's argument. Hankey, of course, could salve his conscience with his *aide-memoire* and the thought that the naval program had not definitely been settled yet, merely postponed till the naval conference. On the other hand, he knew the way the debate was going in British government circles but hid it from the Australians.

Some of Hankey's suggestions, such as a secretariat for the Council of Defence, had merit; others, such as the idea that the Labor Party should be included in it to gain continuity of policy, were idealistic.[22] If Hankey thought that the Labor Party would join the Lyons government in discussing defence in 1934 he was totally out of touch with Australian politics. But a much more basic weakness was his failure to face the implications of British defence decisions. He reported that he had been careful to avoid a commitment to send the fleet to Singapore in an emergency, but that he had pointed out 'as an earnest of intention' that the British had spent lots of money on Singapore and had tremendous interests in the East.[23] The notes of meetings Hankey had with the Defence Committee make it clear that he glossed over the division of opinion within the British government and among the service chiefs and played down British deficiencies in the Far East. He implied that the defences of Singapore would be completed and that Britain would maintain her naval ratio with Japan. He even went so far as to say 'all details . . . for an eventual programme [of naval building] have been worked out, pending the Naval Conference'. When the Australian CGS asked him bluntly if the British would send a fleet out to Singapore, he talked of the completion of the base and added that 'it was not likely that Britain was going to let her vast interests in the Far East go by default' and other nonsequiturs. His long speech in reply gives the strong impression that he was talking his way out of a difficult spot. At the very least he presented a grossly optimistic impression of Britain's ability and intentions.[24]

Hankey spent a week in New Zealand and thoroughly enjoyed himself. 'New Zealand really is the land of my dreams. Everything was perfect for us—the scenery, the people, the accommodation, the weather.'[25] He also enjoyed not having the pressure of business and socialising that had been put on him in Australia. He did not see as much of the New Zealand Cabinet as he had of the Australian, but thought, correctly, that Forbes was not in a good position. Coates, the Treasurer, was the strong man, but in any case an election was imminent. Indeed, the effect of Hankey's visit was lessened because he allowed Forbes to persuade him that it was pointless to see the leader of the Labour opposition, since the party was so uneducated in defence matters.[26] It was a mistake to allow Forbes' prejudices to prevent him from seeing the leader with whom Britain was soon to be dealing in the international scene—and a leader moreover who was capable of holding his own as well as Forbes had done, to say the least.

Hankey's arrival in New Zealand was opportune, in that he could attend a meeting of the new New Zealand section of the CID, formed under his guidance the preceding year. Hankey, however, had been accompanied to New Zealand by three Australians, Senator Pearce, together with the secretary of the Defence Department and the Controller-General of the Munitions Supply Branch. The New Zealand government had invited the Australian Minister for Defence, who was then Pearce, at the same time that they had invited Hankey, presumably as a result of Lyons' letter to them suggesting cooperation between the two countries. As has been seen, although this letter made much of training facilities in Australia and joint exercises, its main motive appears from Australian documents to have been a desire to sell Australian munitions and equipment to New Zealand. The comments of the Australian air, naval and military boards suggest that they did not think they had much to learn from the New Zealanders.[27]

A 'conference' was held in Wellington between 21 and 23 November 1934. On the first day Hankey made a statement on the British defence policy, identical to those he had made to South Africa and Australia, except that this one began with Forbes' statement to the 1930 imperial conference, at which he—primed by Hankey—had urged the importance of Singapore. After that, Pearce made a strong plea for cooperation in defence matters between Australia and New Zealand, especially military or air expeditionary forces, which might go to Egypt or Singapore. The second day began with a formal meeting between Hankey and the New Zealand Cabinet, at which Hankey repeated his theme that the defence of Australia and New Zealand depended on the maintenance of the naval base at Singapore, to which the British could send a fleet in an emergency. Hankey added, in a draft letter to MacDonald, 'My report to Mr. Forbes of what was to be done at Singapore and other ports east of Suez as a result of the Defence Requirements inquiries was, of course, of a reassuring character . . .'.[28] In the afternoon the meeting discussed New Zealand coastal defences and the possibility of sending a garrison to Singapore. Hankey had already been briefed on this ticklish point. The British CIGS had gently rebuffed Sinclair Burgess when he had first made the suggestion. It was admitted to Hankey, however, that the real reason was that the CIGS thought the New Zealand contribution would be small and of doubtful value, but would almost certainly create difficult problems of command, discipline and finance, and even lead to suggestions from South Africa that it could garrison East Africa. When Cobbe, the New Zealand Minister of Defence, 'blurted out something about this' at the Wellington conference, it took all of Hankey's tact to avoid the issue. He got Sinclair Burgess' support by privately informing him of the South

African implications, although Burgess still wished to have New Zealanders trained with British troops to provide a nucleus of instructors for the militia. Pearce then elaborated on possible cooperation between Australia and New Zealand. He had in his conversation with Forbes and Hankey raised the issue of a gift of a warship to Britain, for use in the Pacific, but Forbes had avoided any decision in the absence of Coates. This seems to have been Pearce's pet idea. There had been some opposition to it in Australia; and in New Zealand the naval staff argued against it.[29]

At the final meeting, Hankey asked them how they felt about British defence policy and elicited the obvious response: 'They all expressed great satisfaction and there was not a word of criticism.'[30] This was hardly surprising, since he had hidden the truth so effectively. The conference ended by discussing Australian and New Zealand cooperation once again, and Pearce talked grandly of an Australian expeditionary force of one division, that could sail within three months of an emergency.

Hankey himself thought that though he had not had much time in New Zealand he had 'bucked them all up about their defence a bit'. Once again he tried to use Dominion opinion to bolster his case for a strong British navy. He reported that both Australia and New Zealand were basing their defence expenditure on the assumption that a base would be maintained at Singapore and a British fleet sent to it in an emergency. 'The implication was that the machinations of the Treasury should not be allowed to let these "incredibly patriotic" people down.'[31]

Hankey found the atmosphere in Canada very different. 'After the fervid imperialism of Australia and New Zealand the calculating aloofness of Ottawa strikes a chilly note in more senses than one.' The reasons were straightforward. The political scene was dominated by the fact that an election had to be held in Canada between March and October the following year. There were great problems: the depression; the insolvency of the railways and some of the States; the confusion of parties; the French Canadians—according to Hankey 'one of the most conservative peoples in the world'—and their support for the Liberals. It was generally assumed that Bennett would lose power and be replaced by Mackenzie King. He was therefore fighting for his political life and nervous about the reactions to Hankey's visit. Hankey indeed could hardly have come at a worse time. The Dominions Office had been warned that many Canadians were suspicious that Bennett's government was about to entangle them in another imperialist war.[32]

This suspicion had been increased by Admiral Keyes and Lord Lothian just before Hankey arrived. Lothian had made a speech on 17 October to the Canadian Institute of International Affairs, in which he had raised the possibilities of either creating a Pacific fleet, reaching an understanding with the United States or forming an alliance with Japan. He may have been musing from the Olympian vantage point of London, the centre of the Empire, but as the British High Commission representative reported, 'from the local point of view, the reference to the incidence of the cost of a British Pacific fleet, and to an Imperial Defence Conference next year constituted something of a bombshell in view of the approach of the general election'. The common opinion was that Lothian had been sent to express the official views of the British government, and a special meeting of the Canadian Institute of International Affairs was held to discuss the talk. The meeting, at which Skelton, McNaughton and other members of the Department of External Affairs were present, agreed that Canada was not concerned whether Japan dominated China or not and flatly refused to consider the idea of a Pacific fleet capable of coping with her. Speakers looked to the United States to protect Canada and almost totally ignored Australia and New Zealand. Lothian seems to have merely added to the suspicions of a United Kingdom 'defence plot', without convincing influential Canadians that their country needed to pursue a more active defence policy. The members of the CIIA, of course, were not necessarily typical of Canadian public opinion in general. They tended, according to Hankey, to be intensely isolationist and to place their reliance on the American Monroe Doctrine. Hankey also thought, however, that pacifism was widespread and that talks such as that given by Lothian did more harm than good. He added, 'The mass of Canadians . . . I suspect, do not think very much of these matters. It is probably undesirable that they should'.[33]

This being the situation, it was understandable that Bennett was anxious to avoid any impression of engaging in 'imperial' commitments. The newspapers occasionally tried to stir up defence—or at least imperial—entanglements as an election issue. Accordingly, whereas in Australia and New Zealand Hankey had been shown the defence establishments, invited to their discussions and asked to advise, in Canada he was very definitely not. His visit was confined to Ottawa, instead of ranging all over the country, and he stayed in Government House, in a 'British atmosphere'. Bennett saw the text of the speech he was to make to the Canadian Club of Ottawa and asked him to delete a reference to naval cooperation. Hankey briefly ran over the defence requirements report with him, but since Bennett had been in London recently there was no need to go to great lengths. Bennett agreed with the policy of seeking Japanese friendship to insure against possible trouble in both Europe and Asia. He had accordingly honoured the new British ambassador to Japan on his way through Canada and had given a special luncheon to the Japanese minister.

Bennett supported the British firmly, but other Canadians were clearly anxious that the move towards Japan did not presage hostility to the United States. McNaughton was alarmed by the bad tone of Anglo–American relations and urged that they should be improved. Skelton thought that Britain had not responded to American advances during the Manchurian affair, wanted to know what Hankey meant by 'good relations with Japan' and remarked that 'if Canada had a foreign policy, it was to promote good relations between the United Kingdom and the United States'. Herridge and Arthur Meighen sang the same song. Indeed, Hankey concluded that the visit to Canada had 'brought home to me rather strongly . . . that in cultivating good relations with Japan we must not alienate the United States'. He had not raised the issue specifically in the other Dominions, 'but from incidental remarks made to me I have a strong impression that all the Dominions I visited would attach great importance to the closest possible relations that the peculiar constitution of the United States permits'. This provoked a bitter comment by Vansittart that there was not much prospect of good relations with either Japan or the United States, but that they could not afford to be *un*friendly to Japan just because the Americans insisted on it. 'There is a limit to the length to which we can be blackmailed by the U.S.A. through the less loyal or intelligent elements in Canada.'[34]

Hankey, however, learnt much while in Canada, even for so short a time. Not only did he come to realise the importance of the United States to the Canadians, he also came to see their isolationism and dependence on the Monroe doctrine. After reporting gloomily on the parlous state of Canadian defences, especially the navy ('an almost negligible quantity, in which I could not discover any trace of public interest') and the dominance of McNaughton, he advised that 'it would be wiser not to mention the question of Canadian representation on the Committee of Imperial Defence'. He wrote to Pearce a long letter explaining the Canadian situation and warning him that the idea of joint Dominion battleships in the Pacific was not likely to be taken kindly in Canada. Since South Africa also opposed the idea, it fell through. After Hankey's return to England, the Joint Oversea and Home Defence Committee of the CID, which had been systematically reviewing the defences at various ports, dropped its suggestion to review Canadian ports. Hankey felt that there would need to be an overwhelming case for British entry into a war before Canadians would join her again. Only if the cause were just, if every effort to maintain peace had been exhausted and it was clear that war had been forced on Britain, preferably by aggression, would Canada come in as she had in 1914.[35] This may well have been one slight factor in the later British appeasement of Hitler, though doubtless more immediate British political interests were involved.

Hankey had indeed found a hornets' nest in Canada and, as in South Africa, had to be careful. For example, there was the question which had Bennett 'bothered a lot'—whether Hankey should give any details of the British defence decisions to Mackenzie King. Bennett thought that 'in principle' he should do so, but feared King's use of the information. McNaughton agreed. As it happened, Hankey saw King only briefly, during a crowded luncheon and took King's manner to mean that he desired no confidences.

That Bennett's fears were justified was revealed in January 1935, when King, in the Canadian House of Commons, quoted a London newspaper report that an elaborate scheme of empire defence was being put to the Dominion Prime Ministers by Hankey, and asked Bennett to comment. When Bennett denied this, King returned to the attack three days later. He could not resist the temptation to make political capital out of the visit, even though he must have known that there was little truth behind the report.[36]

Equally tricky was the question to whom and how Hankey should publicly speak. Hankey was reluctant, but some public speech had to be made, to take away the aura of mystery that surrounded his visit. Bennett considered the Canadian Club of Ottawa was the best place, and excuses were made to the others, such as the Empire Club at Toronto and the Canadian Institute of International Affairs. Hankey's speech to the Canadian Club was a *tour de force*. In the typescript, sixteen pages describing his tour and the warmth of his greetings in South Africa, Australia, New Zealand and Canada were followed by a peroration on the intangible ties that knit the Empire together—'the indivisible bonds of Empire'. As he admitted to Harding, 'It is an example of how to talk in public and on the broadcast for half an hour and say nothing at all'. He added that he was 'rather ashamed at talking such stuff' to distinguished Canadians, but was surprised at the warm reception he got. 'So, in the end, the episode I had dreaded most in my trip passed off quite successfully.'[37]

It was a fitting note on which to end the tour. For Hankey had really hidden the truth from those Dominions who were interested in hearing it. He did this not by lies but by half-truths and vagueness. For example, in his introduction to the notes for his talks to the Dominion Prime Ministers, Hankey remarked that since the final decisions concerning the navy had not been taken, the British Cabinet were reluctant to forward an incomplete report. He went on to remark that there had been no alteration in the British policy of peace and disarmament.[38] Such vagueness hid a serious fact—that there had been such disagreement within the ranks of the British

Cabinet that no naval proposals could be agreed upon and instead they had been postponed. Hankey's ambiguities in his talks in Australia have already been noted. His speech to the Canada Club was therefore simply an extreme example of this approach. Hankey also, however, in tight spots sometimes came very near to resorting to such exaggeration as to equal untruth.

There is no doubt that in doing this he was fulfilling exactly the role the politicians in the British Cabinet had desired of him. On other occasions too they had resorted to ambiguities and lies to prevent subordinates or outsiders from challenging basic British thinking and policy. Simon had hedged evasively in telephone conversation with Stimson, and Vansittart had lied outright to the British minister to China, telling him that the United States had not suggested a declaration based on the Nine Power Treaty when the British government had been considering it for the previous thirteen days.[39]

The whole intention of the Cabinet, moreover, had been to use Hankey to save themselves from the necessity of either telling the truth or being forced to commit themselves in writing. They wished to keep the discussion—and certainly the decision—on naval defence expenditure secret from the Dominions. This was revealed on 22 November 1934 while Hankey was actually in the Wellington conference with New Zealand and Australian leaders. For on that date the CID met in London *without* the attendance of Dominion representatives—as Hankey had suggested. In the discussion that ensued, Thomas remarked that the Dominions 'might conclude that our defensive arrangements in the Far East were being neglected' and even consider that the allocation of one squadron of planes to Hong Kong was 'inadequate'. The First Lord of the Admiralty commented that 'the difficulty with the Dominions lay in the fact that they considered Japan to be the primary menace . . .', and added that 'it might be necessary, at some point, to give them the papers, but that it was very undesirable to do so at present'.[40]

In this instance the British hid the truth from Dominion eyes with promises of consultation, which they never fulfilled, and vague generalisations about naval power, when they had little in the Pacific and did not intend to create any more. They also destroyed the usefulness of the CID for the Dominions. If the latter's representatives could be excluded from certain discussions, simply because unpalatable truths might emerge, then they gained nothing from their membership. Canada, who was not a member, was at least not lulled by being in the organisation, as Australia and New Zealand were. It need only be added that the British government hid the truth not only from the Dominions but also from its own parliament. The 'Statement Relating to Defence' issued in March 1935 was completely vague on naval matters. A long rambling dissertation on the role of the fleet successfully hid the fact that the fleet Britain then possessed was too weak to carry out that role, although Baldwin in the Commons debate on 11 March did warn parliament that other powers were building up their naval forces.[41]

Hankey himself in planning the tour seems to have thought of using Dominion opinion as a double-edged sword—against his opponents in the Cabinet. However, when the tour began he found himself the apologist of the British government and committed to placating Dominion fears. Not all of Hankey's listeners, however, were taken in either by his flow of words, or by the formal messages coming from the British government. In Australia Latham, no longer a member of the Cabinet but still in touch with his old colleagues, wrote to Pearce:

> It would be a good thing if Great Britain had a more definite policy about Oriental affairs and if the Dominions actually knew what that policy was . . . Great Britain is quite prepared to say in flowing language what the *objectives* of her policy are—such as co-operation, co-ordination and friendship etc etc with the great nations of the East. Such statements remind me of the noble candidate who states that he will not be deterred from pursuing at all costs the welfare of the people.

Pearce completely agreed with those remarks.[42] As one historian has commented, therefore,

> In retrospect the interest of Hankey's tour lies in its quality as an exercise in public relations. Like many such exercises it was perhaps more reassuring to the salesman than to the clients. While Hankey was warmed by his contact with so many loyal citizens, it is evident that these citizens were not as impressed by the imperial policy he expounded as he supposed.[43]

Nevertheless Hankey could and did try to use 'Dominion opinion' as a buttress for his arguments in the Cabinet, but without any noticeable success. When he reported to the Cabinet on 16 January 1935 it decided to postpone informing the Dominions of the DRC report until the arrival of the Dominion Prime Ministers in London for the Silver Jubilee of King George V that May. Events would show whether the British would be forthright even then.

Aftermath of Hankey: divided policies and weak defence

Hankey's visit had revealed that Dominion interests and attitudes varied widely in 1934. They continued to do so in the first part of 1935, the main difference being between Australia and New Zealand on the one hand, and South Africa and Canada on the other.

In Australia, the argument over defence continued, for it was not to be expected that the army authorities would meekly accept Hankey's verdict. On 5 March 1935 Major General J. B. Bruche criticised

Hankey's report on Australian defence. He argued that though Hankey's opinion should be viewed with respect, because of his experience, the responsibility for defence rested with the military advisors of the Australian government, not the British, who regarded the defence of Australia as merely a minor part of a worldwide problem. Bruche and the Chief of Staff designate, Colonel J. D. Lavarack, 'utterly rejected' Hankey's views. They argued that it was impossible for Australia to be defended adequately from Singapore, apart from the fact that there was no guarantee that a British fleet would be stationed there. Only an 'absolute guarantee' that a British fleet would be sent out in an emergency would justify the Australian government continuing with its naval policy. Another member of the Australian Staff Corps, Major H. C. H. Robertson, in the British *Army Quarterly*, quoted the words of Admiral Sir Richard Webb in November 1930: 'to imagine that we are going to uncover the heart of Empire and send our fleet thousands of miles into the Pacific with only one base, Singapore, . . . is to write us down as something more than fools. Anyway, the British public would never tolerate it.'[44]

The result was stalemate. The Lyons government could never bring itself totally to accept or reject the Singapore strategy. Instead it opted for both policies, and made the army responsible for defence against both raids and full-scale invasion, even though the Singapore naval base was supposed to make such an invasion impossible. Accordingly, the government did not reduce its army organisation, but retained the seven divisions it had before Hankey's arrival. Even more important, the army itself clearly preferred the secondary role the government had assigned to it, and did not send any units to Singapore till February 1941. As one commentator remarks, 'It is difficult to escape the conclusion therefore that the Army was developed between the wars quite independently of the Singapore strategy'. It is also difficult to escape the conclusion that the army in Australia was acting independently of the government, and—as in the matter of the sale of arms to the Far East—was not sufficiently under the control of its political 'masters'. When Admiral Hyde wrote to Hankey, however, informing him of the arguments of the Australian army, Hankey very wisely declined to be drawn back into the debate.[45]

There were some results from Hankey's visit, however. On 9 April the Council of Defence was reestablished. Interestingly enough, the personnel who were to sit on the council were prescribed in the regulations—the Prime Minister, the Minister for External Affairs, the Minister for Defence and the heads of the services, together with other ministers if the Prime Minister coopted them. Sheddon wrote to Hankey: 'It was thought wise to prescribe the regular panel in the regulations rather than leave the constitution entirely at the Prime Minister's discretion for cooption.' The clash between the military and the politicians in Australia continued. Nevertheless, the prerogative of referring matters to the council was retained by the Prime Minister and Minister for Defence. Moreover, rearmament was still slow; by the end of 1935 defence expenditure had still not quite reached the figure for 1928.[46]

In New Zealand, too, slow rearmament was the order of the day. The first review of the New Zealand Sub-Committee of the Chiefs of Staff was produced in March 1935. It urged as large a cruiser squadron and military and air expenditure 'as possible', but given the economic situation this was not specific enough to provoke the government into great activity. The committee's basic premise was that New Zealand was too small to stand on her own and was dependent on British imperial defence, especially the base at Singapore. The Chiefs of Staff therefore warned that if Singapore fell, New Zealand's trade and communications would be cut 'as never before', and at the CID in London the following July the New Zealand High Commissioner urged the start of the second stage of the Singapore defences.[47]

Meanwhile, at long last Forbes rose in the House and made a statement on international affairs. He even had the temerity to remark that it was highly desirable that the parliament and people of New Zealand should be well informed on international movements, as if he had encouraged this during the preceding years. He then made a rambling dissertation on international affairs and one or two quite striking remarks, such as the suggestion that practically every member of the League regarded Japan's action in Manchuria as a breach of the Covenant. He also referred to the use of force, adding that unless every country joined the League and implemented their undertakings, means might have to be found of 'enforcing, if necessary by arms, the application of the principles of the Covenant'.[48]

Forbes seems to have been provoked into making this statement by previous criticism from the opposition, his imminent visit as Prime Minister to London and the suggestion to the disarmament conference of an Air Locarno. It was ironic that it came so late and was so irrelevant to the course of events. Moreover, the ideas were hardly those that Forbes had been pursuing in the preceding four years. One can only assume that, indifferent to foreign policy in general, he did as he had at the 1930 imperial conference and read out a speech prepared by another who had definite ideas. In 1930 Hankey was the guiding force behind Forbes' stand; in 1935 it may have been Berendsen. In the New Zealand archives there is a 26-page document on foreign affairs, written, judging by the internal evidence, in May 1935, which remarked that the ineffectiveness of the measures taken during the Manchurian dispute 'was a grievous blow to the authority of the League and to the efficiency of its police system, and may well prove to have been a major disaster to the world'. After an analysis of the League and the situation of many countries round the world, it remarked that Japan was one of the danger spots, and commented on its rule in Manchuria.[49] This is possibly a forerunner of the later support for the League by the Labour government which was to come to power in New Zealand in 1935.

The other two Dominions, South Africa and Canada, had not changed their attitude to foreign affairs and the British Commonwealth. In South Africa in February 1935 there was a debate in the House of Assembly on the possibility of remaining neutral if Britain went to war, and the subject recurred while the Prime Ministers' Conference was being held in London.[50]

In Canada also there were debates in parliament in which a desire was apparent in some quarters to keep Canada out of war at all costs, together with a suspicion of British policies. The government was therefore embarrassed when the League Council set up a 'Sanctions Committee' in April 1935—as a result of the introduction of conscription in Germany—and included Canada's name on the membership list. As the public announcement was made at the same time that the government was informed, it could hardly refuse to be a member. However, it accepted with such provisos that the Secretary-General of the League objected. The government modified its attitude, but in doing so left the way open for the later misunderstanding with its own advisory officer, Riddell, over oil sanctions against Italy during the Abyssinian crisis.[51]

In May 1935, moreover, the government drifted into a trade war with Japan over the exchange dumping duty which Canada levied on, among others, Japanese goods. The Japanese objected to what they considered to be an imbalance of trade and both sides began to levy duties on the other's exports, contrary to the Commercial Treaty of 1913. This raised a veritable hornets' nest of conflicting interests.[52] It cannot be said that the Bennett government was very happy in its external relations in the closing days of its tenure of office.

In defence matters, the government made some belated moves towards ending the slide to total disarmament. The resignation of McNaughton as Chief of the General Staff in 1935 at least removed the main advocate of air power at the expense of sea power, so the Canadian navy no longer faced the threat of being disbanded. Moreover, when Bennett attended the Commonwealth Prime Ministers' conference in May the British Admiralty warned him that if Japan threatened aggression in the Far East Britain might have to send three-quarters of her fleet there. That would leave her weak against Germany in European waters. The Admiralty therefore laid great stress on the Canadian destroyer squadron for keeping the sea communications open between Canada and Europe. Accordingly, the Bennett government in its estimates for 1935–36 allowed $2 395 000 for the navy, as well as $4 302 900 for the air force.[53]

Nevertheless, Dominion forces still remained pathetically small. The Chiefs of Staff annual review for 1935 lists them, but in doing so gives the impression that somebody was desperately hunting round for *anything* to put in the report. Australia had two 8" (203mm) gun cruisers in commission, a third was being built and a fourth was in reserve. Two sloops were also being built; and a seaplane carrier, survey ship, flotilla leader and five destroyers were all in reserve. Canada had four destroyers and three minesweepers 'in partial commission'; South Africa had scrapped its two trawlers and now simply trained a reserve for the 'African Squadron' of the Royal Navy. The description of coastal defences attempted to hide gross weaknesses by verbiage. As for air forces, Canada had three land plane squadrons; Australia claimed that an expansion of her air force had been approved; New Zealand apparently had an air force of four flights of service aircraft of a general-purpose type (i.e. obsolete). South Africa talked vaguely of 'units of the South African Air Force' and claimed it would have three squadrons in five years. As for regular army units, the truth was that none of the Dominions had them, apart from small bodies of men to maintain camps and stores and act as training cadres for the militia.[54] In short, the Dominion forces were miniscule by world standards and the Dominions in fact survived simply because no power then existed that was interested in attacking them. How long that happy state of affairs would continue remained to be seen.

If the defence of the Commonwealth depended on Britain, its foreign policy was also decided by her government, which usually, as already noted, informed the Dominions afterwards of the situation and policies adopted, but rarely if ever consulted them beforehand. Moreover, in the matter of defence policy the British had tried to hide from the Dominions the extent of their weakness and the significance of recent British decisions. This was illustrated very clearly when the Dominion Prime Ministers met in London for the Silver Jubilee of King George V in 1935.

The Silver Jubilee and the Dominion PMs' meetings, May 1935

As 1935 approached, the British government became determined to celebrate the Silver Jubilee of King George V with as much pomp as Queen Victoria's had been celebrated. The depression and all its woes could be forgotten and the British people united and given an uplift, while the government gained in prestige. The result was the spectacle and pageantry described in the introduction to this book, with their Royal Majesties and their various ministers and servants parading through the streets of London, while throughout the land celebrations occurred.

It was also, of course, an appropriate time to discuss imperial matters. The 1907 colonial conference had agreed that an imperial meeting should take place at least every four years; so since the last conference had been held in 1931 another was then due. Thomas in fact suggested one, but the president of the Board of Trade pointed out that economic questions were sure to be raised and there would most likely be pressure from both the Dominions and British manufacturers to revise the Ottawa agreements. This should be avoided at all costs. The following year, 1936, was not suitable, for a general election had to be held in Britain. In the end, 1937 was chosen for the next full conference. In the meantime, however, less formal and prestigious 'Prime Ministers' meetings' could be held at the time of the King's Jubilee. Only de Valera of Ireland had declined an invitation to this, with the result that from April to May 1935 the leaders of India, the colonies and the other Dominions would be in London.[55]

The problem, however, was how much the Prime Ministers should be told about the British defence situation—let alone the decisions which had been made. The Dominions Office, to its credit, suggested that the Premiers should be personally supplied with Foreign Office 'D' prints, but the Foreign Office objected on grounds of security: they could see the 'D' prints in their High Commission Offices. Other ways of informing them were discussed, even of providing them with the Foreign Office weekly summary. This last was considered too dangerous, since the summary included blunt references to many things that the Foreign Office did not think the Dominions Office or other British government departments should see, let alone the Dominion leaders.[56]

A desire for secrecy was evident among some British officials and was revealed by the sequel. It was decided that a series of memoranda would be provided. The idea was sound in itself; but unfortunately the British deeply disagreed among themselves. For example, the Foreign Office's estimate of the 'situation in the Far East' began by admitting that Japanese ambition was the dominating feature, but then went on to remark that Japan was tied up in Manchuria, where she was threatened by Russia as well. Her main interest lay in China, and although domination was probably beyond her she would make that country her major market. As for Britain, 'our interests seem . . . to be best served by cultivating friendly relations with both China and Japan'.[57]

The British service chiefs were not impressed with this optimistic assessment. The Admiralty flatly disagreed and thought the situation in the Far East was potentially very dangerous, Japan probably regarded Britain as a major obstacle to her progress, and, as the author of the memorandum put it, 'It is difficult to avoid the feeling that the outcome will be a Japanese domination of Northern China . . . which must, sooner or later, clash with our interests'. Britain and the United States were weak in the area and the Admiralty concluded that Japan had every intention of pursuing a policy of domination in China and the neighbouring regions. Danger in Europe made matters worse. For its part, the War Office decided simply to describe the strategical situation and ignore Foreign Office optimism.[58]

Accordingly, when the CID met on 16 April the service chiefs were very pessimistic, especially concerning the possibility of war in the Far East and in Europe at the same time. The Secretaries of State for War and the Colonies and the First Sea Lord stressed this, but Chamberlain remained unimpressed. He still thought that 'by prudent diplomacy we ought to be able to avoid embarking on a war with Japan alone'; and if Britain went to war with Germany and Japan took advantage of it they would just have to stand on the defensive in the Far East. 'Financial implications prevented the provision of maximum needs for each eventuality.' The old clash remained: the leaders of the services and their supporters stressed the terrible weakness in the Far East but were overborne by Chamberlain once again, using the trump card of economic and fiscal necessity. This deep, indeed vital, disagreement was hidden from the Dominions, none of whose representatives were present at the meeting.[59]

The matter was similarly disguised in the Chiefs of Staff annual review for 1935, which, prepared with the Dominion Premiers in mind,[60] was extremely uninformative. It began with the same statement of international developments as the earlier reviews, adding only brief accounts of recent happenings. It then printed the usual passage on imperial commitments, with the same wording as before and going over the same outdated possibility of war with either France or Germany. It then, despite all that Chamberlain had said, repeated as a maxim that Britain should be able to send a fleet to Singapore to provide cover against Japanese forces and at the same time retain in Europe a force sufficient to maintain control of Britain's vital sea areas. It did have the grace to conclude that Britain should direct her diplomacy to prevent the need to fight Germany and Japan simultaneously, but added that if France were Britain's ally then all would be well, 'and the main British fleet would be available to defend our Empire in the East'. The British thus completely hid from Dominion representatives the bitter argument that they had been engaged in, together with Chamberlain's views on expenditure and the defence of the Far East. The review completely confused benevolence with intentions and capability, and attempted to blind the Prime Ministers with vague generalisations and technical detail. For example, after admitting that 1936 was a dangerous year, it repeated verbatim the section on naval responsibilities printed in the 1933 review! (Indeed, whole sections of the rest of the document had likewise been lifted from that review.) In Appendix 5 it gave a table comparing the size of the United States, Japanese, French, Italian and German fleets with that of 'the British Commonwealth'. This looked very fine: fifteen Commonwealth capital ships as compared with nine Japanese; six aircraft carriers as compared with four; 50 cruisers against 34; 169 destroyers to 104. Only in submarines were the Japanese superior, having 57 to the British 49. Yet this, of course, gave a totally false impression of British strength, for, as has been mentioned before, the British forces were scattered over the world, and by 1935 were heavily concentrated in European and Mediterranean waters. The appreciation of Admiral Dreyer, the C-in-C China station, the following August was somewhat different. He noted then that British Far Eastern forces compared with Japanese were no battleships to nine, one aircraft carrier to four, no seaplane carriers to two, four 8" (203mm) cruisers to twelve, no 6" (152mm) cruisers to four, one smaller cruiser to eighteen, ten destroyers to 102, and fifteen submarines to sixty-five.[61] It was not only that if Dreyer's figures were accurate the Chiefs of Staff had grossly underestimated some of the Japanese forces, it was also that by giving general strengths without reference to their disposition they had given a false impression that all was well.

In summary, the Chiefs of Staff review of imperial defence for the 1935 PMs' conference was not a serious and deep reassessment of imperial forces and dangers, but a rehash of previous reviews, designed to give an optimistic picture of the situation. The Dominion Premiers, however, could have seen through this manoeuvre, if they had been aware of danger, if they had correlated all the facts at their disposal, and if they had carefully analysed the material. For example, several hints had been given to the Dominions that all was not what it seemed. In November 1933 and April 1934 Hankey had written to Casey, then Australian Treasurer, informing him of the Defence Requirements Committee and moves in Germany. Lothian, in his speech to the Canadian Institute of International Affairs in October 1934, had said bluntly that 'at a time when trouble was brewing in Europe the British public would not with equanimity watch their fleet sail away to the Pacific'. If this was a true estimate of British public opinion, it cast in doubt the whole British Singapore strategy. This point was made even more bluntly to Bruce in London during meetings on the proposed naval conference. The First Lord of the Admiralty remarked that to send a battle fleet to the Far East Britain had to have a large enough fleet to enable her to leave sufficient strength behind. 'The representatives could quite well envisage the public outcry if our whole naval strength departed to the Far East.' Bruce, if he noticed the significance of this remark, did not comment.[62]

These hints in fact did not seem to have had an effect. Lothian's comment was made to the Canadians, who did not care, and was unlikely to have reached the attention of observers in Australia and New Zealand. Casey, if he drew any moral from Hankey's guarded language, does not seem to have passed it on to his Cabinet colleagues. As for Bruce, he regarded himself as representing the Australian government in London, but hardly as being always answerable to it. On other occasions he had kept his counsel, and, as McCarthy says, regarding the remark of the First Lord of the Admiralty, 'there is no evidence to show that Bruce reported the conversation to Canberra'.[63]

The British Prime Ministers' meetings, which occurred between 30 April and 23 May 1935, were therefore a last opportunity before Mussolini began the major series of European aggressions to draw out the truth about British power and policy. Once again the Dominion representatives had numerous hints provided for them. Simon's address to the conference, according to Barnett, revealed 'the hopeless inconsistencies' of British policy, which wished to maintain friendship with China, Japan, Russia and the United States.[64] The Foreign Office memorandum 'The Situation in the Far East' had been circulated before the meeting. However, it had been strengthened at the end, presumably as a result of the criticism levied against it. In a final paragraph it remarked that

> . . . the aggressive and ambitious spirit of Japan is a reality which only compelling obstacles can ultimately keep within bounds. There is no genuinely moderate party in Japan, and she is likely to grasp at as much as she feels capable of reaching at any given moment. From a naval and military point of view, it is therefore necessary to give serious consideration to the possibilities of Japanese aggression against British possessions and interests, even though for the moment at least it may not be likely to take a very active form, unless events in other parts of the world were to oblige us to concentrate all our efforts elsewhere.

And if that were not enough, Chamberlain, at the second meeting on 7 May, remarked that as Chancellor of the Exchequer he had to provide funds for defence, 'some of which were largely related to the Far Eastern situation. It seemed to him that it would impose a very formidable burden on this country if, in addition to Europe, provision had also to be made for the Far East'. This was a really revealing remark, yet none of the Dominion Premiers took him up on it.[65]

It seems, therefore, that the Dominion Premiers had been given several clues that the British were weak in the Far East and not likely to send their fleet there, but that they still did not see the light. As McCarthy says, 'Both Lyons and Menzies refused to piece all the evidence together in order to draw the obvious and logical conclusion: that if a two-front war did occur any time up to 1939–40 then a British fleet certainly would not be sent to Singapore'.[66]

The reasons for the failure of the Dominion leaders to elicit this fact is interesting. To start with, the Prime Ministers of South Africa and Canada were little concerned with the implementation of the Singapore strategy. Hertzog, after Chamberlain's comment, turned the debate on to what concerned him much more, the policy the British government was pursuing towards Germany. His impassioned defence of that country provided just the red herring the British needed and turned the discussion safely away on to general lines.

Nor was Bennett any better. He asserted that the main point at issue was whether British policy had aimed at securing lasting peace. He thought it had. This general reflection prevented him from looking closely at the strategic situation in which the Empire found itself and at the concrete policies it adopted in order to meet that situation. In the third meeting he thought that Britain had consulted the Dominions as fully as possible, seeing that there were occasions when the British government had to take action on its own initiative. He was, however, concerned at the extent of British disarmament. Perhaps some inkling of what was happening had got through to Bennett: if so he did not become specific.

Even more striking are the statements of the representatives of the two Dominions that *were* vitally concerned with the Pacific. It could at least have been expected that Lyons or Menzies would have questioned the assumptions of the British. As we have seen, if ruthlessly analysed the annual review of imperial defence would have provided a number of interesting points for discussion, and Menzies was a lawyer who should have been capable of reading between the lines of a document. Hankey had assessed Lyons as 'a charming old boy who will agree with you all the way . . . but I would not count on him for doing a thing. The man you ought to get hold of is Menzies'.[67] Yet at these meetings Menzies, who was ignorant of foreign and military policy and inexperienced at such gatherings, failed totally to see the relevant points. Lyons was not present on the occasion when Chamberlain made his remarkable statement and Menzies, instead of seizing on its implications, let the matter pass. In the second meeting, when Forbes raised the question of Singapore, Menzies said that he was not familiar with the matter and perhaps they could come back to it. He then began a discussion on the trade negotiations between Australia and Japan. Later in the same meeting, when Bennett raised the issue of Britain's disarmament to the point of weakness, Menzies turned the discussion on to the treatment of Germany. On two occasions, therefore, Menzies failed to realise the importance of points that were being raised and, by introducing irrelevancies, saved the British from embarrassing moments. It was either ignorance on his part or a desire to be pro-British. One suspects that inexperience was the main reason. Bruce, however, who also attended, was anything but inexperienced. However, in that company, he possibly felt that his loyalty lay with 'imperial'—i.e. British—interests. He did not guide his Prime Minister or Menzies so that they could be more effective.

Lyons was the most effective of the Australian delegation—a fact that says much. In the third meeting he requested fuller information about British policy towards Japan, mentioning the Latham mission. He thought, however, that in Manchuria the Japanese had brought order out of chaos—a Latham idea. He suggested that it might be better to recognise Manchukuo and negotiate some sort of pact for the security of 'all the nations bordering on the Pacific Ocean'. The appeasement of Japan and some sort of Pacific Pact were ideas to which Lyons would return in the following years. Simon pointed out that they should act as League members, MacDonald that the Japanese, not Britain, had obstructed a pact.

Lyons also, however, asked about the defence of Singapore, and at his request the CIGS made a statement on it at the last meeting. The matter was regarded as so secret that it was not included in the record, which is a pity. One suspects, however, that it was a muted and vague report. The notes for his talk by the Chief of Air Staff, which have survived in the Air records,[68] suggest that he revealed the lack of squadrons at Singapore and that Britain's main concern in the air was Germany. That particular part of his notes may not have been used, however, since at the meeting, according to the minutes, he was apparently only asked to talk on Singapore.

Even more odd, however, is the conduct of Forbes at the meetings. At the third meeting he expressed satisfaction with the progress of Singapore and made the almost incredible remark that the matter was not one of special concern to New Zealand adding that there was good feeling between New Zealand and Japan. This has caught the attention of New Zealand historians, who seem at a loss to explain it. Wood thinks that New Zealand alarm at the Manchurian affair had tapered off by then, though Lissington comments that though Forbes' statement may have represented public opinion at that time in New Zealand, it 'was a complete misrepresentation of the view of New Zealand's military advisors and gave an entirely false impression of the Government's own view of the Far Eastern scene'. MacGibbon suggests that Forbes was being diplomatic[69]—though why he should be so at a meeting of Commonwealth Prime Ministers remains a mystery. He certainly seemed confused, for at the last meeting, when little except backslapping was in order, he mixed commendation for British policy with misgivings lest Britain be 'less well equipped than New Zealand might wish to see her' and added that defence measures were a necessary form of insurance. When it is remembered, however, that Forbes' earlier strong statements on Singapore and foreign policy were the work of others, his comments at the Prime Ministers' meetings appear less remarkable; he simply seems to have echoed the opinions of those who had last seen him. Perhaps Hankey and some of the Chiefs of Staff had had a word with him before the last meeting, so that he felt constrained to insert a word of caution.

In short, the Dominion Prime Ministers were not sufficiently statesmanlike to realise the drift the Commonwealth was taking. Some may not have cared, but those who did were not shrewd enough. All too often their irrelevant remarks clouded the point at issue and the debate drifted from one Premier's pet theme to another. This was made worse by the fact that the Dominions had different interests from one another and so did not present a cohesive front to the British. The latter could play one off against another. When this is admitted, however, it must also be added that those Dominion leaders whose countries *were* concerned with the Far East did not show a sufficient grasp of essentials to enable them to play an intelligent part in the discussions. They must have exasperated Hankey, who had looked on them for support for the navy. They proved a broken reed.

The British government, however, was also responsible. It had hid the truth by vague phraseology and imperialist clichés, and had deliberately avoided telling the Dominions about its decisions. And it masked this attitude with sweeping generalisations. For example, MacDonald said in the fourth PMs' meeting that the British government 'had no other objective than the maintenance of peace, and . . . all efforts were directed to this end'. As a sentiment it was impeccable—and untrue. For the British government surely had other objectives, or ought to have had—such as the maintenance of the British Empire/Commonwealth. Nor, despite all the rhetoric of Empire, were the British any more forthcoming in 1935. The Chiefs of Staff reports were only given to the Prime Ministers at the last meeting, when it was too late to influence discussions, when Bennett had already returned home and Bruce was absent, and when the nostalgia of parting had put an 'Old Lang Syne' euphoria over the representatives. Even then, the paper which was circulated to the British representatives at this meeting reminded them that the Cabinet had decided that the Defence Requirements Committee report had been held over till the arrival of the Premiers in London, and 'in view of the comprehensive nature of the review by the Chiefs of

Staff . . . and the developments in the situation since [then] . . . the Prime Minister does not, as at present advised, propose to circulate to the Prime Ministers of the Dominions the Reports on Defence Requirements'.[70] In other words, the Premiers were still not to be told what the British had decided! So much for Dominion 'consultation'.

The meetings therefore broke up, as the British had planned, with fulsome praise for British policy. That outcome, indeed, had been inherent in the very idea of the Prime Ministers' meetings from the beginning. Nothing else could be expected, seeing that they were being held concurrently with the Silver Jubilee. The Prime Ministers were overwhelmed by the ceremony, the protocol, the glorification of Empire, the splendour and pageantry of the occasion, and emotions of loyalty to the now aging monarch. It was not an appropriate time for close analysis and grim heart-searching. The British had chosen their time well to raise fleetingly, and then dismiss, imperial defence. It was wholly to be expected, therefore, that Lyons should make a long and sycophantic speech, remarking, among other things, that he had feared that Britain was not being conciliatory enough, but was now convinced by British judgment. He went on to express gratitude and loyalty to Britain, to defend Germany, and to declare that Australia stood behind the 'Mother Country', in her effort for security. As one cryptic commentator has remarked, 'Neither the existing state of British sea power nor its predicted development warranted such an expression of solidarity'.[71] Forbes was not as fulsome as Lyons and seemed to have a few reservations, which were swept aside by the emotion of the occasion and the effect of Lyons' speech. Bennett had left previously, but also had apparently had some doubts of Britain's preparedness. Hertzog rounded off the meeting with general talk about the celebrations.

It was a sad commentary on the Commonwealth that after the crises of Manchuria and Shanghai and the heart-searching and analyses of the service staffs and some politicians the meeting of Premiers had not reassessed the strategic and foreign-policy situation that faced them, but instead indulged in little more than ceremonial waffle. Some belated and slight rearmament was taking place, but the Commonwealth was neither united in policy nor strong in arms when the next international crisis, which was brewing even while the Premiers were meeting, broke upon them. On 3 October 1935 Mussolini invaded Abyssinia; the League was face to face with another direct challenge to its peace-keeping authority and the Commonwealth with a threat to its sea communications.

7 The Commonwealth fallacy exposed

> *What experience and history teach is this—that people and governments never have learned anything from history, or acted on principles deduced from it.*
>
> HEGEL, *PHILOSOPHY OF HISTORY*

For the British Commonwealth, as for the world in general, the Manchurian and Shanghai crises were ominous. For Britain they revealed an expansionist Japan in the Far East, a Japan moreover whose interests were liable to clash with Britain's own. For by 1933, with the rise of Hitler in Germany, the British had potential enemies at opposite ends of the earth. This had been the fear of many Australians from 1906 onwards, but in the early thirties the nightmare recurred with even greater menace, since the British could no longer hide behind an Anglo–Japanese alliance. Even had they been as heavily armed as in 1918 they could not have easily fought a combination of Japan and Germany. Yet because of the after-effects of the First World War—a revulsion from war combined with a failure to analyse its causes clearly and a resultant public opposition to armaments—they had disarmed to a dangerous extent. For the Commonwealth, the crises posed the questions raised in the preface to this book: whether the constitutional changes in the Empire meant that the British had changed their habits and intended to consult with the Dominions; whether there were common Commonwealth interests that made such consultation worthwhile and enabled a common foreign policy to be formulated; and whether the Commonwealth could take heed of the warning and could recreate effective defence forces.

The divergent Dominions
One result of the crises was to throw a clear light on the divergent interests and attitudes of the various Dominions. Hankey's tour in 1934 only emphasised what was well known before: the Dominions did not have common interests. South Africa was concerned with her position and policies on the African mainland. Canada, basking in the sun of the United States' protection, felt she need spend no money on defence and merely had to keep away from British and European entanglements. On the other hand, Australia and New Zealand, isolated in the South Pacific, feared the new aggressive

Japan that had been seen so recently in Manchuria and Shanghai, and therefore wished to inveigle British defence spending into their area. These differences were noted in 1932, when it had been suggested in the Dominions Office that the CID paper, 'The Defence of Australia', was satisfactory for that country, but the wording would have to be changed if it were circulated, so as not to offend South Africa. A common policy, organised by a common secretariat of the whole Empire, was impossible.[1]

The significance of League failure

Any pretence of a common attitude to world affairs, therefore, depended on support for the League of Nations. For it alone, in Watt's words, 'provided . . . [the Dominions] with an external frame of reference on which their policies could converge'[2]—hence the great stress laid by the Dominions Office on the League. That organisation's weakness in the Far East therefore posed serious problems for the British Commonwealth. The Japanese had revealed not only a capacity to dominate the East and exclude the white nations from a sphere of influence there, but also the continuation of the old game of power politics.

> The good old rule,
> . . . the simple plan,
> That they should take, who have the power,
> And they should keep who can.

This immediately put in question the ability of the League to maintain peace. For it remained an organisation of independent sovereign states and did not have military strength of its own to coerce a recalcitrant nation. If force had to be applied, it would have to be by one of the other major powers. None of them, however, had been either able or willing to intervene in an area which was neither strategically convenient nor involved their immediate interests. And without the backing of force behind it 'world public opinion' had been powerless.

This raised the question of the future application of sanctions: perhaps either economic or diplomatic pressure would force aggressors to accept League decisions. Yet the United States remained outside the League and its businessmen would almost certainly break any boycott which that organisation imposed. Moreover, the designation of an 'aggressor' was a legalistic decision and the Japanese had revealed that aggressors could confuse the issue by specious pleas, historical complexities and provocation of the victims. It was a technique that Hitler was to use later with devastating effect.

This situation brought into the open differences of opinion and interest among the Dominions, and a rift appeared between them at Geneva in the debates in 1932. Canadian policy during the period wavered between criticism of China and apparently strong support for the League. This had been due to Cahan's performance and the government's subsequent overreaction—which was later to have repercussions during the Abyssinian crisis. As for the Manchurian affair, the Canadian government had disarmed to the point of impotence and could not have affected the issue even if it had wished to do so. However, despite its legation in Tokyo, the government was oriented to the eastern seaboard and, although it disapproved of Japanese action, did not feel greatly threatened. It remained anxious to adapt its policies closely to those of the United States, but, since it had as Prime Minister the pro-British Bennett, did little except waver between the ideas of Stimson and Simon. As the policies of Britain and the United States both involved as much non-interference with Japan as possible, cognisant with formal condemnation, this provided few problems for Canada. The Americans would have loudly adopted a more righteous attitude than the British—that was all. Neither government had the naval power or the will to force the Japanese to leave Manchuria. Canadians, however, secure under the United States 'umbrella', were inclined to pacifism and isolationism—fearing involvement in 'decadent' Europe and the wiles of the British empire. In that, they resembled the Boers in South Africa. The Irish, who have featured only occasionally in this study, went further, supporting the League and expressing outright hostility to Britain. De Valera ungraciously declined the invitation to the Silver Jubilee with the remark that 'Ireland has been incorporated into the Commonwealth by force; her territory has been partitioned against her will without regard to justice . . .'. The Foreign Office suspected that confidential information from Britain was being leaked to the Nazis through the Irish Free State government.[3]

The two Pacific Dominions, on the other hand, regarded themselves as representatives of the British race in the southern hemisphere and remained loyal to the 'mother country'. On his way to the Silver Jubilee, Forbes told Canadians that when Britain was at war, New Zealand was too: there was no need to summon parliament.[4] In fact this roused debate in New Zealand, and the Labour leader, Savage, though he supported the Commonwealth, insisted on the right to discuss foreign policy in parliament. A slightly more independent and pro-League policy would soon be adopted by New Zealand. Forbes' remark must have been regarded with amazement in Canada however.

Australian opinion is difficult to gauge exactly, since loyalty to Britain and lack of independent leaders prevented much being said. Yet fear of Japan undoubtedly existed. Pearce had criticised the

British, both publicly and privately, for failure to provide a fleet for the Pacific in 1912 and 1913; he was unlikely to have been very happy about the situation in 1932. However, the Australians not only felt great loyalty to Britain, they also had great respect for British wisdom and authority. Their conservative politicians therefore found it difficult publicly to criticise the British. Deakin in 1910 had remarked, 'there are Pacific problems in which the Australian interest is inexpressible; which, though they may not be made the subject of public debate, should be perpetually and consistently considered . . . by . . . those charged with the foreign affairs of the Empire'. But it had taken J. Cook, the great champion of imperial cooperation, three months to bring himself to counter the Admiralty's arguments in 1914.[5]

In the 1930s, the only publicly vocal member of the government was the aged 'Billy' Hughes. His book, *Australia and War Today: The Price of Peace* drew some morals from the Manchurian episode. Together with Pearce and Latham he was inclined to be glad that Japan had invaded Manchuria, since it would be too busy there to move southwards. Pearce, indeed, told the United States Consul-General in 1935 that with British naval strength reduced below the safety point Australia had no other policy open to it but to try to be friendly, 'and to rejoice (irrespective of the moral aspect) every time Japan advanced more deeply into Manchukuo and North China. He hoped that her energies would be absorbed there for a generation . . .'.[6] Hughes, Pearce and Latham were unusual, however, and their pessidmistic attitude to power politics jarred on their colleagues. Most government members, and especially Prime Minister Lyons, preferred to hide behind polite platitudes and to avoid nasty decisions.

League weakness, however, had serious repercussions. To start with, it threw decisions on foreign policy back to the various members of the Commonwealth. Differences of opinion were bound to come into the open, especially in matters like a declaration of war. The possibility of Dominion neutrality was thereby raised. All these questions were nightmares for constitutional lawyers and imperialists. It was no wonder that they rallied round the only policy, apart from support for the League, that seemed to solve all their problems—appeasement.

Even more vital to the continued existence of the Commonwealth, however, was the problem of defence. For, like a giant with feet of clay, the Empire sprawled across the earth. Dominion and British politicians talked of 'imperial defence'—as if military forces could be reduced to pure numbers and the digits added up like a simple sum in arithmetic. Moreover, both Britain and the Dominions looked on the

Empire as a source of strength and protection, not a demand on their resources.

The statesmen of the Commonwealth were slow to wake from the dream of international amity that had resulted from the events of the late 1920s—the Locarno and Kellogg Pacts and the disarmament conference. Even after the Japanese had struck in Manchuria and at Shanghai they ignored the warnings of their service advisors and concentrated on hopes for disarmament. In Britain, Australia, Canada and New Zealand the story was the same. The British were most intimately involved, since they were, at least in theory, responsible for the foreign and defence policies of the Empire. The National government Cabinet, however, was both nervous of public opinion and, on the matter of rearmament, in agreement with it. Dominated by Chamberlain, it was totally convinced that the way out of the economic depression lay through rigid government economies. It disregarded the arguments put forward by Keynes and the possibility that rearmament would stimulate the economy. The Dominion governments also adopted this attitude. Canada was perhaps the extreme, but she was the least affected directly by the events in the Far East and felt secure under American protection. New Zealand stopped the rot in her defence forces earlier than the others, but still did not increase the minute sums she was spending by very much. The Australian government opted for its traditional reliance on British naval policy, although it realised—or at least some of its members did—the weaknesses of the British in the East. It is perhaps significant, therefore, that Australian pressure, in the person of Bruce, enabled the critics of the British government in the CID to persuade that body to set up the Defence Requirements Committee in November 1933. The immediate reaction of the politicians, however, was to seek a way out of their problems by diplomacy—in Britain by the attempt to come to an agreement with Japan, in Australia by the Latham mission. Only when little progress seemed to have been made did the politicians face the necessity to rearm. Even then they were tardy in action. The Dominions as we have seen did little, while in Britain Chamberlain managed to block the demands for naval rearmament and effected a revolutionary change in British imperial policy: the decision not to send a major fleet out to the Far East but to concentrate instead on British home defences. The Eastern crisis, therefore, was a turning point in Commonwealth defence policy and the minor treatment of it in Mansergh's book *The Commonwealth Experience* is not historically valid. The crisis deserves more than one paragraph.[7]

That decision raised the third issue mentioned in the preface—consultation within the Commonwealth. For if ever there was matter

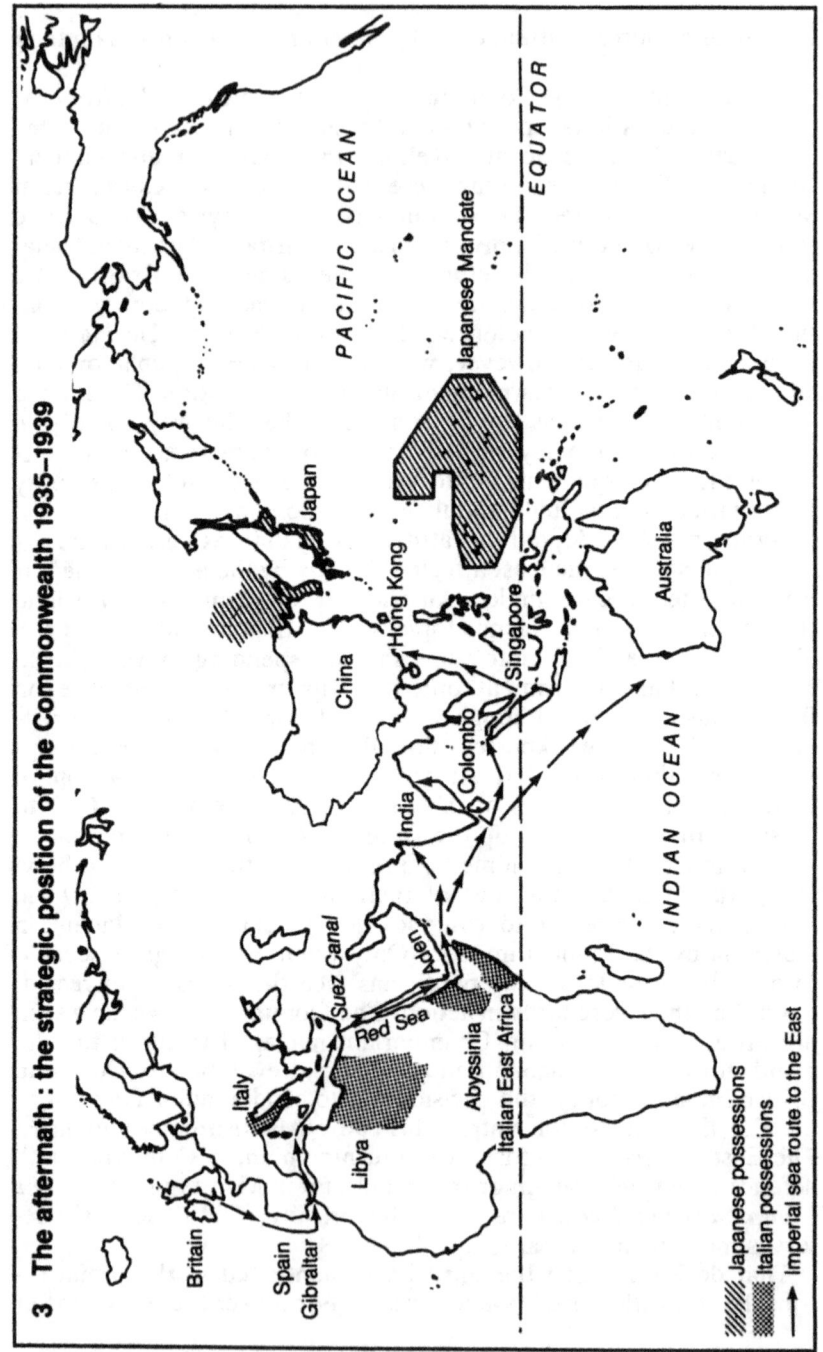

3 The aftermath: the strategic position of the Commonwealth 1935–1939

of vital importance to some at least of the Dominions, this was it. That the British not only did not consult with those Dominions, but went out of their way to prevent them from realising what had happened, reveals that the old wolf of British self-centredness still lived on in the sheepskin of 'Commonwealth Foreign Policy'. At this crisis point in Commonwealth history, not only consultation but even the flow of essential information was restricted by the British. At the same time, however, it must be admitted that Australian and New Zealand leaders were derelict in their duty to their peoples. It was no thanks to them, but rather to luck that the Japanese did not invade their countries during the Second World War.

As for the Australian government, perhaps its leaders did notice what was happening but just did not know what to do about it. Their economic policies precluded spending vast sums on defence; their political stance precluded criticising Britain and relying on an air force to defend Australia. Lyons was totally pessimistic by 1938,[8] yet despite this the Australian government maintained its policy of reliance on the British navy and minimal rearmament. It did not do what was urgently needed—discipline the Defence Department and provide coordinated military and political policies which took account of military realities. Instead, to ease the burden of thought and action on Australian politicians, the situation was allowed to drift.

Even more surprising, however, is the failure to consult and cooperate more closely with New Zealand. Some discussion about cooperation had occurred as early as 1912.[9] Yet with the Axis powers increasing their threat, Australia and New Zealand did not coordinate their defence forces. The two countries had not only governments of a different disposition (by 1935) but also different strategic outlooks. Australia looked to its south-east coast, the Indian Ocean and the Suez canal; New Zealand looked to the Pacific and the Panama canal. So combined naval exercises continued to be the main form of inter-Dominion cooperation, and it was not until the Pacific Defence Conference of April 1939 that any attempt was made to coordinate the defence preparations of the two countries.

Both Dominions were to blame. The New Zealand government was annoyed at the roundabout way the details of the Australian coastal defence preparations got to her, via the CID. Yet papers prepared by the New Zealand Chiefs of Staff went to London but not to Canberra. Even at the Pacific Defence Conference in April 1939 the Australians were still reluctant to discuss with New Zealand general matters, as distinct from technical questions. They thought that London, not Wellington, was the place to discuss policy, and were unwilling to grant New Zealand a liaison officer in Canberra.[10] A flaw in the organisation of the Commonwealth, in that the Dominions dealt with the centre rather than with each other directly, remained.

Weakness in the heart of Empire
A major weakness, however, was undoubtedly at the centre itself, in the Dominions Office and its head J. H. Thomas. He and his office failed to bring the interests of the Dominions before the British Cabinet and did not protect them from the machinations of British politicians. Worse, they failed to coordinate the policies of the Empire and remained a minor department which had little weight in government counsels. The Empire/Commonwealth was thus not only militarily weak and strategically divided, it was also intellectually leaderless in the late thirties. This was revealed by the continuing failure to face the need to build up naval strength in the Far East. The Defence Requirements Committee was reactivated in 1935; but once again it was under the control of the politicians, who made political criteria paramount,[11] and it failed to face the implications of recent events in the Far East. In 1936 the British Cabinet accepted the need for a 'new naval standard' yet effectively postponed any action. In the middle of the same year the Admiralty told the Cabinet that it could not defend Singapore unless it had eight battleships in the Far East, yet nothing was done and no formal defence scheme was drawn up with the Dutch for the East Indies. The result was that in March 1938 the Chiefs of Staff warned that, if Britain were involved in a protracted struggle with Germany to defend Czechoslovakia, she could not defend her possessions against Italy and Japan.[12]

The reasons for British tardiness in rearmament were clear enough: the weakness of their industries, which did not have the technological ability to rearm quickly; the depressed state of their economy, so that the government was reluctant to spend money on rearmament; the reaction to the First World War, especially pacifism and the hope that by reasonableness the problems with the aggressive powers could be overcome. Together with all these went a lack of intellectual rigour on the part of British politicians. Their economic theories made the depression worse; their attitude to armaments made the military situation worse. To them, armed forces existed to perform imperial policing duties and as a precaution against war, not as an instrument of diplomacy. Accordingly they overlooked the part the possession of force plays in diplomatic exchanges and weakened themselves unnecessarily in the great crises ahead. It was a mistake that Hitler never made.

This weakness, moreover, embarrassed the British in their dealings with the Dominions, for in truth they could not defend the Pacific countries with their forces in the Far East. Faced with a resurgent

Germany, they chose to neglect the defences of the East and to try to talk their way out of trouble with Japan. However, if it came to choosing between British security in Europe and Australian and New Zealand security in the Pacific, British politicians would not have hesitated to choose their own security. This was very natural; but they tried to avoid saying as much to the Dominions, even though they admitted it, on rare occasions, to themselves. In October 1935, for example, Sir Warren Fisher, in the Defence Requirements Committee, remarked that 'a proper defence of the heart of the Empire was only provided at the expense of the security of its outlying constituents'.[13]

The 'newspeak' behind consultation
The British politicians, in short, had not changed their habits of thought or attitude to the world with the Balfour Report. To them, the centre of civilisation remained London and they viewed international events from that vantage point. They remained insular in their outlook, revealing on occasion a lack of sympathy for the Dominions and an inability to put themselves in imagination into their position. Even an 'imperialist' such as Hankey was capable of writing about Australian opinion in December 1934, 'Everyone seems to have the wind up about Japan. They are astonishingly ignorant about principles of defence and imagine all kinds of dangers'.[14] That Australian fears were not totally unreasonable was revealed in 1941.

There seems, therefore, to be little basis for the assertion by Watt that British governments were psychologically vulnerable to representations from the Dominions, or his even more incredible statement regarding the development of Commonwealth machinery, that it imposed on those who formulated British policy the need 'continuously' to consult Dominion representatives, or, where that was impossible, 'to operate within the limits of what they thought the Dominions would accept'.

All the evidence gleaned during this study suggests that the opposite was true. The British government followed its own policy and consulted the Dominions, if at all, after the event and reluctantly. It did use the Dominions, however, in a way suggested by Watt himself towards the end of his article, as a reason for a policy that it intended to pursue on other grounds. Indeed, the Dominions had little chance of forcing the British to adopt a policy they disliked. As Mansergh says, 'What evidence there is suggests that, while it was comparatively easy for the dominion governments to exert a negative, restraining influence on United Kingdom policy, they would have had no small difficulty in persuading the United Kingdom to embark on new or unknown paths'.[15]

As it was, the British did not encourage the Dominions to enter into a dialogue with them on general foreign-policy issues, as distinct from the disarmament conference. This was to be revealed in 1935 when, in response to questions in the British parliament and criticism of the imperial system of consultation, Thomas remarked that no Dominion had expressed dissent of any kind from the policy of the British government. This provoked the Canadian government into sending a strong cable to Britain. After admitting the difficulties of the British government and the flow of information it had provided for the Dominions, the Canadian government went on:

> It is not, however, considered that the sending of information regarding policies which have been adopted or in some cases actions which have been taken, constitutes 'consultation(s)' in the proper or usual sense of the term . . . [and] erroneous inferences are apt to be drawn by people in Canada and elsewhere from the statement that there has been no dissenting from the policy adopted . . .

The British answer to this was somewhat pedantic, ending with the distinction between consultation in cases likely to involve active obligations and communication of information on developments.[16] The distinction was a rather fine one, for the Manchurian crisis—and certainly the Shanghai one—if they had got out of hand, might well have involved Australia and New Zealand in 'active obligations'. When the South African High Commissioner requested more personal conversations with the British while the government was deciding its policy, Sir Harry Batterbee of the Dominions Office pointed out that the British government had suggested periodic talks between the Foreign Secretary and the High Commissioners, but that the Dominions had objected. Some did not give much responsibility to their High Commissioners and others—one of which, incidentally, was Canada—did not seem to want to be consulted beforehand. The Foreign Office came into the discussion and strongly supported Batterbee on the issue, stressing the need for the High Commissioners to be responsible spokesmen for the Dominions.[17]

It seems, indeed, that there were faults on all sides in the discussion of 'consultation'. Many of the parties to it had reservations. Australia and New Zealand were keen, since they needed security and wanted to ensure that British policy was protecting their interests. South Africa was concerned about Germany and Canada was concerned not to be involved. In a way, 'consultation' was a shibboleth to which all paid lip service, but not without some silent provisos. The British government and Foreign Office too, for all their talk about the High Commissioners, were not completely honest. They had no intention of handing over vital policy decisions to discussion by the Dominions. They were quite capable of deciding in the CID in May 1939 that the German and Italian fleets would have to be contained before any forces could be spared for the Far East, and at the same time sending 'grandiose words of assurance to the Australian Prime Minister'.[18] In the period covered by this book, as we have seen, the embargo on the sale of arms to the Far East was born out of panic and immediate political expediency, and the government did not pause in order to consult its own representative on the arms trade in Geneva, let alone the Dominions. Even worse, in 1934 it went to considerable lengths to hide from the interested Dominions—Australia and New Zealand—the fact that it was concentrating on rearmament for Britain and ignoring the defences of the Far East.

Britain, Australia, Canada and New Zealand: the future
The basic weakness behind talk of consultation lay in the failure to realise or accept that the various parts of the Empire/Commonwealth had radically different interests. As early as 1914 the Australian F. W. Eggleston had remarked on 'the "two ocean" dilemma which now confronts the Empire'.[19] Geopolitics was pulling it apart. Canada's future was bound up with that of the United States, South Africa's with her own continent, Britain with Europe and Australia and New Zealand with the southern Pacific and south-east Asia. The interests were separate; the attitudes and views of the world were different. Indeed, in 1924 Bruce himself had spoken in the Australian parliament on the danger that Britain would concentrate on her immediate defence 'to the detriment of the outlying parts of the Empire'.[20]

The crises of 1931–34, therefore, should have provided a warning for the statesmen of the Empire/Commonwealth of what was to come: for Canadians, that their isolationism and pacifism would not suffice and that they had to become involved in world affairs; for Australians and New Zealanders that they could no longer rely on Britain in the Far East; for the British themselves that they were desperately weak, and needed to rearm as quickly as possible. For all of them, there was a need to provide a far-sighted policy, supported by military force, to protect the Empire/Commonwealth and to deal with aggression. Despite the euphoria of the Jubilee, this should have been very clear by 1935. For the Japanese moves in the Far East did provide, as the British Chiefs of Staff had written in February 1932, 'the writing on the wall'.

Appendix: Comparative naval strengths in April 1931

	US	France	British Commonwealth	Italy	Japan	Germany	Russia
Capital ships	15	9	15	4	9	8	4
Aircraft carriers	4	1	6	–	4	–	–
Heavy cruisers	16	12	19	10	16	–	–
Light cruisers	13	?	40	?	22	–	–
Destroyers	259	103	173	104	107	38	32
Submarines	103	110	63	70	71	–	21
Naval aircraft (sea)	689	45	261	25	115	–	10
Naval aircraft (shore-based)	311	266	–	117	296	–	130

Source: PRO CP 100(31) CAB 24/220

Endnotes

Abbreviations used:

AA	Australian Archives
ANL	Australian National Library
CID	Committee of Imperial Defence
COS	Chiefs of Staff
CPD	*Commonwealth Parliamentary Debates* (Australia)
DBFP	*Documents on British Foreign Policy*
DCER	*Documents on Canadian External Relations*
DCOS	Deputy Chiefs of Staff
DO	Dominions Office
FO	Foreign Office
NZA	New Zealand Archives
NZPD	*New Zealand Parliamentary Debates*
PAC	Public Archives of Canada
PRO	Public Record Office (London)

Preface

1 Carter, 1947: ch. 5; Bassett, 1952
2 Thorne, 1972
3 Chester and Willson, 1968
4 Garner, 1978. He was appointed to the Dominions Office in 1930 and after being private secretary to a succession of Secretaries of State for Dominion Affairs, became Deputy High Commissioner for Britain in Canada and India and crowned his career by becoming Permanent Under-Secretary of State at the Commonwealth Relations Office and the Commonwealth Office. *Who's Who* 1974. Lord Garner clearly has had to use his memory more in the earlier section of the book, because of the lack of documentary material. He is more detailed on the Commonwealth Office.
5 Feiling, 1947:362; Wrench, 1955:374; *The Times*, 1952:922, 949, 1003, 1005
6 Watt, 1961–63:266, 272

7 Carlton, 1972:59–77; Ovendale, 1975. The latter appears, however, to rely too heavily on British sources and is not always either accurate or reliable on the Dominions—at least Australia.

Introduction

1 The source for the Silver Jubilee celebrations is *The Times* 7 May 1935. For the writing on the wall, see Daniel chapter 5, the Moffatt translation of the Bible.

Chapter 1

1 Barnett, 1972:72
2 The general history of the idea of a 'Commonwealth' is taken from Mansergh, 1969:19–25. Mansergh dates the beginning of the Commonwealth from the period between the Durham Report and the British North America Act—i.e. between 1839 and 1867. This seems to me to be the final stage of *imperial* development, not the beginning of a new era, which I place in the last decade of the nineteenth century and the first of the twentieth.
3 Kendle, 1967:34–35
4 Sales, 1971
5 Judd and Sliner, 1982:19
6 W. Y. Elliott, reviewing A. Berridale Keith's book *The Sovereignty of the British Dominions* in *American Political Science Review* 24, 1930:981; Holland, 1981:58
7 Mansergh, 1969:238
8 This and the following quotation come from Barnett, 1972:202, 207
9 ibid:36, 43 and 60. e.g. '. . .the generation of boys who were to reach leading places in British life in the 1920s and 1930s were the products of the public school at this period of greatest regimentation, stuffiest self-satisfaction and conformity, and most torpid intellectual life. . .' (p. 36).
10 Gallagher, 1982:128, 84. Hughes to Cook 15 July 1921 quoted in Poynter, 1970:241
11 Barnett, 1972:213–15. In 1930 German route mileage was 17 900 miles, compared with 23 005 miles for the British Empire. The Germans carried 93 126 passengers, the British Empire 58 261.
12 Carlton, 1972:73–74
13 Lissington, 1972:72
14 PRO DO 114/32 no. 321; 41 no. 225
15 PRO DO 114/49 and 52 and FO 627/51 and 52. For George V, Simon Papers 14 June 1934 FO 800 289/130–135
16 Imperial Conference 1930 E(30) Series Memoranda E(30)41. Summary of Proceedings Section VI(h) PRO CAB 32/81
17 Garner, 1978:10–14
18 PRO FO 627 U556/556/750 (vol. 58). For a discussion of the value of the meetings, see Garner, 1978:76–78. It was symptomatic of the tensions within the Commonwealth which weakened it that, due to Mackenzie King's opposition, weekly meetings of the High Commissioners in

London were discontinued after 1926 until the deterioration of the European situation in the late 1930s.
19 Palmer, 1934:16
20 Garner, 1978:34; see also Holland, 1981:72-73
21 Palmer, 1934:18
22 Holland, 1981:41-45, 56, 72
23 Interview with Lord Garner, 10 December 1974. See also his book, 1978:29-30 and Holland, 1981:45-46
24 Middlemas and Barnes, 1969:671
25 Blaxland, 1964:170, 242
26 Interview with Malcolm MacDonald, 15 October 1974. Interview with Lord Garner
27 Thorne, 1972:93
28 Blaxland, 1964:262-63; Mackintosh, 1965; Harkness, 1970:208; Middlemas and Barnes, 1969:683; Garner, 1978:19-25, 29, 140-42, 145-47, 173; Holland, 1981:172; interview with Lord Garner
29 ibid. It may be that the closure of some important Dominions Office files is partly intended to cover up the deficiencies in the office as well as to keep silence on touchy matters. In either case the closure is disgraceful. See PRO DO 121, a series of files which cover correspondence with British government representatives overseas, minutes of meetings held with the PM, etc. There are more files 'closed' in this section than in any other I have found. DO 121/2, simply dated 1933-B, is 'closed for 50 years'.
30 Letter to the author from Richard Snelling 25 February 1974
31 PRO FO 371 A6447/359/2
32 PRO FO 627 U679/679/750 (vol. 45)
33 Palmer, 1934:38
34 The section on Skelton is derived from Hillmer, 1973:46-48; Mackintosh, 1965; Veatch, 1975:19
35 Skelton to Keenleyside 27 April 1934 PAC Department of External Affairs Papers, vol. 1608
36 PAC Bennett papers, vol. 247:164784; 217:141647, and passim
37 PAC Bennett papers, vol. 218:142540; 217:141684-85, 141691-92; Rowell papers, vol. 8:6059-62
38 PRO AIR 8/114, Imperial Conference 1930, Stenographic Notes of Plenary Meetings, First meeting 1 October 1930; Williams, 1971:38-39; Wood, 1940:101-6; 1948:13-14
39 Ross, 1972:28-29, from which the immediately following account is taken
40 PRO CID 358-C 'Imperial Defence as Affecting New Zealand' CAB 5/7
41 MacGibbon, 1971:51-52; Lissington, 1972:21-24
42 For Wilford, Scholefield, 1940: vol. 2, 507-8; MacGibbon, 1971:85, 87-88; interview with McCombs. The New Zealand High Commissioner did not get copies of communications between the New Zealand government and the British (via the Governor-General) unless he was required to take some specific action. As a result, he was cut off from a close knowledge of his government's policy. New Zealand governments seemed to repose little trust in their High Commissioners. Palmer, 1934:47

43 Neale, 1975: Appendix 2; Palmer, 1934:42
44 *CPD* 136:1496–97, 21 October 1932
45 Interview with Lord Garner
46 Barnett, 1972, from which the following account is taken. For quotations see pp. 74, 80 and 232.
47 PRO CAB 21/736; Higham, 1962:266; Johnson, 1960:195
48 Stacey, 1981:132–33
49 Meaney, 1976:passim
50 McCarthy, 1976:8–9, 152 n.7
51 For Jellicoe, Bassett, 1952:289–90. For Wilford, NZA PM 111/17/8(i) 10 February 1930; 111/17/5 (i)
52 'Naval Appreciation of the Situation in 1931' 7 April PRO ADM 116/2826
53 PRO CP 100(31) CAB 24/220, Appendix I
54 PRO CID 358-C CAB 5/7
55 Thorne, 1972:209; 68–69; Postan, M. M. (1952) *British War Production (History of the Second World War; United Kingdom Civil Series)*, London: HMSO and Longmans, p. 5; Webster C. and Frankland N. eds. (1961), *The Strategic Air Offensive Against Germany 1939–1945 (History of the Second World War; United Kingdom Military Series)* vol.IV, London: HMSO, Appendix 7, p. 103; Taylor, 1965:229, 331
56 PRO CAB 21/368 29 October 1930
57 PRO ADM 116/2986 and 2787
58 PRO AIR 9/56 no.17; 5/1130 *Historical Narrative of Eastern Air Command RCAF* p. 27; McCarthy, 1976:21–32, 42; PRO AIR 9/56 no. 21
59 PRO ADM 116/3204; New Zealand *Appendix to the Journal of the House of Representatives* 1932, III, H-19; Barnett, 1972:217–18
60 ibid:205; *NZPD* 234:326
61 *Round Table* 24, 1934:711; Young, 1952:177; Middlemas and Barnes, 1969:744–46; Heller, R. (1971) 'East Fulham Revisited', *Journal of Contemporary History* 6, 3, pp. 172–96; Shay, 1977:57 n.25
62 PRO ADM 116/3391
63 McIntyre, 1974:2 from which much of the immediately following material is taken
64 PRO ADM 116/2582
65 Meeting of 16 October 1930 PRO CAB 32/91;
    Meeting of 28 November 1930 PRO CAB 32/81;
    PRO CID 354-C, also 1082-B pp. 4–5 CAB 5/7
66 Hankey to Harding 29 November 1934 PRO CAB 63/78;
    PRO Imperial Conference 1930 'E (30)' Series Memoranda, CAB 32/81

Chapter 2
1 Thorne, 1972:42–43; Carter, 1947:167; Keith Officer in the Australian Department of External Affairs 11 November 1931 AA A981 China 114 pt.1, folder 5/12
2 Mowatt, 1955:386–412, 669–70
3 Thorne, 1972:149. See also ibid:150–52 for British governmental opinion.

4 ibid:92. See also Mowatt, 1955:414; Marquand, 1977:693–701.
5 Barnett, 1972:67
6 Middlemas and Barnes, 1969:689. See also 742–43, 880.
7 Macleod, 1960:163
8 ibid:164; Thorne, 1972:94
9 ibid:95
10 Kordt to Dirksen 29 August 1938 Dirksen, H. von (1948) *Dirksen Papers* Moscow: International Publications, vol. 2, no. 5
11 Quoted by Feiling, 1947:249
12 Watt, 1961–63:270
13 Mowatt, 1955:417–19; PRO CAB 23
14 PRO Cabinet 75 (31) CAB 23/69
15 Lord Reading impressed on Sir Francis Lindley in Japan that in making representations it did so 'on the understanding that other friendly governments were acting similarly' and on the initiative of the French, not itself. PRO FO 405/269, no.36. See Simon's speech to the House of Commons 25 November 1931 Bassett, 1952:613
16 Simon to MacDonald 17 November 1931 Simon Papers, PRO FO 800/285; Thorne, 1972:191; PRO CP 294 (31) CAB 24/224; Cabinet 81 (31) CAB 23/69
17 Thorne, 1972:152 (for quotation), 191–92. The Cabinet minutes for the 15 November meeting are odd. They simply mention 'a short discussion' without details and then give a long resumé of Simon's memorandum. For opinion on sanctions, Drummond to Simon 24 November 1931 *DBFP* Second Series VIII/773; Cecil to Simon 13 November 1931 PRO FO Simon Papers 800/285; Hankey 23 February 1932 PRO CAB 21/368
18 Bassett, 1952:72–90: Mowatt, 1955:421
19 Thorne, 1972:211–12, 244–46; Middlemas and Barnes, 1969–729: Roskill, 1974:29–30.
20 Sinclair, 1959:247; interview with T. H. McCombs, High Commissioner of New Zealand in London, 21 October 1974. See Forbes' entry in *Who's Who in New Zealand* (n.d. but c.1932), p. 168. This goes into great—not to say amusing—detail about his farming activities.
21 Oliver, 1960:178
22 Berendsen to Knowles 4 May 1932 NZA FA 264/2/7 (vi)
23 Letter 20 October 1931 NZA FA 268/2/11(i)
24 NZA PM 111/12/8(ii)
25 Interview, cited
26 Lissington, 1972:81, 84
27 *Round Table* 23, 1933:662, 663
28 Clark to Thomas 23 February 1932 PRO FO 371 F2521/1/10
29 *Round Table* 23, 1933:663
30 PAC Department of External Affairs Papers, vols. 1606–8; Bennett Papers, vol. 245:163287–89; PRO DO 114/32, p. 125
31 The quotations come, in order, from *Round Table* 23, 1933: 401; Wilbur, 1969:5; Stacey, 1981:122. For a caricature of Bennett and a contemporary analysis of him, Bothwell and Hillner eds., 1975:85–87
32 Hillner, 1973; Pearson, 1973:75–76; Stacey, 1981:123–24
33 1 February 1932 PRO FO 371 W1265/10/98

34 Marler to Skelton, 22 February 1932; PAC Department of External Affairs Papers, vol. 1606; Marler to Bennett, 1 August 1931, PAC Bennett Papers, vol. 249:166408–10
35 Letter, 11 June 1931, PRO FO 627, vol. 750
36 Letter to Mackenzie King, 1 August 1935 and despatch 25 October 1935. PAC King Papers, vol. 208:179461–65 and 179554–59; K. P. Kirkwood 'Diplomatic Journal' 1934, p. 84; Kirkwood Papers, vol. 5. For Marler's appointment PRO DO 35/76 and 77. For the trade commissioners PRO FO 627, vols. 35 and 36 and PAC Bennett Papers, vols 216–18:142916–51; also Holland, 1981:84–85
37 PAC Department of External Affairs Papers, vol. 1606; Bennett Papers, vol. 247: 164625–67
38 PAC Bennett Papers, vol. 247; 164702–42
39 Skelton to Marler, 23 January 1932, PAC Department of External Affairs Papers, vol. 1606
40 Kirkwood 'Diplomatic Journal' 6 June 1932
41 PAC Department of External Affairs Papers, vol. 1606
42 *CPD* 132:709 cf. 272, 1074–75
43 Harrison Matley, 1969:74
44 Hankey to Harding, 28 November 1934, PRO CAB 63/70
45 Report by Malcolm MacDonald, January 1935, PRO Simon Papers, FO 800/290 pp. 147–48
46 Cowen, 1965:9
47 ibid:58
48 Edwards, Melbourne *Herald* 25 July 1964, p. 5
49 24 July 1930 AA MP 1049/5-1824/3/9
50 *DBFP* Second Series VIII/526 cf. AA A981 China 114 pt.1, folder 5/9
51 AA A981 China 114 pt.5. Interview with Lord Garner cited. Garner remarked that Bruce was an able man, who was nevertheless inclined to be abrasive with people and say things which, though true, gave unnecessary offence. He seemed insensitive to people's feelings.
52 AA A981 China 114 pt.1, folder 3/29 and 30; pt.2, folder 7/41; China 165 pt.1, folders 1/48, 2 and 3/15; China 166 pt.1, folder 1. MP 729/2-1877/7/46
53 Memoranda for 23 September, 28 October, 6 and 12 November 1931, 5 January 1932, in AA A981 China 114 pt.1, folders 3, 5 and 7
54 *Sydney Morning Herald* 9 January 1932, p. 11. Britain *Parliamentary Debates, House of Commons* vol. 262, col. 205
55 Thorne, 1972:208–9
56 Bassett, 1952:65
57 Thorne, 1972:206
58 Trotter, 1975:3
59 Journal of Admiral Kelly, p. 122
60 Parkes, O. (1932) *Janes Fighting Ships* London: Low
61 Thorne, 1972:64, 66, 206
62 *DBFP* Second Series IX/238 n. 2
63 Journal of Admiral Kelly, p. 120; PRO ADM 116/3112
64 PRO ADM 116/3615; Thorne, 1972:70; McCarthy, 1976:129–30
65 PRO CID 1082-B CAB 4/21

66 Simon to MacDonald 29 January 1932 PRO PREM 1/116. For Austen Chamberlain in parliament, Britain *Parliamentary Debates, House of Commons* vol. 262, col. 1514
67 1 February 1932 AA CP 360 pt.5
68 Riddell Diary; PAC Department of External Affairs Papers, vol. 1606; Bennett Papers vol. 217; 141352; PRO FO 371 F2206/1/10
69 PRO FO 371 F2521/1/10
70 For the debate and Bennett's statement, see Canada, House of Commons *Debates* 1932, vol. I, 19 February 1932:360 ff, 366–68
71 PAC Rowell Papers, vol. 8: 6056–66. For Perley at the Disarmament Conference, see PRO FO 411/15; Riddell Diary 13 February 1932
72 *DCER* 5/298–300, 304; PAC Bennett Papers, vol. 218: 142571
73 *DBFP* Second Series IX/600, 615 and 640. Price to Batterbee 29 February 1932 PRO FO 371 F2206/1/10
74 PAC Bennett Papers, vol. 218:142546–85
75 PAC Bennett Papers, vol. 247:164896–98
76 Veatch, 1975:115–17
77 AA A981 China 114 pt.2, folder 7/55; pt.3, folders 9/7, 9/27 and 13/1
78 *CPD* 133:76, 560–61; AA CP 360/7, 23 February 1932
79 *DBFP* Second Series IX/640 n.2; PRO CP 89(32) CAB 24/228; Britain *Parliamentary Debates, House of Commons* vol. 261, cols. 270, 827; *DCER* 5/303
80 25 November 1931 PRO Cabinet 81(31) CAB 23(69)
81 27 February 1932 CID 1083-B, 'Economic Sanctions and Japan', PRO CP 92(32) CAB 24/228
82 PRO Cabinet 14(32) CAB 23/70; CAB 27/482
83 PRO Cabinet 12(32) CAB 23/70
84 PRO CAB 2/5
85 Roskill, 1974:27
86 Riddell Diary
87 Telegrams on 26 and 27 February 1932, PAC Department of External Affairs Papers, vol. 1606
88 PRO CAB 27/482
89 Thorne, 1972:233

Chapter 3
1 Watt, 1961–63:272
2 AA A981 China 166 pt.1, folder 3 of 28 August 1932
3 PRO Cabinet 27/448; 21/344–47; Cabinet 79(31) CAB 23/69; remarks by Thomas 19 March 1931 CID 252/7 CAB 2/5
4 There were at least two meetings in January 1932, seven in February, three in June and three more in July. PRO ADM 116/2944, 2940 and 3272. Also FO 371 W1265-2294/10/98 and 5913/8382/1466/98. More meetings occurred in November 1932 and in 1933. Riddell Diary for 1933
5 *NZPD* 235:770 (28 February 1933); Knowles to Berendsen 5 March and Berendsen to Knowles 20 April 1932, NZA PM 111/12/18 pt.2; Wood, 1948:29; Ross, 1972:38

6 PRO Simon Papers FO 800/290
7 AA A981 China 114 pt.3 folder 11; *Sydney Morning Herald* 5 February 1932, p. 9
8 *CPD* 136:1516–17; Melbourne *Herald* 28 September 1932; Officer 22 February 1932 AA A981 China 114 pt.3, folder 13/2
9 Riddell, 1947:24–27
10 PAC Bennett Papers, vol. 245: 269341; Mackintosh, 1965:72
11 Mason, 1974:2–3
12 Canada, House of Commons *Debates* 19 February 1932:368
13 Carter, 1947:141; PRO DO 114/119–21
14 Cecil to Simon, PRO Simon Papers FO 800/285; Ministerial Committee on the Far East PRO CAB 27/482; Cabinet 17(32) CAB 23/70; Roskill, 1974:39
15 Skelton to Marler 23 January 1932 PAC Department of External Affairs Papers, vol. 1606; to Miss A. MacPhail 4 March 1932 Norman Robertson Papers, vol. 10, sheet 100; for Perley, Bennett Papers, vol. 245: 269342–44
16 AA A981 China 114 pt.4, folder 14/3, 7 March 1932; PRO FO 371 F8312/1/10; *DCER* 5/303, 305
17 *DBFP* Second Series IX/667
18 Thorne, 1972:213
19 *DCER* 5/307–8; Perley to Skelton 8 March 1932 PAC Bennett Papers, vol. 217:141995; Riddell Diary 8 March 1932
20 For this and the previous quotation, Thorne, 1972:213
21 Riddell Diary 7 March 1932; PRO FO 371 F2427/1/10; PAC Bennett Papers, vol. 218: 142491–93; *DCER* 5/309
22 PRO FO 371 F2427/1/10
23 Riddell to Skelton 11 March 1932 PAC Department of External Affairs Papers, vol. 1607. Riddell Diary 12 March 1932; Perley to Bennett 14 March 1932 PAC Bennett Papers, vol. 249:271911–15
24 Price to Batterbee 14 March 1932 PRO Simon Papers, FO 800/286, pp. 416–20; FO 371 F3453/1/10; Cabinet 18(32) CAB 23/70
25 Britain *Parliamentary Debates, House of Commons* vol. 263, cols. 257–58
26 Thomas' memorandum can be found in PRO CP 95(32) CAB 24/228. For the quotation, Mason, 1974:13–14
27 PRO FO 405/270 no. 168; Britain *Parliamentary Debates, House of Commons* vol. 263, col. 928
28 Carter, 1947:151
29 Report on the League Assembly 30 March 1932 NZA FA 264/2/7(v); Wilford to Forbes 5 July 1932 NZA PM 111/12/18(ii); 26 July 1932 FA 114/3/2(v); Forbes to Wilford 13 August 1932 PM 111/12/18(iv)
30 Forbes to Wilford 21 July 1932 NZA FA 114/2/2(ii); 114/7/2; Knowles to Berendsen 23 September 1932 PM 111/12/8(ii)
31 Keith Officer circulated a memorandum on the matter on 26 April 1932. AA A981 Japan 101
32 9 March 1932 AA A981 China 114 pt.3, folder 14/7; A981 Japan 148 for Duffy's covering letter 9 May 1932 and the Australian copy of CID 1083-B 'Economic Sanctions Against Japan' March 1932; PRO CP 92(32) CAB 24/228

33 PRO FO 371 W8382/1466/98 dated 22 July 1932
34 *CPD* 133:1225; AA A981 China 165 pt.1, folder 3/33; 166 pt.1, folders 2/7, 3/17, 22 and 24
35 The Australian cable can be found in PRO FO 371 F6200/1/10. For the debate on the wording of the reply, PRO DO 114/40, pp. 177–78. The reply is in *DBFP* Second Series X/626.
36 PRO DO 114/40 pp. 178–80
37 AA A981 China 166 pt.1, folder 3/32; Japan 148 pt.1
38 AA A981 China 165 pt.1 folder 3/34 (2 September); 166 pt.1, folder 3/41 (6 September), folder 4 (19 and 20 September); PRO FO 371 F6784 and 6919/1/10; *CPD* 136:2167
39 Canada, House of Commons *Debates* 7 April 1932:1825–26; 25 May 1932:3435–40; Mansergh, 1952:114 n.1
40 Marler still supported the Japanese and thought that the Lytton Report was unfair to them. Marler to Bennett 25 October and 9 December 1932 PAC Bennett Papers, vols 216: 141240–43 and 248:165274–318
41 'The Lytton Report, Japan and the League of Nations' 19 November 1932 *DBFP* Second Series XI/53; for the Cabinet, PRO Cabinet 62(32) CAB 23/73
42 PRO FO 371 F8312/1/10. The incident is partly covered in *DBFP* Second Series XI/58 and 63 and printed in DO 114/40 pp. 180–82. The *aide-memoire* can be found in PRO FO 371 F8265/1/10. For Simon's memorandum, see *DBFP* Second Series XI/53.
43 PAC Bennett Papers, vol. 217:141432
44 Wilford to Forbes NZA FA 114/3/2(v) 21 November 1932; PRO FO 371 F8338/1/10; 8365/1/10; Wood, 1948:16
45 PRO Cabinet 64(32) CAB 23/73
46 PRO FO 371 F8616/1/10
47 Bassett, 1952:288–89. Bassett gives the full text of the speech in an appendix, pp. 627–33
48 Thorne, 1972:332–33
49 Carter, 1947:159
50 Cahan to Bennett 9 December 1932 PAC Bennett Papers, vol. 429: 272783
51 PRO FO 371 8220/1/10. PAC Bennett Papers, vol. 217: 141825–33; *DCER* 5/325
52 AA A981 Appendix D to League of Nations Special Assembly 1932–1933, General Report by Bruce
53 Thorne, 1972:333
54 Veatch, 1975:119; Riddell, 1947:73–74; Lower, 1941:21–22
55 Mason, 1974:20–21; Riddell, 1947:75; PAC Bennett Papers, vol. 430: 273236–38; King Papers, vol. 338: 29129–35; *DBFP* Second Series XI/89
56 PAC Bennett Papers, vol. 217: 141796; 219: 142504–8; *DCER* 5/317
57 Canada, House of Commons *Debates* 1932–1933, vol. II, 18 and 21 November 1932: 1368–70
58 Cahan to King 23 July 1943 PAC King papers, vol. 338:29129–35
59 *DCER* 5/320, 327; Riddell Diary 7 February 1933
60 *DCER* 5/322; Sheddon AA A981 China 166 pt.2, folder 5/17; Report by Bruce on the Assembly debate 8–11 December 1932 AA A981 League of Nations, Special Assembly 1932–1933, General pp. 51–54; Bruce to

Lyons 8 December 1932 AA China 166 pt.2, folder 5/12
61 Eastman, 1946:93
62 Wilford's report to Forbes 30 December 1932 NZA FA 264/2/7 pt.9; AA A981 China 114 pt.3, folders 11 and 13
63 Lower, 1941:17–21; Veatch, 1975:124; PAC Bennett Papers, vols. 429:272783; 218:42509–10; *DBFP* Second Series XI/113, 161; *DCER* 5/326; Riddell Diary 14 February 1933; PRO DO 35/141(6010-370)
64 Mason, 1974:23–24; *DCER* 5/318, 319; PAC Bennett Papers, vol. 430:273236–38
65 *DCER* 5/327, 330; Riddell, 1947:31,77; Finlayson, n.d:297; Riddell to Skelton 14 December 1932 Department of External Affairs Papers, vol. 1607; Herridge to Skelton 17 December 1932 Department of External Affairs Papers, vol. 723
66 Mason, 1975:114
67 *DCER* 5/326; Mason, 1974:28
68 *DCER* 5/329. For Skelton's problems, ibid:326; Finlayson, n.d:297; Bennett to Riddell 12 December 1932 PAC Department of External Affairs Papers, vol. 1607; Skelton to Riddell 14 December 1932 PAC Papers of the Under Secretary of State for External Affairs, vol. 723
69 Riddell Diary 7 February 1933 *DCER* 5/330; Canada, House of Commons *Debates* 1932–33, vol. II, 30 January 1933: 1664; vol. IV, 16 May 1933:5059–68
70 PRO Cabinet 7(33) and 10(33) CAB 23/75; Simon to Cabinet 11 December 1932 PRO CP 431(32) CAB 24/235; document CP 42(33) CAB 24/238
71 *DBFP* Second Series XI/321, 336; PRO FO 371 F1102/33/10
72 Bruce to the Australian government 22 February 1933 AA A981 China 125 pt.2, folder 22; PRO DO 35/141 (6010-449); Robertson memorandum 18 February 1933 PAC External Affairs Papers, vol. 1608. For Skelton, Veatch, 1975:123
73 PAC Bennett Papers, vols. 217:142166–67; 218:141450, 142176, 142592; *DCER* 5/336,337; *DBFP* Second Series XI/352
74 Riddell Diary 7 February 1933; *DCER* 5/330; Skelton to Riddell 19 January 1933 PAC Department of External Affairs Papers, vol. 1608; Bennett Papers, vol. 217:142171, 142182, 141447–48; PRO FO 371 F1882/33/10; DO 35/141 (6010-449)
75 *DCER* 5/342–3, cf. PAC Bennett Papers vol. 217:142217–19, 142239–48
76 PRO FO 371, vol. 17390; AA A981 China 125 pt.2, folder 22/1, 17 January 1933; *CPD* 38:582, 28 March 1933; AA A981 Japan 101, 26 April 1932 and 13 June 1933
77 Bruce to Prime Minister 30 January 1933 AA A981 China 125 pt.2, folder 22/3
78 AA A981 China 125 pt.2, folder 22; *CPD* 138:139, 9 March 1933
79 This chain of events can be found in AA A981 Manchukuo 7, from which the story is told. See 14 June, 25 July and 10 August 1933.
80 PRO FO 371, vol. 17347; Latham to Bruce 8 July 1933 AA A981 League of Nations 14th Assembly, Agenda
81 *NZPD* 235:770
82 PRO FO 627, vol. 53

83 PRO CAB 63/79; FO F372/T9440 & 9652/557/384 vol. 3006
84 1 February 1934 PRO FO 372, vol. 3006; Canada, House of Commons *Debates* 1934, vol. I, 12 February 1934, p. 492. (For the whole debate, see pp. 486–98); Senate *Debates* 1934, pp. 237–53, 280–92, 326–42, 345–53, 365–68, 374–83, 393–96, 397–99, 406 ff, 434 ff, 447 ff
85 *Round Table* 24,1933:85–90: Harrison-Matley, 1969:337
86 *NZPD* 239:7–15, 7 August 1934; 240:151–54, 26 September 1934
87 The Foreign Office part of the CID Paper, 'Imperial Defence Policy, 1933' 19 May 1933 CID 1112-B, p. 51, PRO CAB 4/22
88 Carter, 1947:137
89 Temperley, A. C. (1938) *The Whispering Gallery of Europe* London: Collins, p. 319
90 Bruce to Minister for External Affairs 23 February 1933 AA A981 China 114 pt.5, folder 24/4 and AA A981 League of Nations 14th Assembly, Agenda
91 Veatch, 1975:123–24, 134–35
92 Carter, 1947:164–65
93 11 December 1932 PAC Department of External Affairs Papers, vol. 1607; Cahan to Bennett 19 October 1932 Bennett Papers vol. 430: 273236–38
94 *NZPD* 240:152, 26 September 1934
95 PRO DO 114/47 no. 4; 26 May 1933, PRO Cabinet 37(33) CAB 23/76
96 Thorne, 1972:141 n.2, 232–33, 294; PRO FO 627 U719/26/750, in vol. 51
97 PRO FO 371 F5189/5189/61. See Letter of Robin Hankey to Sir Maurice 27 September 1934 PRO CAB 63/70.
98 Banff Conference Supplement in the *Journal of Pacific Relations* October 1933; Report to the Foreign Office PRO FO 371 vol. 17148; Trotter, 1975:29–32
99 Watt, 1961–63:273

Chapter 4

1 Thorne, 1972:190
2 Hankey in PRO CAB 21/736; MacDonald 19 October 1932 Cabinet 53(32) CAB 21/72; for the three ministers, 20 April 1934 CP 113(34) CAB 24/249
3 See two long telegrams 16 September 1932 PRO CAB 21/354. For support over the proposals to ban poison gas, Cabinet 61(32) CAB 23/73
4 Meetings of Commonwealth delegates to the Disarmament Conference 9 July 1932 PRO ADM 116/3272; 30 September 1933 PRO FO 411/17. For the controversy over bombers, PRO CID 358-C CAB 5/7; 3–4 June CAB 24/230; 6 June CAB 27/505; Canada at the Disarmament Conference PRO FO 371 W2331/40/98. For Australia, PRO AIR 9/56 nos 20, 22 & 32; 23 May 1932 AIR 2/648; McCarthy, 1971a:24–25
5 10 February 1933 PRO CAB 21/379; Shedden, 19 June 1932 PRO ADM 116/2940; Wilford warned the CID that the Model Treaty Preventing War might lessen the ability of the British navy to defend the Pacific (7 December 1931 PRO CAB 2/5) and in Geneva opposed the American

suggestion that cruiser tonnage should be reduced by a quarter (PRO ADM 116/2940)
6   PRO FO 800/285; ADM 116/2940; FO 371 W7420/1466/98; Simon Papers, FO 800/287; Lyons to Simon 18 August 1932 CAB 21/354; Latham *CPD* 135:1069–79 and Australia *Parliamentary Papers, General, Session 1932–33–34* vol. IV, pp. 329–54
7   Meetings 3–4 June 1932 PRO CP 194(32) CAB 24/230; 1 July 1932 NZA PM 111/12/18 pt. 2; PRO CAB 23/72
8   PRO FO 371 W12575/10/98; 371 W12637/10/98. This can be found also in NZA PM 111/12/18 pt. 2; Simon Papers, PRO FO 800/291, pp. 117–25
9   PRO FO 371 W12547/10/98, W618/40/98, W3378/40/98, W14211/40/98
10 First meeting of the DCOS 8 February 1932 PRO CAB 54/1
11 'The Situation in the Far East', Deputy Chiefs of Staff Sub-Committee PRO CID 1084-B CAB 4/21
12 PRO CID 375-C CAB 5/7
13 PRO CID 1087-B CAB 4/21
14 Roskill, 1974: vol. I, p. 632; vol. II, p. 307 n.1; vol. III, p. 36; Watt, 1965:5–6; Hankey to Cecil 31 October 1933, Cecil of Chelmswood Papers, British Library, 51088
15 PRO Cabinet 19(32) CAB 23/70; CID 255(5) CAB 2/5; 28 July 1932 PRO CAB 21/368
16 PRO Cabinet 50(32) CAB 23/72
17 Barnett, 1972:411
18 COS 107th meeting PRO CAB 53/4
19 31 March 1933 PRO CID 1103-B CAB 4/22; memorandum to MacDonald 5 April 1933 PRO CAB 21/402
20 Eayrs, 1964:275. The following account is taken from Eayrs, unless otherwise stated.
21 PRO FO 273 T4114/439/384 (vol. 3096)
22 Eayrs, 1964:316–17; 1965:134
23 Major Goldenstedt, reported on 7 September 1933 AA A981 Japan 101; Thorne, 1972:398
24 Lissington, 1972:85
25 *The Times* 19 May 1932; PRO CID 1112-B 'Imperial Defence Policy', pp. 99–100, CAB 4/22. See also CID 371-C CAB 5/7.
26 Durnan to Clarke 14 April 1933 PRO CAB 21/414; Lissington, 1972:86–88. She quotes from a telegram in the New Zealand Archives which appears to have been lost; NZA Air 102/1/1
27 NZA PM 156/6/26; *NZPD* 239:872; MacGibbon, 1971:165–66; *The New Zealand Official Year Book 1938* p. 216; Appendixes to the *Journal of the House of Representatives* vols III of 1932, 1933, 1934–35 and 1935
28 NZA Air 102/1/1; Lyons to Forbes 3 October 1933 N22/4/12; MacGibbon, 1971:184
29 R. F. Durnan to Admiral Commanding the New Zealand Squadron 15 October 1934 NZA NA 22/4/13(ii)
30 MacGibbon, 1971:184 and 223
31 ibid:234
32 NZA G5/108
33 PRO ADM 116/3472

34 PRO CAB 63/73
35 Pearce to Hankey 15 February 1932 PRO CAB 63/70; CAB 21/397
36 PRO CAB 63/73; Latham to Pearce 21 April 1932 ANL Pearce Papers, MS 213 Bundle 5 items 125–7; Latham to Hankey 27 May 1932 printed in CID 372-C, Appendix I, PRO CAB 53/22
37 103rd Meeting of the Chiefs of Staff Sub-Committee Minutes PRO CAB 53/4; cf. Latham to Pearce 3 June 1932 ANL MS 213 Bundle 4 item 31
38 'The Defence of Australia', PRO CID 372-C CAB 4/22; also in AA A981 Defence 59 pt. 1. Even in 1905 and 1906 the Colonial Defence Committee and the CID had decided that the maximum scale of attack to be feared by Australia was that of raids by cruisers. Meaney, 1976:138; for parts, PRO CAB 5/7
39 Haining to Macready June and July 1932 PRO CAB 21/397
40 McCarthy, 1971a:21
41 For Bruce's tactful comments to the CID 8 November 1932, PRO CID 257(4) CAB 2/5. For his letters to Pearce 25 November 1932, Australian War Memorial Pearce Papers, Box 121, Bundle no. 4; Hankey to Batterbee 30 September 1932 PRO CAB 21/397; 'Imperial Defence Policy 1933' PRO CID 1112-B CAB 4/22, p. 108
42 256th meeting of the CID, CAB 2/55
43 Hasluck, P. (1952) *The Government and the People 1939–1941* Canberra: Australian War Memorial, p. 40; AA A664/464/401/818A; *CPD* 136:1810–18, 2093–95
44 The British Admiralty as early as 1923 had suggested that Australia develop a northern port, and Darwin had been chosen by 1924, but little had been done. A committee of officers at last inspected the site and produced a report in March 1932. By 1934 some equipment had been shifted from Thursday Island, storage tanks and a permanent garrison provided. AA MP 1049/9-1856/5/198 and 206; 1804/2/2; 667/202/395; MP 341/1-704/1/16; CP 290/14 bundle 1
45 PRO DO 35/182 (6702-10); CAB 63/71
46 PRO ADM 116/2910; Cabinet 1(33) CAB 23/75; DO 35/167 (6254-92); CAB 21/397; McCarthy, 1976:52–54
47 Report of 6 September 1933 PRO CAB 21/397; Harrison-Matley, 1969:342–46
48 ibid:352; *CPD* 142:4712, 17 November 1933
49 AA A981 Defence 275 pt.3; PRO DO 35/182(6702-17)
50 AA MP 431/1-704/1/12
51 Andrews, 1977, from which the following account is taken
52 The story is told from Thorne, 1970; *DBFP* Second Series XI/360; PRO CP(42) 33 CAB 24/238; CAB 21/379; Cabinet 11(33) CAB 23/75
53 Interview with Lord Garner cited
54 Eden told the Canadian Advisory Officer at Geneva, Riddell, that he 'disapproved very much' of the decision. Riddell Diary 1 May 1933
55 PRO DO 114/48 no. 70
56 Eayrs, 1964:313–15
57 PAC Department of External Affairs Papers, vol. 1472:515; Bennett Papers, vol. 217:141852, 141889
58 PAC Department of External Affairs Papers, vol. 1657:247; Bennett

Papers, vol. 250:166533; Canada, House of Commons *Debates* 1 March 1933, p. 2616; *DCER* 5/351
59 ibid., 350, 353; PAC Bennett Papers, vols 217: 142220–25; 250: 166532; 276: 184581–86; Department of External Affairs Papers, vol. 1657:247
60 ibid., vol. 1608, McNaughton memorandum of 8 March; *DCER* 5/356
61 PAC Bennett Papers, vols. 216: 141308–9; 218:142522–24; 248: 165535–37; PRO FO 371 W7296 and W8167/40/98 in vol. 17364
62 PRO FO 371 W12546/10/98; McCarthy, 1971b:167–69
63 Minutes of the Defence Committee 11 April 1930 AA A2031 vol. I; PRO CAB 63/71; Laverack, 1933
64 AA A2031, Minutes of the Defence Committee, vol. 3; MP 729/2-1855/1/65
65 Minutes of CID Meeting 6 April 1933 PRO CID 258(5) CAB 2/5
66 111th meeting of the COS 20 June 1933 PRO CAB 53/4; Cabinet 50(33) CAB 23/77; Chatfield to Hankey 15 September 1933 CAB 21/369; COS Annual Review for 1933 CID 1113-B CAB 4/22
67 CID Meeting 9 November 1933 PRO CID 261(1) CAB 2/6
68 Watt, 1965:85
69 Minutes of the Defence Requirements Sub-Committee PRO CAB 16/109

Chapter 5
1 PRO ADM 116/3121–22; AIR 2/1357
2 Burgess Watson to the Governor-General of New Zealand 28 February 1934 NZA G 48-N/10
3 *Round Table* 24, 1934:686; PRO CID Minutes 264(3) CAB 2/6; *NZPD* 238:199; 239:849–51
4 PRO DO 35/182(6702-20); Letters of 17 November and 13 December 1934 CAB 63/70; Australia, Minutes of the Defence Committee, vol. 3, 2 March 1934 AA A2031; CP 290/14 bundle 1, 10 April 1934
5 AA A1967/309 Box 32 item 3
6 AA A981 Far East 2 (28 June 1932); CP 290/14 bundle 1
7 Melbourne and Fry, Conference of the Queensland Branch of the Australian Institute of International Affairs 20 and 21 October 1934; 'Report on Trade Between Australia and Japan', p. 3, AA CP 290, item 10; PRO DO 35/181 (6635-28, 29 & 33) FO 371 2839/1/10; 627 U184/72/750; Megaw, 1973:251; Willis, 1975: 2; 27 July 1933, Lyons Papers, AA CP 30/3 Box 3, folder 19
8 AA A981 Far East 5 pt. 1 (Lyons to Bruce 13 December 1933); pt. 2 (18 December); pt. 8 (cable to Bruce 30 January 1934); PRO DO 35/181(6635-28, 29 & 33); FO 371 2839/1/10
9 AA A981 Far East 5 pt. 7; *Sydney Morning Herald* 4 December 1933, p. 9
10 AA A981 Far East 5 pt. 16
11 Australia *Parliamentary Papers, Session 1932–33–34* vol. IV, 'Australian Eastern Mission 1934'

12 AA A981 Far East 2 (letter of Lyons 13 February 1934); ibid. 5 pt. 1; PRO DO 35/181 (6635-1, 2); Willis, 1975:3–4
13 ibid; Latham to secretary 21 December 1933 AA A981 Far East 2; ibid. pt 5; Latham, 1962:80; PRO FO 371 F888/1/61; F3638/1/61
14 PAC Bennett Papers, vol. 245:163352–54, 163462–83; *The Times* 11 January 1934
15 *CPD* 144:327–28. PRO DO 35/181 (6635-60). Officer first of all assured the British that Lloyd was 'a kind of publicity officer for the Commonwealth government, having been previously connected with the press'. PRO DO 35/181 (6635-17). When Sir E. Lindley queried Lloyd's secret service work he was assured that it was simply internal, to deal with communists in Australia. FO 371 F662/1/61
16 Megaw, 1973:248–49
17 PRO DO 35/181 (6635–57)
18 Megaw, 1973:250
19 Trotter, 1974a:62
20 Dodd to Foreign Office 12 May 1934 PRO DO 35/181 (6635–57). The Foreign Office decided that this should not be sent to Australia or shown to Keith Officer. The story of Latham and Hirohita is largely taken from this account.
21 Official secret report of the Australian Eastern Mission, AA A981 Far East 5 pt. 16
22 PRO FO 371 F2856/1/61
23 Kennedy, 1969:320, 323
24 Latham, Confidential Report, p. 14; Cable from the British Consul-General in Canton, 12 June 1934, AA A981 Far East 5 pt. 9. See also his speech in Canton praising the Chinese for improved buildings and roads. PRO DO 35/181 (6635-56)
25 Crutchley to Harding PRO DO 35/181(6635-53); 'The Australian Eastern Mission, 1934; Report of the Right Honourable J. G. Latham' Australia *Parliamentary Papers Session 1932–33–34*, vol. IV: 446 and 452 (i.e. 10 & 16 of the report)
26 Dodd 19 May 1934 PRO DO 35/181 (6635-57); Kirkwood, 'Diplomatic Journal 1934', p. 50 PAC Kirkwood Papers vol. 5, 14 May 1934; Bennett Papers vol. 245:16344–61
27 Willis, 1975:5–6, 10; AA A981 Far East 3; PRO FO 371 vol. 18158; Cutlack, 1934
28 *CPD* 144:328
29 AA CP 290/1 item 10
30 Keenleyside to Ottawa 28 June 1934 PAC Bennett Papers, vol. 245:163506
31 Megaw, 1973:258
32 *Commonwealth Year Book* no. 28, 1935, p. 247; PRO DO 35/181 (6635A-3); Sissons, 1976
33 'Report on the International Position in the Far East' 30 June 1934 p. 14, AA CP 290/1 item 10
34 PRO FO 371 vol. 18160; DO 35/181(6635-66); Latham, 1962:81
35 PRO FO 371 F3676/1/61; DO 35/181(6635-66)

36 PRO CP 362(32) CAB 24/234; 11 September 1933 CAB 21/369; Cabinet (57) 33 CAB 23/77
37 PRO DRC 9 CAB 16/109; Roskill, 1974:87; PRO CID 1147-B CAB 4/23
38 Shay, 1977:33; Gibbs, 1976:118–20
39 PRO CP 77(34) CAB 24/248
40 Trotter, 1975:37–38
41 WO comments attached to letter Vansittart to CIGS 12 March 1934 PRO WO 32/2538
42 PRO CP 78(34) and 80(34) CAB 24/248; Cabinet 9(34) CAB 23/78; 19 March 1934 PRO CAB 21/700
43 Trotter, 1974a:65
44 PRO Cabinet 10(34) CAB 23/78
45 PRO Cabinet 18 and 19(34) CAB 23/79; Roskill, 1974:107
46 PRO DC(M) (32) CAB 16/110; interim report of the Ministerial Committee on the DRC report PRO CAB 21/388
47 PRO DC(M) (32) 45 CAB 16/110
48 PRO DC(M) (32) 120 CAB 16/111
49 PRO CAB 21/388
50 Hankey Papers, PRO CAB 63/49
51 Compare the Deputy Director of Military Operations and Intelligence on 88 pages of memoranda produced by the Foreign Office. He suggested that his two-foolscap-page summary was quite sufficient. 'I do not suggest that you read any of them.' So much for the efforts of the Foreign Office! PRO WO 32/2538
52 23 June 1934 PRO CAB 21/388
53 Minutes of the Ministerial Committee on Disarmament PRO CAB 16/110
54 In a letter to Baldwin, 30 July 1934, Hankey mentions he was worried by the remarks of Chamberlain at 'the recent' Ministerial Committee meeting. That would be Friday 27 July. (PRO CAB 21/398). In CAB 27/510 there is a draft copy of the report, with a covering letter that in order to get the report to the Cabinet in time for the meeting on Tuesday 31 July, it was necessary to send it out, even though the Ministerial Committee had not yet had time to consider it. One wonders if a sudden meeting, without minutes, was called.
55 Report by Ministerial Committee on Defence Requirements PRO CAB 27/504; Cabinet 31(34) CAB 23/79
56 Gibbs, 1976:125; Trotter, 1975:92 appears to misunderstand the significance of the decisions.
57 Roskill, 1974:110–11
58 Gibbs, 1976:99–102
59 Trotter, 1974a:71, 75–77; PRO Cabinet 32(34) CAB 23/79
60 PRO CP 223(34) CAB 24/250
61 Thorne, 1972:396
62 PRO FO 371 F6613/591/23
63 PRO DO 121/3; CAB 29/151; Cabinets 40 and 47(34) CAB 23/80
64 Trotter, 1974a:78; 1975:107–9
65 PRO Cabinet 41(34) CAB 23/80; Trotter, 1974a;80; Gibbs, 1976:156
66 PRO Cabinets 4, 5 and 9(35) CAB 23/81. For the Leith Ross mission

and the bureaucratic struggle between the Foreign Office and the Treasury, see Lowe, 1981:150–53

Chapter 6

1 Hankey had written to the Dominions Office, as to other government departments, asking for material to be incorporated in the report. The Dominions Office reply was to provide a couple of pages of general comment, but to advise that any references to the Dominions be kept in the main body of the report. No separate consideration was therefore given them. PRO CAB 21/369. For Lindley, CID 1111-B CAB 4/22; for Foreign Office, memorandum CP 77(34) CAB 24/248
2 PRO Cabinet 17(34) CAB 23/79; CAB 16/110; CAB 21/338
3 PRO CID minutes, 264(1) CAB 2/6. There was therefore a great difference between defence planning and the proposed British guarantee to Belgium, where the Cabinet Committee agreed that they could not make a declaration without consulting the Dominions first. 11 and 21 June 1934 PRO CAB 16/110
4 PRO CAB 21/389; Ministerial Committee on Defence Requirements 17 July 1934 CAB 16/110; Roskill, 1974:148–49. I have been unable to find the record of the correspondence between Lyons and the British government, either in Britain or Australia. It is discussed in a memorandum 30 July 1934 CAB 21/388.
5 PRO CAB 21/398
6 PRO Cabinet 31(34) CAB 23/79; 2 August 1934 CAB 21/398
7 On 3 December 1934 Wing Commander Hodsoll remarked that it was becoming difficult to keep the DRC report secret. PRO CAB 21/398. When this was reported to the Cabinet, however, it decided to postpone any decision until Hankey reported after his tour: . . . the extent, if any, to which the information contained in the Report should be communicated to the Dominions'. PRO Cabinet 45(34) CAB 23/80
8 The story is taken from PRO CAB 63/70; Trotter, 1974b
9 PRO CAB 21/398; Parr to Hankey 18 July 1934 CAB 63/77; minute on Durnan to Clarke 16 May 1933 CAB 21/414
10 PRO Cabinet 31(34) CAB 23/79
11 Hankey to MacDonald 3 August 1934 PRO CAB 21/388; Letters between Thomas and Hertzog over the three Protectorates November 1933 to July 1934 CP 197(34) CAB 24/250; PRO FO 372, vol. 3004
12 Hankey to MacDonald 3 August 1934 PRO CAB 21/388; Hankey to Baldwin 23 August CAB 63/66
13 Trotter, 1974b:324–25
14 PRO CAB 21/398; Britain *Parliamentary Debates, House of Commons* vol. 293, col. 1763; Hankey to Prime Minister 7 September 1934 PRO CAB 21/385
15 Earle Page, for example, merely remarked that the government was 'anxious to avail itself of the unique opportunity presented by the presence of Sir Maurice Hankey in this part of the world'. *CPD* 145:249

16 Hankey to MacDonald 7 September 1934 PRO CAB 21/385, also Diary CAB 63/67. Letters to the British High Commissioner in South Africa 5 July and 2 August 1934 CAB 63/69
17 PRO CAB 63/71; Hankey to Dill 30 November 1934 CAB 63/70
18 Hankey to Parkhill 15 November 1934 PRO CAB 21/386; CAB 63/67; Hankey to Dill 30 November 1934 PRO CAB 63/70
19 ibid.; Hankey to MacDonald 17 November 1934 PRO CAB 63/70
20 Diary PRO CAB 63/70; Hankey to MacDonald 26 October 1934 CAB 21/386; Minutes of the Defence Committee, vol. 3, AA A2031
21 Hankey to CIGS 31 January 1935 PRO CAB 21/386; 'Report . . . On Certain Aspects of Australian Defence' 15 November 1934 PRO CAB 21/386; Defence Committee Minute, no.54/1934 AA A981 Defence 59 pt. 1
22 PRO CAB 21/386; Diary PRO CAB 63/67
23 Hankey to Dill 30 November 1934 PRO CAB 63/70
24 Meetings of 19 October and 5 November 1934, PRO CAB 63/74; Trotter underestimates the element of deceit in Hankey's tour, especially in her book, 1975:94–96
25 Hankey to Harding 29 November 1934 PRO CAB 63/78
26 Hankey to Dill 2 December 1935 PRO CAB 21/414
27 NZA NA 22/4/13(ii); PRO CAB 63/77
28 Draft letter some time in December. This passage was apparently deleted later. PRO CAB 63/78
29 PRO CAB 63/67, 77 and 78; MacGibbon, 1971:186
30 Hankey to MacDonald 12 January 1935 PRO CAB 63/78 also 23 November 1934 NZA G5/67
31 Hankey to Dill 2 December 1934 PRO CAB 63/78
32 Fisher to Marsh 3 September 1934 CAB 63/79; 'Impressions of Canada, December 1934' PRO CAB 63/81
33 ibid.; Archer to Batterbee 1 November 1934 and to Hankey 14 November PRO CAB 63/79
34 Hankey to MacDonald 2 January and Vansittart to Hankey 14 January 1935 PRO CAB 63/81
35 'Impressions of Canadian Defence Policy', 'Impressions of Canada' and Hankey to Pearce 2 January 1935 PRO CAB 63/81; Pearce to Hankey 19 February 1935 CAB 63/70; CAB 36/3
36 PRO CAB 63/67; Canada, House of Commons *Debates* 1935, vol. 1, 21 and 24 January: 14 and 139
37 PRO CAB 63/79; DO 35/187 (7040-23)
38 PRO CAB 63/69
39 Thorne, 1972: 254, 256 n.2, 257–58
40 CID Minutes 266(2 & 6) PRO CAB 2/6 pt. 1
41 Britain, Parliamentary Papers, 1934–1935 *Commons* Vol. XIII, Accounts and Papers (2), pp. 803–812; *Parliamentary Debates, House of Commons* vol. 299, cols, 51–53
42 Latham to Pearce 19 December 1934, Pearce to Latham 21 December 1934: Latham Papers NLA
43 Trotter, 1974b:329
44 McCarthy, 1971a:26–28; Robertson, 1935

ENDNOTES

45 Parkhill to Hankey, 16 August 1935, PRO CAB 21/397; McCarthy, 1971b: 169; Hyde to Hankey, 27 March 1935, CAB 63/70
46 PRO DO 114/60:158–59; *CPD* 146:1088, 1273–74 (9 & 18 April 1935); Shedden to Hankey 27 August 1935 PRO CAB 21/397; Menzies to Minister for Defence 7 August 1939 AA MP 431/1 704/1/67; Long, G. (1952) *Australia in the War of 1939–45, To Benghazi* Canberra: Australian War Memorial, p. 16
47 McIntyre, 1974: 3; PRO CID Minutes 270(5) CAB 2/6
48 *NZPD* 241:79–83
49 NZA FA 101/1/4(i)
50 PRO FO 372 vol. 3098
51 Cables 17 April to 26 May 1935 Riddell Papers PRO DO 114/62 no. 152; Eayrs, 1965:16–27
52 PAC Bennett Papers, vols 249 to 251
53 PRO ADM 116/4080; Eayrs, 1964:278, 301–2
54 COS Annual Review 'Imperial Defence Policy' 1935 PRO CID 1181-B CAB 4/23
55 PRO CP 108(34) CAB 24/248; CAB 32/125
56 PRO FO 372 T3415/492/384 in vol. 3097
57 PRO COS 368 CAB 53/24
58 PRO COS 370 CAB 53/24; COS 141st meeting, CAB 53/5
59 PRO CID Minutes 269(2) CAB 2/6
60 This was stated on the cover, PRO 1181-B CAB 4/23.
61 Appreciation by Admiral Sir Frederick C. Dreyer, C-in-C China Station, 8 August 1935 PRO ADM 116/3338
62 Roskill, 1974: 94–95, 99–100; 17 October 1934 PRO CAB 63/79; 18 December 1934 PRO CAB 29/151
63 McCarthy, 1971a:132
64 Barnett, 1972:349
65 Second Meeting of British Commonwealth Prime Ministers 7 May 1935 PRO CAB 32/125; PM (35) (2) CAB 32/125
66 McCarthy, 1971a:134
67 Hankey to CIGS 31 January 1935 PRO CAB 21/386
68 PRO AIR 8/193
69 MacGibbon, 1971:175; Lissington, 1972:90
70 Hankey 25 April 1935 PRO AIR 8/193
71 McCarthy, 1971a:135

Chapter 7

1 PRO DO 35/182 (6702-3); *Round Table* 24, 1933:42–61
2 Watt, 1965:149
3 PRO DO 114/52 no. 127; FO 627 vol. 58
4 Wood, 1948:33
5 Meaney, 1976:205, 236, 238–39, 246
6 Hughes, 1935; Sissons, 1976:482; Hooker, 1956:30
7 Mansergh, 1969:271
8 Whiskard to Harding 28 November 1938 PRO AIR 9/56 no. 58
9 Meaney, 1976:233–35

10 MacGibbon, 1971:234
11 In May 1935 a Defence Policy and Requirements Committee was brought into existence 'to guide the DRC on the political assumptions on which its programme was to be based . . . '. Point in a lecture by Hankey PRO CAB 21/736. Also note by Hankey CP 187(35) CAB 24/257
12 PRO DPR(DR)9 which became part of CID 215-B in CAB 16/112; Higham, 1962:276; Howard, 1972:119
13 18th meeting of the DRC Sub-Committee of the CID, PRO CAB 16/112
14 Hankey to Howarth 13 December 1934 PRO CAB 63/70
15 Mansergh, 1952:59–60
16 12 and 17 April 1935 PRO DO 114/60 no. 25
17 PRO FO 372 vol. 3097
18 Higham, 1962:277
19 Meaney, 1976:259
20 *CPD* 107:1703

Bibliography

Unpublished official records
Public Record Office, London
DO 114 and 121	DO confidential prints
DO 35/181	Latham Mission to Japan and Debuchi Mission to Australia and New Zealand
DO 35/182	Defence of Australia
DO 35/186	Australia and Japan—Diplomatic
DO 35/187	Hankey's tour of the Dominions
CAB 2/5 and 6	Minutes of CID meetings
CAB 4/20 to 23	CID memoranda
CAB 16/109	Reports etc. of the Defence Requirements Committee
CAB 116/110	Cabinet Committee on Questions of Defence Requirements and the Disarmament Conference of 1932
CAB 16/111	CID—Defence Requirements Sub-Committee, 1934
CAB 16/112	CID—Defence Requirements Sub-Committee, 1935 onwards
CAB 23/68-82	Cabinet minutes 1931–35
CAB 21	Cabinet memoranda
CAB 24	Cabinet documents
CAB 27	Cabinet ministerial committees
CAB 32/125-6	The meetings of the British Commonwealth Prime Ministers, 1935.
CAB 53/22-4	COS memoranda 1930–35
CAB 53/3-5	COS, minutes of meetings 1929–36
CAB 54/1 and 3	Deputy COS minutes and memoranda
CAB 63/44-82	Hankey papers
PREM 1	Prime Minister's Office files
FO 371	General correspondence series
FO 372	'Dominions Intelligence' turning into 'Treaty Dept.' or T files
FO 627	'Dominions Information' or 'U' files
FO 410	Confidential prints (92–95 deal with Japan)
FO 800/285-8	Private papers of Sir John Simon
ADM 116	Assorted Admiralty papers
WO 32/2538	Assessment of the Far Eastern situation
WO 106/132-4	The defence of Singapore
AIR 2/1537	The Singapore Conference

Australian Archives, Canberra
A981   General Correspondence Series

China 49, 50, 94, 114, 125, 165, 166
Far East 5 (Pts 7–9) and 16 (Latham Mission)
Japan 101 Pt 2
Manchukuo 7
League of Nations 13th Anniversary 1932, Agenda, etc.
League of Nations Special Assembly 1932–33, general
CP 360/5 Cables from DO to Australia
CP 360/7 Cables from Australia to DO
A 2031 Minutes of the Defence Committee, vols 2 and 3
Australian Archives, Melbourne
MP 1049 Series 9   Department of the Navy, classified general correspondence 1921–39
MP 431 Series 1   Department of Defence, general correspondence 1931–39
MP 729 Series 2   Department of Defence, classified general correspondence 1906–36
Public Archives of Canada, Ottawa
R. B. Bennett Papers, MG 26K vols 216–18 (China) and 245–51 (Japan) 272, 276, 425, 429, 430, 882, 947
W. L. Mackenzie King papers, MG 26 J4, vol. 117
Papers of the Under-Secretary of State for External Affairs, RG 25 DI vol. 723
Department of External Affairs Papers, RG 25 GI vols 1472, 1606–8, 1657
Rowell papers MG 2711 D13, vol. 8
K. P. Kirkwood papers, MG 27 111 E3 vol. 5
Cahan papers MG 27 111 B1 vols 2 and 7
New Zealand Archives, Wellington
G49/44   New Zealand's attitude to the Disarmament Conference
FA 264/2/7 Pts 1–2 Documents from Britain, the League, etc, and two letters from Sir Thomas Wilford
FA 201/4/85   Relations with Japan
FA/201/4/89   Relations with China (British circulars only)

Published official records

Documents on British Foreign Policy, 1919–1939 second series, vols 9 and 11, London 1965 and 1970
Documents on Canadian External Relations vol. 5, Ottawa 1973
Great Britain *Parliamentary Debates, House of Commons* 1931–35
Australia *Commonwealth Parliamentary Debates*
Canada *Parliamentary Debates*
New Zealand *Parliamentary Debates*

Unpublished unofficial papers, diaries, etc.

K. P. Kirkwood 'Diplomatic Journal' PAC MG 27 111 E3, Ottawa, Canada
Diary of W. A. Riddell, York University Archives, Toronto, Canada

Books and articles

Agar, A. W. S. (1959) *Footprints in the Sea* London: Evans
—— (1962) *Showing the Flag* London: Evans
Andrews, E. M. (1977) 'The Great Temptation: The Australian Government and the Sale of Arms to China during the Manchurian Crisis, 1931–33' *Australian Journal of Politics and History* 23, 3, pp. 346–59
—— (1978) 'The Broken Promise—Britain's Failure to Consult its Commonwealth on Defence in 1934 and its Implications for Australian Foreign and Defence Policy' *Australian Journal of Defence Studies* 2, 2, pp. 102–113
—— (1981) 'The Australian Government and the Manchurian Crisis, 1931–1934' *Australian Outlook* 35, 3, pp. 307–316
Barnett, C. (1972) *The Collapse of British Power* London: Eyre Methuen
Bassett, R. (1952) *Democracy and Foreign Policy: A case history: the Sino-Japanese Dispute 1931–33* London: Cass
Blaxland, G. (1964) *J. H. Thomas: A Life for Unity* London 1964: Muller
Bothwell, R. and Hillmer, N. (eds) (1975) *The In-Between Time: Canadian External Policy in the 1930s* Toronto: Copp Clarke
Carlton, D. (1972) 'The Dominions and British Policy in the Abyssinian Crisis' *Journal of Imperial and Commonwealth History* 1, pp. 59–77
Carter, G. M. (1947) *The British Commonwealth and International Security: the Role of the Dominions, 1919–1939* Toronto: Canadian Institute of International Affairs
Chester, D. M. and Willson, F. M. G. (1968) *The Organization of British Central Government 1914–1964* London: Allen & Unwin
Cowen, Z. (1965) *Sir John Latham and Other Papers* Melbourne: Oxford University Press
Cross, J. A. (1964) 'Whitehall and the Commonwealth: the Development of British Departmental Organisation for Commonwealth Affairs' *Journal of Commonwealth Political Studies* 2, pp. 189–206
—— (1967) *Whitehall and the Commonwealth: British Departmental Organisation for Commonwealth Relations, 1900–1966* London: Routledge & Kegan Paul
Cutlack, F. M. (1934) *The Manchurian Arena: An Australian View of the Far Eastern Conflict* Sydney: Angus & Robertson
Eastman, S. M. (1946) *Canada at Geneva: An Historical Survey and its Lessons* Toronto: Canadian Institute of International Affairs
Eayrs, J. (1964) *In Defence of Canada: From the Great War to the Great Depression* Toronto: University of Toronto Press
—— (1965) *In Defence of Canada: Appeasement and Rearmament* Toronto: University of Toronto Press
Feiling, K. (1947) *The Life of Neville Chamberlain* London: Macmillan
Finlayson, R. K. 'Life with R. B.: That Man Bennett', ms edited by R. J. H. Wilbur in Public Archives of Canada, MG 30 E43, Ottawa
Fitzhardinge, L. F. (1967) 'W. M. Hughes and the Treaty of Versailles 1919' *Journal of Commonwealth Political Studies* 5, pp. 130–42
Gallagher, J. (1982) *The Decline, Revival and Fall of the British Empire* Cambridge: Cambridge University Press
Garner, J. (1978) *The Commonwealth Office 1925–68* London: Heinemann

Gathorne-Hardy, G. M. (1950) *A Short History of International Affairs 1920–1939* London: Oxford University Press
Gibbs, N. H. (1976) *Grand Strategy* vol. I London: HMSO
Haggie, P. (1981) *Britannia At Bay: The Defence of the British Empire against Japan 1931–1941* Oxford: Clarendon Press
Hall, H. D. (1962) 'The Genesis of the Balfour Declaration of 1926' *Journal of Commonwealth Political Studies* 1, pp. 169–93
Harkness, D. (1970) 'Mr. de Valera's Dominion: Irish Relations with Britain and the Commonwealth, 1932–1938' *Journal of Commonwealth Political Studies* 8, pp. 206–228
Harrison Matley, J. (1969) Australia and the Far Eastern Crisis 1931–1933, MA thesis, University of Sydney
Higham, R. (1962) *Armed Forces in Peacetime Britain, 1918–1939, A Case Study* London: Foulis
Hillmer, N. (1973) 'O. D. Skelton: The scholar who set a future pattern' *International Perspectives* September/October, pp. 46–49
Hillmer, N. and Wigley, P. (1980) *The First British Commonwealth; Essays in honour of Nicholas Mansergh* London: Cass
Holland, R. F. (1981) *Britain and the Commonwealth Alliance 1918–1939* London: Macmillan
Hooker, N. H. (1956) *The Moffat Papers: Selections from the Diplomatic Journals of Jay Pierrepont Moffat 1919–1943* Cambridge (Mass): Harvard University Press
Howard, M. (1972) *The Continental Commitment; the dilemma of British defence policy in the era of two world wars* London: Temple Smith
Hughes, W. M. (1935) *Australia and War Today: The Price of Peace* Sydney: Angus & Robertson
Johnson, F. A. (1960) *Defence by Committee: The British Committee of Imperial Defence 1885–1959* London: Oxford University Press
Judd, D. and Slinn, P. (1982) *The Evolution of the Modern Commonwealth* London: Macmillan
Kendle, J. (1967) 'The Round Table Movement: Lionel Curtis and the Formation of the New Zealand Groups in 1910' *New Zealand Journal of History* 1, 1, pp. 33–50
Kennedy, M. D. (1969) *The Estrangement of Great Britain and Japan* Manchester: Manchester University Press
Latham, Sir John (1962) 'Remembrance of Things Past, Mainly Political' *Meanjin Quarterly* 88, March, pp. 78–81
Lavarack J. D. (1933) 'The Defence of the British Empire, with Special Reference to the Far East and Australia' *Army Quarterly* 25, 2, pp. 193–217
Lissington, M. P. (1972) *New Zealand and Japan, 1900–1941* Wellington: Department of Internal Affairs
Louis, W. R. (1971) *British Strategy in the Far East 1919–1939* Oxford: Clarendon Press
Lowe, P. (1981) *Britain in the Far East: A survey from 1918 to the present* London: Longman
Lower, A. R. M. (1941) *Canada and the Far East-1940* New York: Institute of Pacific Relations

MacDougall, R. L. (ed.) (1965) *Our Living Tradition: fifth series; Canada's Past and Present: A Dialogue* Toronto: Toronto University Press

MacGibbon, I. C. (1971) The Blue-Water Rationale: New Zealand's Naval Security Problem, 1919–39, MA thesis, Victoria University, Wellington

Mackintosh, W. A. 'O. D. Skelton', chapter in MacDougall above pp. 59–77

Macleod, I. (1960) *Neville Chamberlain* London: Muller

Mansergh, N. (1952) *Survey of British Commonwealth Affairs: Problems of External Policy, 1931–9* London: Oxford University Press

—— (1969) *The Commonwealth Experience* London: Weidenfeld & Nicholson

Marquand, D. (1977) *Ramsay MacDonald* London: Cape

Mason, A. (1974) Canada and the Far Eastern Crisis, 1931–1933, paper presented to the Canadian Historical Association

—— (1975) 'Canada and the Manchurian crisis', in Bothwell and Hillmer (eds) above, pp. 113–19

McCarthy, J. M. (1971a) 'Australia and Imperial Defence: Cooperation and Conflict, 1918–1939' *Australian Journal of Politics and History* 17, 1, pp. 19–32

—— (1971b) 'Singapore and Australian Defence 1921–1942' *Australian Outlook* 25, 2, pp. 165–80

—— (1976) *Australia and Imperial Defence 1919–39: A Study in Air and Sea Power* St Lucia: Queensland University Press

McIntyre, W. D. (1974) New Zealand and the Singapore Base on the Eve of the Pacific War, paper presented to the Institute of Commonwealth Studies, London

—— (1977) *The Commonwealth of Nations: Origins and Impact, 1869–1971* Minneapolis: University of Minnesota Press

McLintock, A. H. (1966) *An Encyclopaedia of New Zealand* Wellington: Government Printer

Meaney, N. (1976) *The Search for Security in the Pacific 1901–14* Sydney: Sydney University Press

Megaw, R. (1973) 'The Australian Goodwill Mission to the Far East in 1934: Its Significance in the Evolution of Australian Foreign Policy' *Journal of the Royal Australian Historical Society* 59, 4, pp. 247–63

Meyers, R. (1976) 'Britain, Europe and the Dominions in the 1930s: Some Aspects of British, European and Commonwealth Policies' *Australian Journal of Politics and History* 22, 1, pp. 36–50

Middlemas, R. K. and Barnes, J. (1969) *Baldwin: A Biography* London: Weidenfeld & Nicholson

Morley, J. W. (1984) *Japan Erupts; The London Naval Conference and the Manchurian Incident, 1928–1932* New York: Colombia University Press

Mowatt, C. L. (1955) *Britain Between the Wars 1918–1940* London: Methuen

Neale, R. G. (ed.) (1975) *Documents on Australian Foreign Policy 1937–49* vol I. Canberra: AGPS

Nish, I. H. (1963) 'Australia and the Anglo-Japanese Alliance, 1901–1911' *Australian Journal of Politics and History*, 9, 2, pp. 201–212

Ogata, S. N. (1962) *Defiance in Manchuria: the Making of Japanese Foreign Policy 1931–1932* Berkeley: University of California Press

Oliver, W. H. (1960) *The Story of New Zealand* London: Faber

Ovendale, R. (1975) *'Appeasement' and the English Speaking World: Britain, the United States, The Dominions, and the policy of 'Appeasement' 1937–1939* Cardiff: University of Wales Press
Palmer, G. E. H. (1934) *Consultation and Cooperation in the British Commonwealth* London: Oxford University Press
Patrick, K. A. (1970) Armaments and Security: the basis of British policy at the Disarmament Conference 1931–33, MA thesis, Monash University, Melbourne
Pearson, L. B. (1973) *Memoires 1897–1948: Through Diplomacy to Politics* London: Gollancz
Poynter, J. R. (1970) 'The Yo-Yo variations; Initiative and Dependence in Australia's External Relations, 1918–1921' *Historical Studies* 14, 54, pp. 231–49
Primrose, B. N. (1974) Australian Naval Policy, 1919 to 1942: A Case Study in Empire Relations, PhD thesis, Australian National University
Riddell, W. A. (1947) *World Security by Conference* Toronto: Ryerson
Robertson, H. C. H. (1935) 'The Defence of Australia' *Army Quarterly* 30, 1, pp. 15–33
Roskill, S. W. (1974) *Hankey, Man of Secrets* vol. 3 London: Collins
Ross, A. (1972) 'Reluctant Dominion or Dutiful Daughter? New Zealand and the Commonwealth in the inter-war years' *Journal of Commonwealth Political Studies* 10, pp. 28–44
—— (1980) 'New Zealand and the Statute of Westminster' in Hillmer, N. and Wigley, P. *The First British Commonwealth; Essays in honour of Nicolas Mansergh*, London: Cass, pp. 136–58
Sales, P. M. (1971) 'W. M. Hughes and the Chanak Crisis of 1922' *Australian Journal of Politics and History* 17, 3, pp. 392–405
Scholefield, G. H. (ed.) (1940) *A dictionary of New Zealand biography* Wellington: Department of Internal Affairs
Shay, R. P. (1977) *British Rearmament in the Thirties; Politics and Profits* Princeton: Princeton University Press
Sissons, D. C. S. (1976) 'Manchester v. Japan: The Imperial Background of the Australian Trade Diversion Dispute with Japan, 1936' *Australian Outlook* 30, 3, pp. 480–502
Sinclair, K. (1959) *A History of New Zealand* Harmondsworth: Penguin
Stacey, G. P. (1981) *Canada and the Age of Conflict; A History of Canadian External Policies* vol. 2 Toronto: University of Toronto Press
Taylor, A. J. P. (1965) *English History 1914–1945* Oxford: Clarendon Press
The Times (1952) *The History of The Times* vol. 4 London: The Times
Thorne, C. (1970) 'The Quest for Arms Embargoes: Failure in 1933' *Journal of Contemporary History* 5, 4, pp. 129–49
—— (1972) *The Limits of Foreign Policy: the West, the League and the Far Eastern Crisis of 1931–1933* London: Hamilton
Trotter, A. (1974a) 'Tentative Steps for an Anglo-Japanese Rapprochment in 1934' *Modern Asian Studies* 8, 1, pp. 59–83
—— (1974b) 'The Dominions and Imperial Defence: Hankey's Tour in 1934' *Journal of Imperial and Commonwealth History* 2, 3, pp. 318–32
—— (1975) *Britain and East Asia 1933–1937* Cambridge: Cambridge University Press

Veatch, R. (1975) *Canada and the League of Nations* Toronto: University of Toronto Press
Watt, D. C. (1961–63) 'Imperial Defence Policy and Imperial Foreign Policy 1911–1939—a Neglected Paradox?' *Journal of Commonwealth Political Studies* 1, pp. 266–81
—— (1965) *Personalities and Policies; Studies in the Formulation of British Foreign Policy in the Twentieth Century* London: Longman
Wilbur, R. (1969) *The Bennett Administration 1930–1935*, Ottawa: Canadian Historical Association Booklet no. 24
Wilford, Sir T. M. (1928) *New Zealand and the Pacific, with Special Relation to the Singapore Base* London: Empire Parliamentary Association
Williams, P. (1971) 'New Zealand and the 1930 Imperial Conference' *New Zealand Journal of History* 5, 1, pp. 31–48
Willis, S. (1975) The Australian Eastern Mission, 1934, paper presented to the Foreign Policy and Defence History Conference, Sydney University
Wood, F. L. W. (1948) *The New Zealand People at War; Political and External Affairs* Wellington: New Zealand Government Press
—— (1940) *New Zealand in the World* Wellington: Department of Internal Affairs
Wrench, J. E. (1955) *Geoffrey Dawson and Our Times* London: Hutchinson
Yoshihashi, T. (1963) *Conspiracy at Mukden: the Rise of the Japanese Military* New Haven: Yale University Press
Young, G. M. (1952) *Stanley Baldwin* London: Hart-Davis

Index

Admiralty, 28, 30, 31 33; Australia and, 117, 118, 119, 144, 162; Defence Requirements Committee and, 109, 130, 145, 149; Dominions and, 45, 106, 153, 171; Naval weakness in the East and, 57, 108, 114–15, 129, 177–8, 179–80, 192
Aga Khan, 74, 81
Amery, L. S., 11, 12, 13–14, 17, 22
appeasement, 151–5, 182, 188, 189
Australia, xiv, 22, 26, 37, 95; air force in, 32, 120, 176; argument between army and navy in, 116, 127–9, 159, 162, 163–4, 172–3; armaments production in, 114, 121, 124; Britain and, 4–5, 7, 12–13, 18–19, 24–5, 32–3, 100–101, 102, 187–8, 194–5; Canada and, 52–3, 94, 119, 134, 135, 168; China and, 137, 138–9, 140–2, 143; CID and, 27, 115–18, 120, 127–30; Council of Defence established in, 163, 165, 173–4; Country Party in, 136, 163; defence and, 32, 109, 115–20, 126–31, 133–4, 174, 189, 191; Defence Requirements Committee and, 148, 149; Department of Defence in, 120–1, 124, 134; Department of External Affairs in, 24–5, 49, 51–3, 77, 89, 94, 96, 134–5, 137; disarmament conference 1932 and, 67, 105–6; Far East and, 10, 137, 142; fear of Japan in, 28, 52, 98, 119–20, 134, 187, 193; government of Lyons in, 49–53; Hankey's Commonwealth tour and, 159, 160, 161, 162–5; Japan and, 95, 98, 137, 138, 139–40, 142–3, 152, 153, 155, 156, 185, 188; Labor Party (ALP) in, 120, 162, 165; Latham mission to the East, 135–45, 151, 189; League of Nations and, 68–9, 71, 72, 86, 89, 90, 93, 94–6, 97, 98, 100, 143; Manchurian and Shanghai crises and, 61–2, 77–80, 99, 143; messages to Britain, 53, 61, 63–4, 66, 78–80; navy in, 32, 119, 164, 176; New Zealand and, 113–14, 166, 167, 191; recognition of Manchukuo and, 78–80, 95–6; sale of arms to China, 120–26; sanctions and, 78, 95; Singapore base and, 34, 107, 126–7, 132–3, 173, 181; trade with Japan, 37–8, 77–8; US and, 112

Baldwin, S., 26, 33, 38, 39, 43, 122, 158, 160
Balfour, S. M., 5, 6, 7, 9, 156
Balfour, Report, 5, 8, 9, 10, 62, 193
Bennett R. B., 16, 27, 46, 62, 125–6, 152, 187; Commonwealth PM's meetings and, 175–6, 181, 183, 184; Hankey's tour and, 167, 168, 170; League of Nations and, 49, 69–70, 80, 87, 88, 91, 92, 93–4, 98, 100; parliament and, 59, 97, 125; Skelton and, 20, 46, 92
Berendsen, C. A., 44, 174–5
Britain, xi, 8; China and, 76, 81, 99, 145, 146, 147, 151, 152; Commonwealth used as excuse for policies, xi–xii, 62; disarmament, 28, 30–31, 104–6, 185, 192; Dominions and, 100–102, 137–8, 193, 195; Far East, weakness in, 31, 37, 55–7, 58, 60, 107–110, 132, 136, 149, 150, 192–3; government of, 38–43; Japan and, 38, 99, 130, 131, 136, 144–6,

224

147, 151–5, 177–8, 180; League of Nations and, 66–7, 71, 75–6, 84–90, 96, 99, 122; Lytton Report and, 81–2, 84–5; Manchurian and Shanghai crises and, 54–5, 58; Nine Power Treaty and, 78–80, 171; rearmament, 109, 132, 148, 160–1; sale of arms to China, 120–26; sanction and, 75–6, 92; Silver Jubilee, xiv–xv, 176–7, 184, 187; Treasury in, 14, 17, 27, 108–9, 128, 130–1, 145, 147, 154, 167; United States and, 43, 146, 169, 171; War Office in, 146, 178; *see also* Australia; Canada; Commonwealth; consultation; Chamberlain; Dominions Office; Empire, British; Foreign Office; Hankey; imperial defence; imperial foreign policy, New Zealand

Bruce, S. M., 50–1, 52–3, 137; Britain and, 5, 6, 9, 18, 24, 32–3, 101, 106 195; defence and, 118, 122, 123, 124, 127, 129–31, 149, 153, 179–80, 189; League and, 81, 86, 89, 90, 93, 95–6, 100; PM's meetings, 182, 183

Bruche, Major General J. H., 128, 172

Cahan, C. H., 85–92, 93, 94, 100, 101, 187

Canada, xiv, 3, 4–5, 6, 7, 8, 10, 12–13, 15, 16, 22, 26, 37, 51, 99; Australia and, 52–3, 94, 119, 134, 135, 168; China and, 90, 94, 124–6, 168; consultation and, 24–5, 27, 62, 64, 181; defence and, 32, 105, 106, 109, 110–12, 119, 120, 124, 169, 172, 175–6, 187, 189; Department of External Affairs in, 19–21, 24, 46, 48; Hankey's tour and, 159, 161, 167–71; imperial defence and, 31, 118, 157, 169; imperial foreign policy and, 101, 144, 193; Japan and, 45–9, 90, 152–3, 168, 169, 175; League of Nations and, 48, 59, 69–70, 71, 72–3, 74, 75, 80, 85–92, 93–4, 97–8, 100, 175, 187; Legation in Tokyo, 12, 20–21, 40–49, 59–60, 139, 187; Manchurian and Shanghai crises and, 45–9, 58–61, 187; parliament in, 92, 97–8; United States and, 46, 80, 87, 90–1, 102, 112, 125–6, 153, 168, 169, 185, 187

Casey, R. G., 24, 37, 52, 159, 160, 179, 180

Chamberlain, N., 13, 38, 43, 122; defence economies and, 104–5,
108–9, 130, 189; defence requirements and, 129–31, 145, 146–50, 158, 189; dominance of the British cabinet, 39–40, 41, 131, 189; Dominions and, 156, 158; Japan and, 130, 151–5; PM's meetings 1935 and, 178, 180, 181

Chanak crisis, 4, 21, 24, 68

Chatfield, Sir. E., 110, 148

Chiefs of Staff, 27, 56, 57, 109; Australia and, 31–2, 116–18, 129–30, 159; Annual Review by, (1932) 104, 107–8, (1933) 156, (1935) 176, 178–9, 183; Far East and, 107–8, 110, 192

Churchill, W. S., 5, 28, 30, 33–4

China, 37, 42, 76, 81, 86, 89–90, 94, 137, 138–9, 140–2

Clive, Sir R., 139, 151

Coates, J. G., 9, 33, 165, 167

Cobbe, J. G., 113, 166

Commonwealth, British, xiv, 1–36, 66–103, 105–6

Committee of Imperial Defence (CID), 26–8, 35, 42, 77, 104, 108–9; Australian defence and, 115–18, 120, 127–30, 159, 163–4, 191; Dominions and, 10, 12, 27–8, 63, 169, 171, 178; New Zealand and, 22–3, 31, 105, 112–13, 114, 166, 174, 191; Singapore and, 22–3, 133

conferences, (Imperial) 3, 4–6, 11, 12, 22, 24–5, 32–3, 34, 51, 107, 127, 177; (other), 7, 11, 30, 97, 102–3, 104–6

consultation, 3, 5, 8–9, 11–19, 58–65, 106–7, 122–3, 152, 155, 156–9, 176, 177–84, 185, 189–95

Cutlack, F. M., 138, 140, 141

Defence Requirements Committee, 129–31, 132, 145–51, 156–7, 171–2, 189, 192, 193

de Valera, E., 16, 70, 177, 187

disarmament, (imperial) 25–36, 58; (conference 1932) 67, 104–6, 151; (naval treaties) 145, 146, 154

Dominions Office, x–xi, 10, 94, 101–2, 153, 177, 186; arms to the East, 122–3, 124; Australia and, 78–9, 143–4; cables on the crises, 21, 52, 58; creation of, 11, 13–16; Wilford and, 82, 83; defence and, 118, 146, 149; Hankey's tour and, 159, 167; weakness in coordinating the Empire/ Commonwealth, 25, 28, 106, 156, 192, 194

INDEX

Duffy, V. C., 24, 49, 51, 52, 69, 77, 78, 79, 80

Economy, 1, 10, 22, 41
Eden, Sir A., 62, 122–3, 137
Empire, British, x, xiv, 1, 3–6, 10–11, 15, 25–6

Far East; Latham mission to, 135–45; British weakness in, 31, 107–8, 109, 110, 114–15, 129–30, 136, 144, 150, 156, 164–5, 167, 172, 177–9, 192, 195
Fisher, Sir. W., 43, 131, 145, 148, 193
Forbes, G. W., 43–4, 50, 58, 165, 166, 167, 174; Britain and, 21–2, 181, 182–3, 184, 187; defence and, 34, 112–13; League and, 67–8, 77, 82, 90, 96, 99, 174
Foreign Office, 1, 9, 14, 20, 35, 41, 70; Australia and, 24, 79–80, 140, 143–4; defence and, 122; 130–1, 145–6, Dominions and, x–xi, 12, 17–18, 74, 82, 83, 102, 106, 156, 177, 180, 187, 194–5; Japan and, 56, 151, 152, 153; Manchurian crisis and, 42–3, 89, 99

George V, xiv, 10–11, 16, 176
Germany, 110, 129, 130, 131, 132, 134, 145, 147, 152, 193, 195
Great Britain, see Britain

Hankey, Sir M., 35, 42, 43, 50, 71, 109, 110, 112, 113, 115–16, 122, 130, 134, 147, 148–9, 156, 158, 159–74, 179, 183, 185, 193
Harding, Sir E., 81, 82
Herridge, W. D., 90, 91, 92, 125, 169
Hertzog, General J. B. M., 5, 6, 76, 161, 181, 184
High Commissioners for the Dominions, 9, 10, 11, 12, 13, 18, 23, 24, 25, 34, 45, 49, 51, 61, 67, 93, 126, 133, 156, 194–5
Hirota, K., 139–40, 151–2
Hong Kong, 107, 110, 138, 152, 171
Hughes, W. M., 6, 7, 23, 50, 68, 100, 112, 188

imperial defence, 25–36, 116–18, 127–31, 132, 160, 161, 167–8, 170–1, 176, 184, 188–9, 192, 195; see also Defence Requirements Committee
imperial foreign policy, 18–19, 101–2, 143–4, 185–6, 187, 191–2, 195
intellectuals, 97, 102–3, 134–5

Ireland, xiv, 3, 4, 8, 10, 12, 13, 16, 27–8, 31, 70, 72, 73, 84, 85, 88, 99, 105, 187

Japan; Australia and, 28, 34, 37–8, 77–8, 139–40, 141, 142–3; Britain and, 28–31, 40–41, 42, 70, 76, 103, 129–31, 132, 147, 185; Canada and, 45, 60–1, 87–8, 90, 91, 175; expansion, 28, 35, 37, 70, 73, 80, 83, 86, 119, 121, 129, 180, 185; League of Nations and, 85, 92, 96; naval power, 56, 152–4, 179; New Zealand and, 22–3, 37, 82, 83
Jellicoe, Lord, 22, 28, 30, 33

Keenleyside, Dr. H. L., 47–9, 53, 60–1
Kelly, Admiral Sir H., 55, 57
Keynes, J. M., 132, 189
King, W. L., Mackenzie, 4–5, 6, 19, 20, 24, 27, 87, 167, 170
Knowles, C., 83, 85

Latham, Sir J., 50–2, 53, 61, 63, 67, 78, 80, 95–6, 105–06, 115–18, 121–4, 127, 140, 172, 182, 188; mission to the East, 135–45, 151, 189
Lavarack, J. D., 128, 173
League of Nations, 13, 139; Assembly, 70–4, 83, 84–90, 92, 121; Australia and, 68–9, 71, 100, 139; Britain and, 31, 41–2, 64, 75–6, 81–2, 99; Canada and, 48, 59, 69–70, 71, 72, 85–92, 100; Committee of Nineteen, 74, 84, 92–3, 125; Commonwealth and, 3, 35, 66, 73–4, 89–90, 99–100, 103, 186, 187; Lytton commission, 70, 78, 79, 80–4, 86, 88, 92, 95; Manchurian incident and, 37, 41–2, 65, 70, 186; New Zealand and, 67–8, 72, 76–7, 81–3, 100; sanctions, 64, 71, 75–80, 88, 186
League of Nations Union (Australia), 68, 90
Leeper, A. W. A., 18, 24
Lester, S., 72, 73
Lindley, Sir. F., 59, 60, 70, 139, 156
Lloyd George, D., 28, 40, 109
Locarno Treaty, 5, 6
London, stress on by British government, 105, 193
Lothian, Lord, 167, 168, 179, 180
Lyons, J. A., 50, 68, 89, 96, 105–6, 113–14, 120, 121, 124, 136, 137, 141, 158, 162–5, 166, 181–2, 184, 191; see also Australia

INDEX

MacDonald, M., 14, 17, 50, 68
MacDonald, J. Ramsay, xiv–xv, 10, 14–15, 16, 22, 33, 38–9, 40, 101, 104, 108, 110, 118, 121, 122, 146, 147, 150, 157–8, 160, 182, 183
McNaughton, A. G. L., 110, 111, 125, 126, 168, 169, 170 175
Manchurian crisis, x, xii, 31, 35, 37, 38, 46, 49, 50, 55, 67, 104, 107, 139
Manchukuo, 76, 78, 81, 83, 92, 94
Marler, Sir H., 46–8, 53, 59–61, 69, 81, 125, 138, 141
Massey, W. F., 5, 23
Melbourne, Dr. A. C. V., 135, 137
Milner, Lord, 9, 109
Mukden, incident at, 35, 37, 55

Nash, W., 68, 98
New Zealand, xiv, 9, 15, 25, 26, 44–5, 49, 149, 155; Australia and, 113–14, 166, 167, 191; Britain and, 4–5, 9, 11, 12–13, 18–19, 21–4, 101, 132–3, 182, 187, 194; CID and, 27, 31, 112–13, 114, 115, 118; defence and, 10, 27 31, 32, 105–6, 109, 112–13, 172, 174, 176, 189; fear of communism in, 82, 83; Hankey's tour and, 159, 164, 165–7; Japan and, 22–3, 83, 112, 133, 152, 156, 175, 185; League of Nations and, 67–8, 72, 76–7, 81–3, 85, 90, 93, 96, 97, 98–9, 100, 174–5; Manchurian crisis and, 37, 43–5, 76, 99, 102, 174–5; Shanghai crisis and, 58, 59, 64–5; Singapore and, 22–3, 33–5, 107, 174
Netherlands East Indies, 138, 140, 143, 192
Newfoundland, 3, 10
Nine Power Treaty, 53, 73, 76, 78–9, 93

Officer, K., 49, 52, 53, 61, 68–9, 77, 78, 80, 121
Ottawa agreement, 41, 135, 136

pacificism, 104, 121, 146, 168, 185, 187, 192
Parkhill, Sir A., 127, 163
Pearce, Sir G., 78, 100, 113, 114, 118, 119, 120, 121, 159, 162, 163, 166, 167, 169, 172, 187–8
Perley, Sir G., 46, 59, 64, 69, 71, 72–3, 74, 75, 88
Pirow, O., 160, 162
public opinion, appeal to, 39, 109

Riddell, W. A., 58, 63, 73, 86, 87, 89, 91, 92, 94, 101, 126, 175
Rowell,, N. W., 18–19, 21, 59
Ryrie, Sir G., 52, 63, 69, 71, 74

Savage, J., 99, 187
Scullin, J. H., 34, 49–50, 120, 163
Shanghai, 107, 121, 138, 141; crisis, 43, 54–5, 58, 62
Shedden, F. G., 134, 173
Silver Jubilee of George V, xiv, 176–7, 184, 187
Simon, Sir J., 40, 171; defence and, 104–6, 118, 121, 122–3, 146; Dominions and, 62, 64, 72, 74, 79–101, 137, 180, 187; Japan and, 57–8, 145, 151–4; League of Nations and, 40–3, 67, 71, 72, 73, 75–6, 81–2, 83–4, 84–5, 92, 93
Sinclair Burges, Major General W. L. H., 112, 113, 166–7
Singapore base, 10, 13, 30, 33–5, 57, 107–8, 109–10, 131, 192; Australia and, 31–2, 107, 116, 117–18, 126–9, 143–4, 173; Hankey's tour and, 160–1, 164, 165, 166, 167; New Zealand and, 22–3, 33–5, 107, 112, 174; PM's meetings and, 178, 180–1, 182; rationale changed, 148, 158, 179–80, 189
Singapore conference, 132–3
Skelton, O. D., 19–21, 24, 46–7, 92, 168; Britain and, 4, 20, 27, 168; Chinese and, 90, 124; League of Nations and, 48–9, 59, 69–70, 71, 72–3, 75, 87–8, 91, 93–4, 100; Shanghai and, 61, 62, 64
Smuts, J., 3–4, 153, 160–1, 162
South Africa, xiv, 10, 12, 15, 25, 185; Britain and, 3–4, 5, 6, 9, 13, 22, 31, 175, 181, 194; defence and, 118, 169, 172, 176; Hankey's tour and, 159, 160–2, 166–7, 185; League of Nations and, 72, 73–4, 76, 85, 99, 109, 187, 194
Stimpson, H. L., 42–3, 53, 70, 73, 74, 90–1, 187

Ten Year Rule, 30, 107, 108, 109
te Water, C., 72, 73–4, 83
Thomas, J. H., 14–16, 25, 35, 53, 58, 62–3, 75, 81, 101–2, 106, 114, 122–3, 144, 145, 146, 149, 153, 156, 159, 160, 171, 192, 194

trade, 1, 22, 37–8, 41, 44–5, 52, 103, 135–6, 139, 142–3, 155, 175

United Australia Party (UAP), 50–1, 115, 120, 137
United Kingdom, *see* Britain
United States, 1, 12, 42, 43, 46, 79, 80, 84, 87–8, 90–1, 92, 125–6, 186, 187

Vansittart, Sir R., 43, 56, 131, 145–6, 169, 171

Washington conference 1921, 28–30, 154
Wellesley, Sir V., 82, 83
Westminster, Statute of, 10, 35, 51
Wilford, Sir T., 23–4, 30, 37, 44, 76–7, 81–3, 85, 90, 98–9, 112, 133

For Product Safety Concerns and Information please contact our EU representative GPSR@taylorandfrancis.com
Taylor & Francis Verlag GmbH, Kaufingerstraße 24, 80331 München, Germany

www.ingramcontent.com/pod-product-compliance
Lightning Source LLC
Chambersburg PA
CBHW061441300426
44114CB00014B/1778